Cultural Mélange
in Aesthetic Practices

Annjo Klungervik Greenall & Domhnall Mitchell (Eds.)

Cultural Mélange in Aesthetic Practices

Copyright © 2015 by
Fagbokforlaget Vigmostad & Bjørke AS
All Rights Reserved

ISBN: 978-82-450-1721-2

Graphic production: John Grieg AS, Bergen

Typeset by Type-it AS
Cover illustration: Johnny Yen

This book is published with funding from the Department of Language and Literature and the Faculty of Humanities at NTNU.

Inquiries about this text can be directed to:
Fagbokforlaget
Kanalveien 51
5068 Bergen
Tel.: 55 38 88 00
Fax: 55 38 88 01
e-mail: fagbokforlaget@fagbokforlaget.no
www.fagbokforlaget.no

All rights reserved. No part of this publication may be reproduced, stored in a retrieval system, or transmitted, in any form or by any means, electronic, mechanical, photo-copying, recording, or otherwise, without the prior written permission of the publisher.

Preface

The chapters in this volume are revised versions of papers given at a workshop entitled "Cultural Mélange in Aesthetic Expressions" held at the (former) Department of Modern Foreign Languages at the Norwegian University of Science and Technology (NTNU), Trondheim, Norway, 11–12 February, 2013. The initiative for the workshop was taken by members of Translating Cultures, one of three prioritised research groups based at (what is now known as) the Department of Language and Literature at NTNU. The workshop aimed to draw on group members' collective research interests in addressing and sharing views on a topic that - also in Scandinavia - is becoming increasingly relevant in today's globalized society, namely the cultural-linguistic mixing and blending that is an increasingly significant part of our daily experience. In addition, the workshop saw the beginnings of a sustained process of networking with international scholars working on similar issues: three distinguished colleagues, Christiane Fioupou, Henrik Smith-Sivertsen, and Riitta Oittinen, from France, Denmark and Finland, respectively, were invited to contribute to the workshop and subsequently to the volume. The fact that they come from fields as different as African studies, musicology, and translation studies testifies to the interdisciplinary nature of the workshop as well as of the current volume. Mélanges of a broadly cultural (linguistic, generic, discursive) kind have been discussed, in this work, using a variety of literary, theatrical, musical, linguistic and translational approaches, and it is our belief that the topic at hand benefits greatly from – or perhaps even requires – such a diversity of treatment, it being the case that all of these aspects are often intertwined in one and the same (textual or non-textual) aesthetic practice. A single angle will just not do.

We would like to extend our thanks to the members of the Translating Cultures research group and to the invited contributors of this volume for their hard work, enthusiasm and endless patience. Thanks are also due to the Faculty of Humanities at NTNU and the Department of Language and Literature for hosting and helping to fund the workshop and this publication, and to the editorial team at Fagbokforlaget for their kind input and guidance.

Contents

1 Cultural mélange in textual and non-textual aesthetic practices: Some considerations 9
Annjo K. Greenall

Part I Literary and Theatrical Practices

2 Friction, facts and fiction: Hybridity in Jean Potocki's 'Oriental' travelogues 25
Marius Warholm Haugen

3 From Victor Hugo and Juliette Drouet to the rest of the world: A mélange of genres 39
Nelly Foucher Stenkløv

4 Wole Soyinka's 'armoury of creativity': Cultural mélange from *Opera Wonyosi* to 'Guerrilla Theatre' 53
Christiane Fioupou

5 A 'jazzy literature': Cultural hybridity and multilingualism in Mongo Beti's *Trop de soleil tue l'amour* 69
Inger Hesjevoll Schmidt-Melbye

6 Franglais as an example of cultural mélange 81
Sophie Vauclin

7 The mélange of multimodality: Picture books in translation 95
Riitta Oittinen

Part II Textual-Musical Practices

8 Travelling nationalisms? US hip hop and the French connection 115
Priscilla Ringrose

9   The sound of (good) music: Cultural and linguistic hybridity in the
    Scandinavian popular music soundscape.   131
    Henrik Smith-Sivertsen

10 Norwegian-English code-switching in popular music lyrics 1960s –
    2000s.   149
    Annjo Klungervik Greenall

11 'Your multilingual business friend might make you a better reader':
    Multilingualism and song lyrics in Kjartan Fløgstad's prose   171
    Anne Karine Kleveland

12 'Famous Blue Raincoat' in translation.   189
    Anja Angelsen and Domhnall Mitchell

Contributors   207

1 Cultural mélange in textual and non-textual aesthetic practices: Some considerations

Annjo K. Greenall

The OED defines *purity* as 'The state or quality of being free from extraneous or foreign elements, or from outside influence; the state of being unadulterated or refined; clarity'.[1] The concept is of course deeply value-laden: while the first part of the definition emerges as relatively neutral, bar the possible negative connotations of 'foreign' and 'outside', the latter part is a distilled expression of centuries of desire: who wants adulteration, non-refinement, non-clarity? Still, the history of human creation is replete with examples that purity is an illusion. Dictionaries showcase languages as entities often composed of other languages; local literatures from all over the world are framed by genres hailing from ancient cultures such as those of Greece and Italy, France and Spain; musical expressions such as jazz and blues have African roots. A large majority of aesthetic practices tend to constitute *mélanges* of form and content, emerging either as smooth ensembles or as collections of sharply defined, even discordant components.[2] Decades of modern and postmodern aesthetics accompanied by accelerating globalization have caused a situation where non-purity, as it were, is now both generally accepted, and nothing less than ubiquitous: to find an example all you need to do (in very many cases) is grab the

---

1 'purity', *Oxford English Dictionary Online* <http://www.oed.com/view/Entry/154916?redirectedFrom=purity#eid> [accessed 6 January 2014].
2 Mélange is italicised here because this is its first appearance: since it is a word that has now more or less passed into English usage, it will be represented in roman type for the rest of this volume.

book nearest to you. For me, this social-media-inspired experiment provided me, for the purposes of this chapter, with Norwegian author Heidi Linde's latest novel *Nu, jävlar* [literally: *Now, devils*; in dynamic translation: *Fuck it, I'm ready*].[3] A novel about the lives of four relatively unassuming characters in the small Norwegian town of Kongsvinger, it starts out borrowing elements from the crime novel (in the form of an italicised preface depicting the quiet life in a small police precinct which is shattered when they receive a phone call from a witness giving evidence about a crime having been committed). It continues, however, as a predominantly psychological novel, exploring the effects of the past on the characters' present. Borrowing and mixing are also evident on the level of theme: Virginia Woolf's *A Room of One's Own* looms in the background throughout the character Therese's plot line.[4] Therese has two small children and is heavily pregnant with a third, and the novel finds her grieving for lost opportunities in life and longing for some untainted time she can spend exclusively in her own company. Structurally, the novel is anchored in an event involving an outside cultural figure, namely the news about Barack Obama's Nobel Peace Prize nomination. Partly as a result of this, the novel contains, in addition to the Swedish loan expression used in the book's title (*Nu, jävlar*), prominent borrowings from English: the Obama mantra 'Change', for example, heads one of the book's subsections.

This example illustrates many aspects of cultural mélange that are relevant for this volume. Above all, it demonstrates how mélange is a function of choices made at several different levels of a text and/or (other) aesthetic practice. Mixes and blends take place between genres, between and among literary works, fact and fiction, languages, and also, as one of the contributions to this book will show, between and among different textual modalities (the visual, verbal, and aural). More often than not, these blends have a cultural dimension: an intruding genre may be seen to properly belong elsewhere, intertextual references, items and events, as well as languages are often borrowed from outside. It would, however, be a mistake to approach each individual element in such

---

3 Heidi Linde, *Nu jävlar* (Oslo: Gyldendal, 2011).
4 Silje Stavrum Norevik, 'Denne boka bør du lese i vår: Skarpt skrevet fra søvnige Kongsvinger'. *Dagbladet*, 4 March 2011, Reviews section <http://www.dagbladet.no/2011/04/03/kultur/bok/litteratur/litteraturanmeldelser/anmeldelser/16033544/> [accessed 6 January 2014].

blends with the expectation that they should be somehow original and pure. Academic literature past and present abounds with an insistence that cultural and/or textual purity does not in principle exist: postcolonial theorist Edward Said's much quoted claim that no culture 'is single and pure, all are hybrid, heterogeneous'[5] is echoed by more recent theorists such as Marwan Kraidy's 'all cultures are to some extent hybrid'.[6] Cultural historian Peter Burke draws our attention to the fact that 'Martin Luther, anticipating modern linguists, once remarked that '[a]ll languages are mixed',[7] and we recall Russian literary scholar Mikhail Bakhtin's insistence that the word is always half someone else's.[8] Thus, any element of a given mix is also always in itself a mix, and so on, indefinitely. Despite this, an artistic work or practice is still, borrowing some terms from gestalt psychology, often perceived in terms of figures (extraneous elements) against grounds (more – to perception – unified home bases). In Heidi Linde's novel, for example, the genre of crime fiction, which plays only a small part in the book, is likely to be perceived as a figure in a predominantly psychological novel constituting the ground; the Swedish and English language insertions will be perceived as figures against a Norwegian-language ground, and so on.

The current volume contains eleven empirical studies that together richly illustrate the multi-level nature of mélanges and the complex ways in which the various elements are interwoven. The contributions discuss the historical points of departure for, the political repercussions and the aesthetic functions of, a number of artistic works and practices from different parts of the world, with the main focus on Europe. Before introducing these studies further, however, it is necessary to take a closer look at the leading concept of this book, namely mélange.

---

5   Edward W. Said, *Culture and Imperialism* (London: Vintage, 1993), p. xxix.
6   Marwan M. Kraidy, *Hybridity, or the Cultural Logic of Globalization* (Philadelphia: Temple University Press, 2005), p. 119.
7   Peter Burke, *Cultural Hybridity* (Cambridge, UK: Polity, 2009), p. 46.
8   Mikhail M. Bakhtin, *The Dialogic Imagination*, trans. by Caryl Emerson and Michael Holquist (Austin: University of Texas Press, 1981), p. 345.

Mélange vs. hybridity

Above all, the choice of the term mélange needs to be discussed above all because of the existence of another, more commonly used term – hybridity – which might intuitively seem to be appropriate for discussing many of the phenomena discussed in the contributions to this volume. The latter term has its roots in the field of biology, where it denotes a cross between two different species, and where it is often used to designate something that is not acceptable (cf. impure breeds).[9] Within linguistics and discourse analysis the term has been used as a label for texts that display features of more than one genre or text type (ibid.), but most notably, it has been used extensively within postcolonial theory, social science and cultural studies as a label for the cultural blends that arise as a result of colonisation and globalization. In postcolonial studies the term is traced back to Homi K. Bhabha, who refers to hybrids as 'intercultural brokers in the interstices between nation and empire',[10] in other words people, typically expats from previously colonized countries, who live and write through and in a colonizing culture and language. Within postcolonial studies, hybridity is a deeply political concept, pointing above all to issues of unequal power, conflict and tension. This endows it with certain connotations that makes it useful, according to Haugen (this volume), for discussing blends also outside the postcolonial context, since the latter is obviously not the only context where cultural-linguistic juxtapositions can cause jarring and tension.

Two of the contributors to the present volume, Fioupou and Schmidt-Melbye, write about typical Bhabhaian hybrids – Nigerian playwright Wole Soyinka, and Cameroonian Francophone author Mongo Beti, respectively. The hybridity that is played out in their works cannot, however, be said to be solely due to the postcolonial situation of their countries of origin. Wole Soyinka's play *Opera Wonyosi*, for example, also has clear intertextual ties to Bertolt Brecht's *The Threepenny Opera*, a work emanating from Germany, a country that never colonized Nigeria. Adopting a more long-term, historical perspec-

---

9   Christina Schäffner and Beverly Adab, 'The idea of the hybrid text in translation: Contact as conflict', *Across Languages and Cultures*, 2.2 (2001), 167–80 (p. 168).
10   Jan Nederveen Pieterse, *Globalization and Culture: Global Mélange* (Lanham: Rowman & Littlefield Publishers, Inc., 2009), p. 79.

tive on globalization,[11] we could say that the hybridity in such works is due to globalization projects, including colonialism and various other forms of cultural contact, recently intensified by increased travel and encounters through media and technology. Within the social sciences and cultural studies the idea that globalization results in cultural hybridity (understood as ongoing mixing) is now becoming the cornerstone of a leading, postmodern hybridity paradigm[12] which has displaced two older paradigms associated with modernism (the ideas of cultural differentialism (that differences between cultures will always remain), and cultural convergence (that cultures will grow increasingly similar)). Hybridization, according to globalization theorist Jan Nederveen Pieterse, is associated with notions such as travelling culture,[13] and can be defined as 'the ways in which [cultural] forms become separated from existing practices and recombine with new forms in new practices'.[14] For Nederveen Pieterse, studying hybridization becomes a matter of coming 'to terms with phenomena such as Thai boxing by Moroccan girls in Amsterdam, [and] Asian rap in London'.[15] These are examples of objects of hybridity, which Burke distinguishes according to three types: artefacts, practices, and people.[16] Within the sub-category of artefacts, Burke lists architecture, furniture, images, texts and literary genres.[17] Hybrid practices, he continues, 'may be identified in religion, music, language, sport, festivals and other cultural domains',[18] and he draws particular attention to music and language as arenas where we find many striking examples of cultural hybridization.[19] The current volume supports this observation, insofar as the entirety of the second half is dedicated to contributions that deal with song lyrics, and two of the contributions (Smith-Sivertsen, and Greenall) focus on language mixing or code-switching.

---

11   Ibid., pp. 15ff.
12   Ibid., p. viii.
13   Ibid., p. 44.
14   William Rowe and Vivian Shelling, Memory and Modernity: *Popular Culture in Latin America* (London: Verso, 1991), p. 231.
15   Nederveen Pieterse, *Globalization and Culture*, p. 75.
16   Burke, *Cultural Hybridity*, p. 13.
17   Ibid., p. 17.
18   Ibid., p. 21.
19   Ibid., p. 23, 26. See also Kraidy, *Hybridity*, p. 141ff.

Within social sciences and cultural studies, the term hybridity has had a neutral, even positive flavour, and has been criticized by some for offering an overly harmonious image of something that often does not deserve that label.[20] The stark contrast to how the notion is often interpreted in the context of postcolonialism draws attention to the fact that the concept's extensive use in a multitude of different contexts has made it problematically ambiguous.[21] A number of alternative concepts have been employed to denote the same or similar cultural processes and products, such as mosaic, bricolage, palimpsest, borrowing, creolization, métissage, localization, glocalization, syncretism, crossover, appropriation, accommodation, cultural translation, and so on. Most of these are, however, less overarching in nature than hybridity insofar as each tends to emphasize a different aspect of the processes and products in question: mosaic points to a juxtaposition of pieces where each individual piece retains its integrity but assists in creating a new whole; palimpsest indicates, perhaps, a more deeply integrated mix; borrowing accentuates provenance, appropriation[22] highlights receptive agency, and so on. *Mélange* does not yet figure as an established concept on this list[23] and has thus been chosen here because of its potential to yield a fresh start – it is simply intended to denote a blend of elements belonging to categories that are somehow experienced as different from each other, and functioning in relation to each other (strongly or weakly) as figures vs. grounds.

The role of translation

Two of the contributions to this volume (Oittinen, and Mitchell and Angelsen) have translation as their main focus, and many of the remainder also touch on the role of translation in the creation of mélange, or on the challenges of translating culturally mixed source texts. Exploring hybridity (their term) in trans-

---

20 Burke, *Cultural Hybridity*, p. 7.
21 Ibid., p. 13.
22 Ibid., pp. 54–5.
23 Although it has been used, most notably in Nederveen Pieterse's book *Globalization and Culture*, where 'mélange' is used as a simple synonym for hybridity. In his book, the label seems mainly to have been brought in for its ability – in the context of an English-language text – to illustrate what it designates.

lation, Schäffner and Adab define hybrid texts as ones that 'show features that somehow seem "out of place"/"strange"/"unusual" for the receiving culture'.[24] Such texts can be original texts produced in a cultural space-in-between,[25] or they can be translations.[26] As regards the latter, Schäffner and Adab distinguish between true hybrids, the results of positive translatorial decisions, and texts that emerge as peculiar merely because of the translator's lack of competence.[27] According to Schäffner and Adab, not *all* translations are hybrids. This view is contested by others, e.g. Neubert,[28] who argues that a translation, any translation, cannot help containing features of the original, and is therefore, by definition, always hybrid. A similar point is made by Haugen (this volume).

For Schäffner and Adab, translation-induced hybridity is seen to reside at the levels of genre, text and/or language.[29] Within translation studies, it is generally acknowledged that the adoption of genres and text types through translation causes hybridization, which may eventually give rise to new genres and text types.[30] The challenge of genre translation emanates strongly from Stenkløv's contribution, which examines the play *Victor Hugo, My Love* and its projected translation into Norwegian. Two other major issues to do with translation and mélange are also touched upon in the volume. The first concerns original texts that are culturally hybrid: what happens to these in translation? This is one of the questions asked in Fioupou's chapter on Soyinka's *Opera Wonyosi*. It is an important question that has yet to be empirically resolved – do translators tend to function as gatekeepers between languages, or as contributors to mélange? Some scholars[31] are adamant that hybrid texts mostly if not always become dehybridized in translation, while others claim the oppo-

---

24 Schäffner and Adab, 'The idea of the hybrid text in translation', p. 167.
25 Schäffner and Adab, 'The idea of the hybrid text in translation revisited', *Across Languages and Cultures*, 2.2 (2001), 277–302 (p. 279).
26 Ibid., p. 277.
27 Schäffner and Adab, 'The idea of the hybrid text in translation', p. 167.
28 Albrecht Neubert, 'Some implications of regarding translations as hybrid texts', *Across Languages and Cultures*, 2.2 (2001), 181–93.
29 Schäffner and Adab, 'The idea of the hybrid text in translation revisited', p. 288.
30 This point is made, e.g. in Sonja Tirkkonen-Condit, 'EU project proposals as hybrid texts', *Across Languages and Cultures*, 2.2 (2001), 261–64.
31 E.g. Anthony Pym, 'Against praise of hybridity', *Across Languages and Cultures*, 2.2 (2001), 195–206.

site.[32] The second issue, which is represented in the contribution by Oittinen, concerns plurisemiotic/multimodal texts in translation. The complexity of these texts makes them a particularly interesting case, insofar as they contain modal hybridity as well as other forms of hybridity, adding an additional layer to the mix. They also contain elements – notably visual elements – that to a greater degree than the accompanying text tend to remain unchanged in translation, something which often causes interesting cultural mélanges to arise.

The contributions

'Since "everything is hybrid"', states Nederveen Pieterse, 'hybridity is an avalanche and discussing examples of hybridity is like drinking from a fire hydrant. It follows that only those forms of hybridity are worth discussing that illuminate the variety, spread, depth and meaning of hybridity, or that shed light on history, past or future'.[33] Unified by their focus on globalization-induced mélange, the different case studies presented here, which deal with travel literature, theatre, picture books, music lyrics, and so on, certainly illustrate the great variety of possible objects of hybridity within the field of art and popular culture. Furthermore, they shed light on the spread of the phenomenon: studies on cultural hybridity have, because of the urgency in addressing postcolonial issues, tended to be focused on the Americas, Africa and Asia, and although a couple of the contributions to the present volume also have those areas as their focus, the majority take us into geographical regions hitherto little explored with respect to hybridity or mélange, namely Western, Eastern and Northern Europe. Especially novel is the focus on Scandinavia. This is an area with no recent colonization history, which means that it has previously been considered of little interest in regards to issues such as the ones addressed here. It is, however, an area that has been experiencing extremely rapid hybridization in the last few decades, due to more recent phases of globalization, which have brought with them, among other things, consid-

---

32 See Rainier Grutman, 'Multilingualism and translation', in *Routledge Encyclopedia of Translation Studies*, ed. by Mona Baker (London: Routledge, 2001), pp. 157–60 (p. 160).
33 Nederveen Pieterse, *Globalization and Culture*, p. viii.

erable anglification. Another aspect that sets the book apart is its interdisciplinarity. Bringing together contributions from literary studies, discourse analysis, sociolinguistics, musicology and translation studies, it aims to illuminate the 'depth and meaning' of mélange by considering it from various perspectives.

The first part of the book, Literary and Theatrical Practices, begins with a chapter by Marius Warholm Haugen on the eighteenth-century travel memoirs of the Polish, French-speaking author Jean Potocki. In it, Haugen demonstrates that Potocki's texts are composite entities and suggests that hybridity might in some cases be genre-defining, insofar as a mixing of genres, blurring of fact and fiction, and borrowing genres and texts from a foreign source (often in translated form), seem to be recurrent features of travel memoirs. Haugen also draws attention to hybrid aspects of the practice of writing travelogues: authors would often hybridize themselves by dressing up to look like the inhabitants of the places they visited in an attempt at cultural immersion, to ensure an unhampered understanding of the culture. In chapter 3, Nelly Foucher Stenkløv examines French playwright Anthéa Sogno's *Victor Hugo, My Love* (2009), a play based on the historical love affair between the great author Victor Hugo and Juliette Drouet. Stenkløv focuses on the play's mix of genres (letters, poems, dialogue), addressing the consequences of this kind of mélange for the play's translation. Drawing on a cognitive framework, Stenkløv demonstrates what goes on in the process of intrusion of one generic form into another, and how the resulting generic cocktail necessitates *cultural* processing, which poses obvious challenges for potential translators of the play. Chapter 4 continues the focus on theatre; Christiane Fioupou discusses Wole Soyinka's *Opera Wonyosi*, a satire of inequity and corruption in Nigeria following the 1970s oil boom. The play combines various genres (dialogue, music, song and dance), elements from European theatre (*The Beggar's Opera*, and *The Threepenny Opera*) and British songs (e.g. 'Who Killed Cock Robin'; 'Mud, Mud, Glorious Mud'), in addition to a collection of cultural elements and languages stemming from Nigeria's colonial past. Fioupou highlights artistic resourcefulness as a source of mélange, showing how Soyinka founded the Guerilla Theatre Unit, a form of protest that 'was taken to the streets, markets and other open public places as *agit-prop*, "Guerilla" or "Shotgun" theatre'. Like Stenkløv, Fioupou comments on the challenges of translating a composite work, focusing on how the translation process will add another level to the mélange. Chapter 5 examines the novel *Trop de soleil tue l'amour* (1999), written by Cameroonian Francophone author Mongo Beti. The chapter's author, Inger Hesjevoll Schmidt-Melbye, investigates the author's narrative style, looking especially at linguistic mélange, showing how Beti combines a 'constant play with French language and culture', African oral elements, and code switching between French, English and local languages. Schmidt-Melbye questions whether such a use of mélange must always have a predominantly political purpose, and sets out to investigate its aesthetic effects. In chapter 6, Sophie Vauclin extracts material from a contemporary French novel, *Les Morues* by Titiou Lecoq, using it to conduct a sociolinguistic study of the phenomenon of "Franglais", a (highly negative) term used for the borrowing of English words and expressions into the French language. Vauclin looks at a number of English loanwords in terms of their understandability among different age groups within the French population, taking understanding as a measure of a word's level of integration into the French language. Vauclin's study draws attention to two important ideas; firstly, that foreign elements are integrated to varying degrees in a language and (by extension) in texts, and secondly, that the nature and depth of a given mélange may differ among different audiences. A similar issue underlies chapter 7, which deals with the translation of multimodal texts. Riitta Oittinen looks at Finnish author and illustrator Mauri Kunna's picture book adaptation of the Finnish national epic *The Kalevala*, viz. *Koirien Kalevala*, and its translation into Swedish (*Hundarnas Kalevala*) and English (*The Canine Kalevala*). In both translations cultural mélange is the result as the original illustrations have been retained while the actual text has been adapted to the new culture. The contrasts between illustration and text are less marked, however, for the Swedish readership than the British, since the familiarity with Finnish culture is much greater in Sweden than in Britain. In the words of Oittinen: '[a]ll in all, verbally, visually, and aurally, the different versions depict and form different cultural mélanges'.

The second part of the book – Textual-Musical Practices – opens with a chapter by Priscilla Ringrose, who looks at the re-territorialization and interpretation of US hip hop culture in France in the 1980s and 90s. Ringrose looks at the extent to which the two main community-forming strategies used in the USA – black militant nationalism with an Islamic thrust and Afrocentrism – were deployed on French soil. She shows how these movements were transposed from American inner cities to the French *banlieues* by virtue of imitation of their proponents' cultural-historical styles, but also by virtue of indigenization, in the form of a focus on recent, French colonial history, expressed in the discourses and lyrics of various French rap groups. Chapter 9 revolves around cultural and linguistic hybridity in Scandinavian popular music. Henrik Smith-Sivertsen takes as his point of departure modern technologies which lead to increasing cultural contact and Anglophone dominance within popular music in Denmark and Scandinavia. Smith-Sivertsen traces the development of different kinds of cultural-linguistic mélanges (German/Danish, English/Danish) in the period from the early twentieth century up until today, demonstrating the deeply complex nature of hybridity within this field – involving, for example, the frequent co-presence in Danish charts of original artists singing in English and Danish artists singing the same songs in English or Danish (with original or translated lyrics). Anglophone dominance within popular music and code-switching between a Scandinavian language and English is also the topic of chapter 10. Here, Annjo K. Greenall shows how the use of code-switching in Norwegian song lyrics has evolved from its early emergence in the 1960s up until today, relating these developments to changes in the status and role of the English language in Norway during the same period. Greenall analyses a number of lyrics, showing that while the earliest instances of code-switching are sparse, with English insertions first and foremost playing a role as part of the narrative, later examples show English serving more of a text-structuring and/or identity-building function, with artists aiming to connect with audiences both intranationally and internationally. In chapter 11, Anne Karine Kleveland continues the focus on song lyrics. However, in this study, the lyrics are not embedded in a socio-musical context, but in a literary one. Kleveland shows that song lyrics (real-life or made up, translated or untranslated) in the prose fiction of Norwegian author Kjartan Fløgstad often punctuate the text, causing cultural and linguistic compositeness. English is the most frequent language inserted, but other languages, such as Spanish, German and French, are also represented. Kleveland shows how these insertions contribute to Fløgstad's literary language in causing high semantic density, providing a ludic element, and creating an overall estranging style that forces a specific kind of reading, perhaps demanding a certain type of reader. The chapter that rounds off the volume, by Domhnall Mitchell and Anja Angelsen, targets song translation more specifically, presenting a study of the lyrics for Leonard Cohen's song 'Famous Blue Raincoat'. Tracing not only the translation but also the mediation of these lyrics into three Nordic languages and cultures, Norwegian, Swedish and Danish, this contribution keenly illustrates how mélange in an original text is often transformed and intensified through translation. According to the authors, 'the song's referential landscape is inherently hybrid [...] it contains elements of Eastern and Western religions, European popular culture in a mediated form, contrasting topographies and social history (in the shape of open relationships and sexual liberation, social and spiritual experimentation and the rise of feminism during the sixties)'. The chapter traces the journey of some of these references to Scandinavia through translations that either retain and transform them by virtue of inserting them into a target context where they acquire new meanings, or get rid of them, instead creating other forms of mélange due to conscious cultural transplantation. By virtue of its focus on translators' choices, the analysis offered in this chapter strongly challenges the idea that mélange should be anything as simple as a *result* of globalization processes. Like the other contributions to the volume, this final contribution rather suggests that mélange is a consistent, active *part of* those processes, driving them dynamically forwards, constantly taking part in shaping the *réalités mixtes* that constitute our lives.

Bibliography

Bakhtin, Mikhail M., *The Dialogic Imagination*, trans. by Caryl Emerson and Michael Holquist (Austin: University of Texas Press, 1981).
Burke, Peter, *Cultural Hybridity* (Cambridge, UK: Polity, 2009).
Grutman, Rainier, 'Multilingualism and translation', in *Routledge Encyclopedia of Translation Studies*, ed. by Mona Baker (London: Routledge, 2001), pp. 157–60.
Kraidy, Marwan M., *Hybridity, or the Cultural Logic of Globalization* (Philadelphia: Temple University Press, 2005).
Linde, Heidi, *Nu jävlar* (Oslo: Gyldendal, 2011).
Nederveen Pieterse, Jan, *Globalization and Culture: Global Mélange* (Lanham: Rowman & Littlefield Publishers, Inc., 2009).

Neubert, Albrecht, 'Some implications of regarding translations as hybrid texts', *Across Languages and Cultures*, 2.2 (2001), 181–93.

Norevik, Silje Stavrum, 'Denne boka bør du lese i vår: Skarpt skrevet fra søvnige Kongsvinger', *Dagbladet*, 4 March 2011, Reviews section <http://www.dagbladet.no/2011/04/03/kultur/bok/litteratur/litteraturanmeldelser/anmeldelser/16033544/> [accessed 6 January 2014].

Oxford English Dictionary Online <http://www.oed.com/view/Entry/154916?RedirectedFrom=purity#eid> [accessed 6 January 2014].

Pym, Anthony, 'Against praise of hybridity', *Across Languages and Cultures*, 2.2 (2001), 195–206.

Rowe, William and Vivian Shelling, *Memory and Modernity: Popular Culture in Latin America* (London: Verso, 1991).

Said, Edward W., *Culture and Imperialism* (London: Vintage, 1993).

Schäffner, Christina and Beverly Adab, 'The idea of the hybrid text in translation: Contact as conflict', *Across Languages and Cultures*, 2.2 (2001), 167–80.

Schäffner, Christina and Beverly Adab, 'The idea of the hybrid text in translation revisited', *Across Languages and Cultures*, 2.2 (2001), 277–302.

Tirkkonen-Condit, Sonja, 'EU project proposals as hybrid texts', *Across Languages and Cultures*, 2.2 (2001), 261–64.

PART I
Literary and Theatrical Practices

2 Friction, facts and fiction: Hybridity in Jean Potocki's 'Oriental' travelogues

Marius Warholm Haugen

The travel memoirs of the Polish Francophone author Jean Potocki (1761–1815) are remarkable documents that put into literary form the circumstances of intercultural encounters in the late eighteenth century. They are remarkable both in their awareness of the issues attached to such encounters, and because of their composite nature, generically and linguistically. Can the term *hybridity* bring something new to our understanding of these texts?

There is certainly something about hybridity that is immediately appealing to many literary critics. Postcolonial criticism, especially, has made extensive use of the term, linking it to 'the idea of cross-fertilisation between [the] constitutive elements' of a postcolonial culture.[1] In the almost proverbially globalized world of the postcolonial era, where intercultural encounters, and conflicts, are repeatedly subject to ideological as well as critical debates, hybridity is often evoked to account for and to analyse their creative potential.

However, could a term closely linked to this specific school of literary and cultural criticism be pertinent for analyses of texts from an early modern setting? For Gesa Stedman, author of a recent publication on cultural exchange in seventeenth-century France and England, the answer appears to be no. Categories such as 'third space' and hybridity seem 'too closely tied to the par-

---

1 Bill Ashcroft, Gareth Griffiths, and Helen Tiffin, eds., *The Post-Colonial Studies Reader* (London: Routledge, 1995), p. 184.

ticular needs of the historical moment in which this field was first opened up – the later decades of the twentieth century' and 'are not effective enough for the analysis of early modern development'.[2] When used to study cultural exchange, such categories would not be sufficiently exact to account for the historical specificities of this period, according to Stedman.

Contrary to this view, I would argue that hybridity could indeed be a fruitful tool, if not for a broader cultural analysis, then at least in analyses of individual works from the early modern period. This is because it has the advantage of being applicable to several aspects of a text, on a generic and linguistic level as well as a cultural. Hybridity allows a critic to approach a text from different angles, while at the same time keeping to a common, thematic perspective. It could, in fact, prove quite appropriate to speak of hybridity in the context of the eighteenth century, at a time when writers increasingly concerned themselves with otherness, through a rising interest in non-European cultures, languages and literatures. And it seems even more appropriate when we take into account that a large amount of texts from this period appear as generically composite entities. In this respect, travel literature has some especially interesting qualities, as we shall soon see.

Moreover, the term hybridity has a history that stretches far beyond the horizon of postcolonial studies, thus evoking semantic layers that may in themselves be fruitful for a hermeneutical analysis. Initially a biological term referring to a *bastard*, often a breed of a wild boar and a pig, it has been used throughout history to describe different forms of composite objects, outcomes resulting of meetings between two (or indeed several) entities. These entities could be biological, linguistic, literary and cultural. From the seventeenth century on, it was used particularly as a linguistic term, applied to words composed from different languages, especially Greek and Latin.[3]

Could an analysis that departs from such a context even give something back to our understanding of the term itself? When applying the term on to

---

2   Gesa Stedman, *Cultural Exchange in Seventeenth-Century France and England* (Aldershot: Ashgate, 2013), p. 11.
3   This is the use of the term that appears in Diderot and d'Alemberts Encyclopédie. See the entry *hibrides* in *Encyclopédie, ou Dictionnaire raisonné des sciences, des arts et des métiers* (1751–1772) <http://portail.atilf.fr/encyclopedie/> [accessed 22 April 2013].

a cultural sphere, using it metaphorically as it were, we need to ask what distinguishes hybridity from other metaphors for meetings applicable on cultural objects, such as the mélange, the mosaic or the puzzle. Whereas mélange, for example, gives certain connotations of seamlessness and even organic blends, there is a significant element of friction contained in the notion of hybridity. And where both mosaic and puzzle refer to a harmonious whole comprised of different parts, hybridity is associated with monstrosity, as in the case of the Greek *Chimera*. In the *Encyclopédie*, Diderot even describes linguistic hybrids as *monstres*.[4] Hybridity seems thus to refer to something that is disturbing, or at the very least highly confusing, to the viewer or to the reader. I would therefore claim that the great benefit of applying hybridity as an analytical tool – regardless of the historical frame of the text in question – is that it allows us to highlight the frictional and disturbing aspects of, and between, elements that make a composite text.

This, however, remains to be tested, and we shall do so by turning to two travelogues of the Polish count Jean Potocki, originally written in French. It was with his journey to Turkey and Egypt in 1784, at the age of 23, that Potocki the traveller for the first time coincided with Potocki the author. The memoirs from his journey, taking the form of a series of letters addressed to his mother, were published in Warsaw in 1788, revealing the unmistakable talent of a minute observer and a brilliant stylist.[5] He returned to the African continent in 1791, with a journey to Morocco that would give him the opportunity to further assert himself as a writer, not only of factual prose, but also of fiction.

What characterizes these two memoirs is precisely their composite nature. In neither of them does the author confine himself to observations and descriptions of the countries he is visiting. He also gives historical accounts, adds fictional tales and quotes long passages from other authors. In the case of the

---

4   Ibid.
5   As François Rosset and Dominique Triaire point out in their introduction to Potocki's travelogue, we cannot know for sure whether the letters that form the text really were sent, or even written, to his mother prior to their publication. Anne Thérèse Potocka is nonetheless presented as the addressee of the letters, and the published travelogue is dedicated to her. See François Rosset and Dominique Triaire, 'Présentation', in Jean Potocki, *Voyage dans l'Empire de Maroc, suivi du Voyage de Hafez* (Leuven: Peeters, 2004), p. 7.

Voyage dans l'Empire de Maroc [*Travels in the Moroccan Empire*], Potocki cites entire pages of a report written by a local chronicler, describing the reign of the current emperor, Moulay Yazid: 'Ce que je vais écrire sera donc le mémoire que cet homme m'a donné, & que j'accompagnerai seulement de quelques commentaires'.⁶ The report is incorporated in Potocki's text without markers, and he also keeps the first person form of the original narrator. As for Potocki's own commentaries, they are embedded in the report also without markers, with the effect that the reader must stay alert to be able to distinguish between the two voices, the 'je' of the author of the report and the 'je' of Potocki.

Even more voices are to be added to the choir, for when the report has been exhausted, the Polish author turns to other, unnamed sources:⁷

> The European consuls residing in Tanger came together to Tetuan to present themselves before the Emperor, who received them very badly. The report does not say anything else about it, but having made enquiries elsewhere, I shall give the full report of His Majesty's dialogue:
>
> The Emperor. Which one of you is the English consul?
> The Qaid. Here he is.
> The Emperor. I'm friend of the English. Which one is the consul of the Ragusians?
> The Qaid. There isn't one, & there has never been one.
> The Emperor. That doesn't matter, I'm friend of the Ragusians. Where is the consul of Spain?
> The Qaid. Here he is.
> The Emperor. You shall leave my States, and so shall your merchants. I give them six months to settle accounts.
> The Qaid. And the other consuls?
> The Emperor. Let them go dine with the Spaniard. (p. 148)

The approach is quite astonishing, almost theatrical, as the author distributes lines in direct speech to the two 'main characters'. Some pages earlier, Potocki has used a similar technique when presenting a dialogue between the late

---

6 Jean Potocki, *Voyage dans l'Empire de Maroc, suivi du Voyage de Hafez* (Leuven: Peeters, 2004), p. 146. 'What I'm going to write is the report that this man has given to me, and I shall accompany it only with a few commentaries'. This, and all subsequent translations of Potocki's texts are mine. I have kept the original ortography in all the French quotations.
7 Due to the length of the quotation, only the English translation is given here.

emperor Sidi Mohammed ben Abdallah (1720–1790) and one of his subjects, creating what appears almost as the script to an historical reenactment (p. 135). In other words, in his attempt to understand the history and the political life of Morocco, and in order to transmit his knowledge to the reader, the future novelist employs techniques belonging to the domain of the *belles-lettres*. The text appears, at least to a modern reader, as a fictionalization of factual events.

Thus the text seems to blur the border between fact and fiction in a way that would become a constant in Potocki's writing, in later travelogues as well as in his plays and prose fiction.[8] The protagonist of his novel *Manuscrit trouvé à Saragosse* [*The Manuscript Found in Saragossa*], for instance, is deeply troubled when he reads a fictional account identical to his own story, revealing to him his own fictional nature.[9] And in the travelogue from Potocki's journey to China in 1805, factual *personae* would appear in fictionalized form, as veritably novelistic characters.[10] In this way, hybridity may also be applied as a metaphor for the mix of discourses belonging to different sides of the fact-fiction border; the friction of the matter, or even the monstrosity of it, is the result of the unease that is brought about when fiction invades reality.

The composite nature of the text is also striking in the *Voyage en Turquie et en Égypte* [*Travels in Turkey and Egypt*], published a few years before the Moroccan journey. In this case, Potocki adds to his own text two tales that he claims to have heard in Constantinople from a local storyteller:

> Un conteur de profession rapporte l'aventure la plus nouvelle, en l'ornant de tous les agréments de l'élocution orientale; en voici une que j'entendis raconter hier dans un Café du fauxbourg de scutari, & que j'ai mise aussi-tôt par écrit; elle pourra vous donner une idée de leur manière de s'énoncer.[11]

---

8   Potocki's *Œuvres* have been published in five volumes (volume IV consists of two books) at Peeters, Leuven, 2004–2006, edited by François Rosset and Dominique Triaire.
9   Jean Potocki, *Manuscrit trouvé à Saragosse (version de 1810)* (Leuven: Peeters, 2006), p. 134.
10 Jean Potocki, *Mémoire sur l'ambassade en Chine* (Leuven: Peeters, 2004). Dominique Triaire has analysed this aspect of Potocki's travelogue in his article 'De la "difficulté de s'entendre" ou l'apparition de l'imbécile', in *Wiek Oświecenia*, 28 (2012), 72–83.
11 Jean Potocki, *Voyage en Turquie et en Égypte* (Leuven: Peeters, 2004), p. 23. 'A professional storyteller gives the most recent adventure, embellishing it with all the charm of Oriental eloquence; here is one that I heard yesterday in a café in a faubourg of Shkodër, and which I immediately put in writing; it may give you an idea of their way of expressing themselves'.

It is difficult to determine whether the storyteller in question spoke French or whether the tales were translated either by an interpreter or by Potocki himself. According to Daniel Beauvois, the count did possess a certain degree of understanding of both Turkish and Persian.[12] It is most likely, therefore, that Potocki translated the tales – as he also claims himself a few pages further on (p. 25) – although perhaps through the help of an interpreter.[13] In any case, what is important in this context is that the tales are embedded into the running text of the published version, adding to the impression that there is something fundamentally hybrid about the text, when it comes to form and genre.

There is of course also an intercultural element at play here. Potocki's text creates a meeting between two genres belonging to different cultural spheres, the Oriental tale and the Western travelogue. Furthermore, the tales that the author shares with his readers are more than just a curiosity for him, for they are at the core of his project of understanding the culture he is visiting. In Constantinople, the Polish adventurer takes care to criticize other European travellers who show no interest in the Turkish parts of the city, being content with visiting its Greek monuments (p. 19). He makes claim to a very different approach:

> Nourrie par l'étude de l'histoire & de la littérature des orientaux, ma curiosité m'a fait suivre une autre marche. Depuis près d'un mois, je passe les journées entieres à parcourir les rues de cette Capitale, sans autre but que de me rassasier du plaisir d'y être.[14]

Knowledge of Oriental history and literature stimulates the traveller's curiosity, and naturally enhances the capacity to understand the culture. Potocki is acting as an ethnologist *ante litteram* in considering storytelling and other forms of amusement as a privileged source of cultural understanding: 'J'ai employé deux lettres entières à vous parler des amusements des Turcs, parce que j'ai

---

12 Daniel Beauvois, 'Introduction. Jean Potocki, voyageur', in Jean Potocki, *Voyages en Turquie et en Égypte, en Hollande, au Maroc* (Paris: Fayard, 1980), pp. 14–15.
13 It was in Constantinople that he acquired the services of Ibrahim, a Turkish servant who would remain with him until Potocki died in 1815. See François Rosset and Dominique Triaire, *Jean Potocki – biographie* (Paris: Éditions Flammarion, 2004), p. 98. It is possible that Ibrahim served as an interpreter.
14 Ibid. 'Nourished by the study of the history and the literature of the Orientals, my curiosity has made me follow a different path. For more than a month now, I spend the entire days running about the streets of this capital, without any other goal than to take satisfaction in the joy of being here'.

cru qu'un peuple s'y peignoit mieux, que dans toutes les autres circonstances de sa vie privée'[15] (p. 37). If Potocki's travelogue appears as a hybrid text, both generically and culturally, it is partly because it is driven by a project of understanding the Other, as well as by a desire to share this understanding with the reader.

The sort of hybridity we find in Potocki's memoirs is quite a common characteristic of the genre of travel memoirs. Travelling has often given birth to a form of writing that operates with mixed generic traits, blending observations and descriptions of customs and events with dialogues and reflexions, and quite frequently combining factual prose with fiction.[16] If we take a quick detour to look at one of the great travel writers of the twentieth century, Bruce Chatwin, we may observe some interesting similarities with Potocki's text. In his breakthrough book, *In Patagonia*, from 1977, the British author systematically mixes the account of his own journey with stories and legends, both of people that he encounters and of historical figures that have been shaped by the land. In a similar way to Potocki, Chatwin creates fictitious dialogues between historical persons, fictionalizing historical events in order to make them become real in the mind of the reader.[17]

Chatwin's book is not a randomly chosen example, for it is symptomatic of the difficulties in determining the genre of a certain kind of travel writing, difficulties stemming from the disparate literary discourses contained in these texts. When *In Patagonia* was released in 1977, the critics had a hard time classifying it, and would turn to such labels as 'mosaic', 'puzzle' and 'collage'.[18] I would like to suggest that precisely *hybrid* might be a better term, in the sense that it entails the blending of parts that do not, in the mind of the reader, initially belong together, and for that reason might be perceived as frictional, or even troubling.

---

15   'I spent two full letters talking to you about the amusements of the Turkish, because I deemed that a people is thus better portrayed than in any other circumstance of its private life'. Inversely, a knowledge of customs and culture is a prerequisite for properly understanding foreign literature. In Morocco, Potocki notices how his direct observations allow him to better understand certain passages of his beloved *Mille et une nuits*. See *Voyage dans l'Empire de Maroc, suivi du Voyage de Hafez*, p. 111.
16   This is one of the central arguments of Arne Melberg's excellent book on travel writing: *Resa och skriva: en guide till den moderna reselitteraturen* (Göteborg: Daidalos, 2006).
17   Bruce Chatwin, *In Patagonia* (London: Vintage Books, 2005). See for instance p. 23.
18   Melberg, p. 11.

One of the elements to cause trouble is the question of generic determination that we see both in Chatwin and Potocki. If we are to believe Arne Melberg, determining the genre of this kind of travel writing is something that continues to trouble critics and other readers (p. 52). Even more troubling might be the uncertainty created as regards the relationship between factual and fictional elements in texts that aspire to say something about the real world. In fact, it is perhaps less the generic blend than the blending of different voices, hard to discern, and the blurred borders between fiction and reality, that trouble us when reading the travelogues of Potocki as well as of Chatwin.

If travel literature tends to be of a composite nature, and to play with uncertain boundaries between factual prose and fiction, it is also, by its very nature, regularly confronted with questions regarding language and translation. A traveller is necessarily forced to deal with differences of language or dialect, something that often resurfaces in the text.[19]

In Potocki's case, the linguistic element becomes particularly visible when we consider the Turkish tales embedded in the travelogue, which he claims to have translated himself into French. From a certain theoretical point of view, translation may in itself be seen as a sort of hybridity. The French poet and theorist Emmanuel Hocquard, for example, suggests a definition of translation as an 'entre-deux' ('half-way') between two languages,[20] something that is neither here nor there, neither this nor that.[21] If we look at one of the few passages where Potocki mentions his own practice of translating, we see that he reveals a certain awareness of this aspect of translation:

> J'ai donné le nom de récit à ce genre de composition, parce qu'il m'a paru répondre à celui de Hykaïet, que lui donnent les Lettrés de l'Orient. J'ai cherché de même à rendre avec exactitude leurs figures et leurs expressions ; & si j'y ai changé quelque chose, c'est en ôtant à leur richesse plutôt qu'en y ajoutant.[22]

---

19 Often, also, the very absence of linguistic commentary reveals a strategy of obscuring the fact of translation, in order to, in the terms of Michael Cronin, 'create the illusion of linguistic transparency'. Michael Cronin, *Across the Lines: Travel, Language, Translation* (Cork: Cork University Press, 2000), p. 3.
20 My translation.
21 Emmanuel Hocquard, Ma haie (Paris: P.O.L., 2001), p. 526.
22 *Voyage en Turquie et en Égypte*, p. 25. 'I have chosen to call this kind of composition 'story' [récit], because it seems to correspond with the word Hykaïet, by which the Oriental men of letters name it. I have likewise sought to render with exactitude their figures and expressions; and if I have changed something, I have done so by reducing their richness rather than adding to it'.

The passage is revelatory of the author's intuition that something goes missing in the transition from one language to the other, in this case the 'richness' of the Oriental manner. Aiming for 'exactitude' in his translation, Potocki seems nonetheless to sense the friction of the matter.

Potocki then moves to imitation when, inspired by his translations, he takes a shot at the genre himself. Four pastiches of 'Oriental tales' authored by the Polish count are included in the *Voyage en Turquie et en Égypte*, again in the running text, adding yet another aspect to its hybridity. In this case, the author's confidence in his own capacities, and in the possibilities of a seamless intercultural transference, is striking:

> Je ne sais trop comment vous trouverez les apologues des Orientaux; pour moi je raffole de leur maniere, & je m'y suis essayé: les lectures que j'ai faites depuis près de deux ans, m'ont rendu si riche en pensées orientales, que je n'ai eu que la peine d'en groupper quelques-unes & de leur donner des cadres. Je suis bien sûr d'avoir réussi à conserver à mes figures leur physionomie orientale, mais je ne suis pas également sûr que cette physionomie réussisse en Occident.[23] (pp. 26–27)

As we see, there are several concerns involved in this imitation: both the success of authentically rendering the nature of the characters, and the success these characters would have in pleasing Western readers. Whereas the latter is chiefly a literary concern, the former is also ethnological and epistemological. Have I succeeded in capturing the essence of the Other, Potocki seems to be asking – and responding affirmatively.

So we see how his project of understanding has shifted in strategy: the author is not only trying to translate the literature of the Orientals, but also somehow to put himself in their place, by way of imitation. If we were convinced by Potocki's self-confidence, we would perhaps be inclined to conclude that this has less to do with hybridity than with a sort of *total immersion*, a perfect adoption of the style and manner of the Other that completely obscures the original

---

23 'I don't know how you'll find the apologues of the Orientals; for my part, I relish in their style, and have made an attempt at it myself: the things I've read for more than two years now have made me so rich in Oriental thoughts, that I've only had to group some of them and put them within a frame. I'm quite confident of having been successful in conserving the Oriental physiognomy of my characters, but I'm not equally confident that this physiognomy would succeed in the West'.

identity of the Self. But this would mean ignoring the linguistic aspect of the matter: Potocki's French text, however successful it might be in capturing the 'Oriental manner', remains a translation, with all the difference this entails.

Moving from the level of language to the practice of travel itself, we may observe some interesting parallels. Writing Oriental tales was not the only attempt at immersion made by Potocki during his journey. Preparing to go to Egypt, the adventurer chose to put on a disguise:

> Je me prépare actuellement à ce voyage, que je dois faire dans cinq ou six jours. Déjà vous ne me reconnoîtriez plus. Je porte un grand turban à la Druse; j'ai la tête rasée, & des habits à l'Egyptienne, qui sont un peu différents de ceux de la Turquie.[24] (p. 45)

Dressing up like the locals is a quite common move in travel literature, and is usually described in theoretical approaches to the genre as a strategy of *going native*.[25] According to Arne Melberg, this is not just a practical move, but also a 'theatrical and symbolic act', an attempt to see the Other on her or his own premises (p. 62).[26] In Potocki's case, *going native* is both theatrical and literary, the disguise and the imitations of Oriental tales being different attempts at obtaining cultural immersion.

The success of the disguise seems first to be attested by the author's affirmation that it would fool even his own mother, who, as mentioned, is presented as the addressee of the letters that form the basis for the text. Again, however, Potocki experiences a noticeable degree of friction, this time in an encounter with an Egyptian mob:

> [...] malgré le soin que nous avions de nous tenir cachés derrieres des especes d'auvents, nos turbans à la Druse & notre air étranger nous avoient attiré l'attention de quelques jeunes Mamelucs, qui, d'un toit voisin, nous lançoient des oranges vertes & des pierres [...].[27] (p. 50)

---

24 'I'm preparing at the moment for the journey, which I have to make in five or six days. At this point you wouldn't have recognized me. I'm carrying a large turban in the Drusean style; I have shaved my head and am wearing Egyptian clothes, which are a bit different from the Turkish ones'.
25 Melberg, p. 73.
26 Ibid., p. 62.
27 '[...] despite the care we had taken to keep hidden behind some sort of canopy, our Drusean turbans and foreign appearance drew the attention of some young Mamelukes who, from a neighbouring roof, started throwing green oranges and stones at us [...]'.

Far from allowing Potocki to immerge seamlessly into the culture of the Other, his disguise appears precisely as theatrical, and as such draws attention to itself. Like his translations, like all translations perhaps, Potocki's disguise is a sort of 'half-way', between languages, customs and cultures. An appropriate term for this might be *going native*. He might even be well enough disguised to have passed unrecognized by his own mother. The result, however, is once again a hybrid, this time in the sense of an intercultural encounter revealing the friction of unsurpassable otherness.

When applied to this context, hybridity seems therefore to be linked to an epistemological concern that was central to the late Enlightenment era: the conflict between, on the one hand, the aspiration towards certain knowledge, and, on the other, the experience of the futility of this quest. The friction stemming from Potocki's attempt to understand the Other may have been revelatory of the limits of knowledge, quite disturbing for someone who lived by the maxim of 'Il faut d'abord savoir',[28] you first and foremost have to know.

If the overall tone of Potocki's travelogues remains rather optimistic with regard to the possibilities of knowledge, he emblematically concludes his Moroccan travel with a fictional tale that undermines the epistemological optimism of the factual prose. In this 'Oriental tale', entitled *Le Voyage de Hafez*, [*Hafez' Journey*] the eponymous protagonist sets out on a journey in order to seek the truth of the world and of the Other, in a way similar to the young Polish count himself. His travel companion, a wise dervish, concludes the story by exposing the futile nature of the quest.[29]

The conflict of optimism and scepticism is thus translated into a hybrid form, with a fictional travelogue that appears as a *mise en abyme* of the factual one, and which brings to the surface the frictions and the epistemological doubts that remained more implicit in the latter. As a matter of fact, the source of friction is double here, for it not only appears in the conflict between scientific optimism and scepticism, but also arises from the uncertain and blurry

---

28 Jean Potocki, *Écrits politiques* (Leuven: Peeters, 2004), p. 351. On the conflict between epistemological optimism and scepticism in the works of Potocki, see chapter 2.2 of my book *Jean Potocki: esthétique et philosophie de l'errance* (Leuven: Peeters, 2014).
29 Hafez's quest for knowledge makes the dervish characterize him as 'insensé', insane. *Voyage dans l'Empire de Maroc, suivi du Voyage de Hafez*, p. 196.

territory that separates fiction from reality. Although in this case not embedded in the running text, but added as an appendix, the fictional tale nonetheless invades the factual prose and threatens to overthrow its *raison d'être*: the search for the truth of the Other.

We have seen how hybridity operates on multiple levels in Potocki's travelogues: generic, linguistic, cultural and literary. As an analytical tool, the term allows us to bring out the frictional and disturbing elements of the text, and to discuss certain distinctive issues of this kind of travel literature, noticeably the problem of approaching and understanding otherness. The hybrid travelogue appears as the arch stone of an epistemological project aimed at understanding otherness; at the same time, hybridity reveals the limits to this very project.

Finally, *Le Voyage de Hafez*, the 'mirror-travelogue' that concludes Potocki's Moroccan journey, presents the notion that travel may in fact turn the traveller himself into a hybrid, by alienating him from his point of origin: 'Mes amis vous voyez le malheur des voyages: L'on y connoît des hommes selon son cœur, & il faut les quitter: Et tandis que vous rompez ces nouveaux liens, vous allez retrouver les anciens relâchés par l'absence & par l'inhabitude'[30] (p. 196). In other words, travel has its own disturbing features – the feeling of exile it creates, a sense of loss that comes from an alienating of the Self, as well as from the unsurpassable distance to the Other. What it also creates, perhaps from this very sense of loss, is the text.

Bibliography

Ashcroft, Bill, Gareth Griffiths and Helen Tiffin, eds., *The Post-Colonial Studies Reader* (London: Routledge, 1995).

Beauvois, Daniel, 'Introduction. Jean Potocki, voyageur', in Jean Potocki, *Voyages en Turquie et en Égypte, en Hollande, au Maroc* (Paris: Fayard, 1980), pp. 14–15.

Chatwin, Bruce, *In Patagonia* (London: Vintage Books, 2005).

Cronin, Michael, *Across the Lines: Travel, Language, Translation* (Cork: Cork University Press, 2000).

---

30 'My friends, you see the misfortune of travel: You get to know people according to your heart, and then you have to leave them. And while you tear these new bonds, you go to find the old ones loosened by absence and disuse'.

Diderot, Denis and Jean le Rond d'Alembert, eds., *Encyclopédie, ou Dictionnaire raisonné des sciences, des arts et des métiers* (1751–1772) <http://portail.atilf.fr/encyclopedie/> [accessed 22 April 2013].

Haugen, Marius Warholm, *Jean Potocki: esthétique et philosophie de l'errance* (Leuven: Peeters, 2014).

Hocquard, Emmanuel, *Ma haie* (Paris: P.O.L., 2001).

Melberg, Arne, *Resa och skriva: En guide till den moderna reselitteraturen* (Göteborg: Daidalos, 2006).

Potocki, Jean, *Écrits politiques* (Leuven: Peeters, 2004).

Potocki, Jean, *Manuscrit trouvé à Saragosse (version de 1810)* (Leuven: Peeters, 2006).

Potocki, Jean, *Mémoire sur l'ambassade en Chine* (Leuven: Peeters, 2004).

Potocki, Jean, *Voyage dans l'Empire de Maroc, suivi du Voyage de Hafez* (Leuven: Peeters, 2004).

Potocki, Jean, *Voyage en Turquie et en Égypte* (Leuven: Peeters, 2004).

Rosset, François and Dominique Triaire, *Jean Potocki – biographie* (Paris: Éditions Flammarion, 2004).

Rosset, François and Dominique Triaire, 'Présentation', in Jean Potocki, *Voyage dans l'Empire de Maroc, suivi du Voyage de Hafez* (Leuven: Peeters, 2004).

Stedman, Gesa, *Cultural Exchange in Seventeenth-Century France and England* (Aldershot: Ashgate, 2013).

Triaire, Dominique, 'De la "difficulté de s'entendre" ou l'apparition de l'imbécile', *Wiek Oświecenia*, 28 (2012), 72–83.

3 From Victor Hugo and Juliette Drouet to the rest of the world: A mélange of genres

Nelly Foucher Stenkløv

Victor Hugo, mon amour ou 'Aimer c'est plus que vivre' [*Victor Hugo, My Love or 'Love is More than Life'*], a play penned by Anthéa Sogno, charts the momentous love affair between Victor Hugo and Juliette Drouet which spanned half a century.[1] The text of the play is both the starting point and the corpus of this article. Largely ignored in Hugo's bibliographies, the correspondence between Hugo and Drouet, an actress, amounted to over 23,000 letters and ended on her death in 1883 at the age of 77. Drawing on this immense reservoir of letters and poems at the start of the twenty-first century, the playwright, actress and theatre director Anthéa Sogno produced a historically accurate play which has been performed more than 500 times in 130 French and Swiss cities to over 70,000 spectators since it premiered in 2009.

With reference to theories from cognitive science and genre studies, I focus on the complexities of generic hybridity in *Victor Hugo, My Love*. I begin by describing my first experience of the play, before situating it in relation to the theoretical concept of hybridity (or blending) as applied to genres, with particular attention to the works of Martina Allen,[2] Malrieu and Rastier,[3] and

---

1 <http://www.victor-hugo-mon-amour.fr/boutique-victor-hugo-mon-amour/> [accessed 1 October 2012]. All further references are to this online edition and are given parenthetically by scene number after quotations in the text. Unless otherwise noted, all translations in this chapter are my own.
2 Martina Allen, 'Against "hybridity" in genre studies: Blending as an alternative approach to generic experimentation'. *Trespassing Journal: An Online Journal of Trespassing Art, Science, and Philosophy* <http://trespassingjournal.com/Issue2/TPJ_I2_Allen_Article.pdf> [accessed 2 June 2014].
3 Denise Malrieu and François Rastier, 'Genres et variations morphosyntaxiques'. *Traitement Automatique des Langues*, 42.2 (2001), 548–77 [accessed 22 January 2013].

Rastier.[4] Secondly, I show how both thematic and stylistic aspects of *Victor Hugo, My Love* illustrate the difficulty of defining and labeling genres. Finally, again with reference to Allen and Rastier, I provide an exploration of the cognitive processes triggered by unexpected generic intrusions in the play, which in turn opens up for wider questions regarding generic hybridity, of which some will be discussed in some depth.

Victor Hugo, My Love

I saw the play for the first time in February 2012, at the Comédie Bastille in Paris. The play is set in 1833, when the young bestselling author, Victor Hugo, stages his play *Lucrezia Borgia*. Juliette Drouet, a dazzling and daring young woman is given a small role. While the ensuing love affair between writer and actress is portrayed as marked by fits of jealousy, tears and break ups, these passionate episodes do not propel the relationship towards a tragic *denouement*, but are rather seen to strengthen it. Juliette soon chooses to abandon her career as an actress in order to live as a recluse, in the shadow of her successful lover. In the play, Sogno draws heavily on the 23,650 letters exchanged by the lovers over the fifty years of their relationship (over 20,000 of which were written by Juliette), but while these lift the veil on the couple's secrets, they leave unresolved the question as to which of the two lovers fulfilled the role of muse for the other.

Observing the performance of the play, I was struck by the degree to which Sogno redistributes generic categories (letters, poems, speeches, and theatre), creating a seemingly harmonious mélange of voices and styles – but whether this allows the play to be categorized as 'a true mélange of genres' remains to be seen. In light of the heterogeneous corpus at hand, I have chosen to focus on a cognitive revisitation of the concept of hybrid genres, where the idea of generic mental spaces is central.

---

4   François Rastier, 'La traduction: interprétation et genèse du sens'. *Texto!* <http://www.revue-texto.net/Lettre/Rastier_Traduction.pdf> [accessed 23 January 2013].

Generic hybridization

According to David Duff, generic hybridization can be defined as the 'process by which two or more genres combine to form a new genre or subgenre; or by which elements of two or more genres are combined in a single work' (qtd. in Allen, p. 3). Although the definition may appear straightforward, it is flawed because it encompasses a too-vague view of the concept of genre. In fact, depending on what is assumed to be a genre in this definition, it is equally possible to speak of the genre of comedy as it is of the genre of drama even though the former is defined by the themes and the dialectics of the text (What is the text about? How is the text structured?), whereas the latter depends on the dialogical and tactical frames of the text (Who is talking to whom? What are the spatial and temporal frames of the plot?). Following from this, I can assert that *Victor Hugo, My Love* is a comedy, because it has a happy ending. But I can equally assert that it is a theatrical play because the story is dramatized in front of an audience, by actors who employ a combination of speech and gesture.

In other words, generic identification is blurred because the definition of the concept of genre itself is unstable, and the criteria by which genres can be identified are not clearly specified. In instances like these, both genres become fully compatible, merging into the subgenre of theatrical comedy. Contrary to Duff's view, however, I will claim that theatrical comedies are not the result of generic hybridization, in the sense of a process that brings together elements that can or should not be mixed. In the discussion of hybridization that follows, my argument will be developed in four stages. First, I will define the process as a dynamic cognitive one that originates in the human capacity to associate elements in order to meet practical, cultural and linguistic challenges. Secondly, I will apply this very general assumption to the study of genres. Each genre corresponds to a mental space. The phenomenon of hybridization thus assumes input from one mental space into another. For this reason, I prefer to use the terms 'mélange' or 'cocktail' since they give a concrete picture of the actual act of blending separate elements. Third, I show how this input or insertion functions as a type of intrusion which may have a powerful effect on the audience – creating something resembling a shock. By using the concept of generic components from a model introduced by Malrieu and Rastier (2002), I argue that these shocks are due to a confrontation between different generic expectations. Finally, I use examples from *Victor Hugo, My Love* to illustrate how mélange, brought about by a process involving separate mental spaces with input travelling from one to the other, often necessitates cultural disambiguation, which will favour audiences familiar with a given cultural reference.

A cognitive revisitation of the process of mélange

In a critique of the notion of hybridity in genre studies (2013), Martina Allen draws a parallel between literary and generic studies. 'Saying that [...] a [given] combination constitutes a hybrid is like saying that a motorbike is a hybrid because it combines the notion of "bike" with that of a motorized vehicle, or that a house cat is a hybrid because it can be classified both as a predator and as a pet' (Allen, p. 6). Whereas Allen seems to think that the lack of a clear boundary between the conceptual categories these notions belong to makes it problematic to define hybridity, Fauconnier and Turner take a somewhat different tack:

> We can bring two things together mentally in various ways. Blending them is one subset of those ways, and the blends that satisfy the governing principles are a much smaller subset. An even smaller subset consists of those core compression patterns that are entrenched in a culture. The next subset down consists of those entrenched compression patterns that have associated grammatical forms.[5]

In the light of Fauconnier and Turner's claim that human beings have developed a unique capacity for 'double-scope blending', I will argue that the phenomenon of joining words in expressions such as 'motorbike', 'wildcat' or 'car-boot' can be applied to the field of genre studies. Assuming with Fauconnier and Turner that genres can be conceived of as 'mental spaces' facilitated by textual constructions, the concept of 'blended genres' becomes both more practical and scientifically relevant than the concept of 'hybrid genres' because it implies a dynamic: What enables us to assert that a text facilitates

---

5   Gilles Fauconnier and Mark Turner, *The Way we Think: Conceptual Blending and the Mind's Hidden Complexities* (NY: Basic Books, 2003), p. 353.

generic mélange is that it causes the actual intrusion of one mental space into another (input space). Bridges are then required between these spaces in order to create a 'partial cross-space mapping [which] connects counterparts in the input spaces' (Allen, p. 12). However, no matter how tight those connections might be, the cognitive approach emphasizes that the process of blending or mélange nevertheless involves a confrontation between generic expectations.

Confrontations between generic expectations

In order to apply the idea of input spaces to the field of genre studies, I draw on the model developed by Denise Malrieu and François Rastier (pp. 548–54). This model is of interest here because it combines generic criteria that involve cognitive dynamics that are compatible with the idea of mental spaces. According to Malrieu and Rastier, 'one can conceive of the production and the interpretation of texts as a non-sequential interaction of autonomous components'.[6] Some of these 'autonomous components' are particularly relevant to my argument. They are the following:

- THEMATICS: The themes reflect the contents, i.e. the semantic universe implemented in the text. In terms of production and interpretation, this involves identifying the main notions the given text deals with.
- DIALECTICS: Dialectics reflect the time frame shown, and the given sequence of events and states.
- DIALOGICS: Dialogics refers to the way that the overall communication works in a text (who speaks to whom). It assumes that utterances involve the interaction of diverse perspectives and that they are embedded in a socio-historical context.
- TACTICS relate to the order in which semantic units appear in a text and the order in which they are processed.

---

6 'To establish the conceptual framework of a typology, you can design the production and interpretation of texts as a non-sequential interaction of autonomous components'. In Malrieu and Rastier (2002), p. 549.

Malrieu and Rastier define the concept of genres in relation to the above four variables, with each specific genre varying in terms of its particular combination of variables, each of which may apply differently according to the genre. As such, the tactics of an epistolary work are chronological, while those of a scientific report are tight and rigorous. The dialectics of political speeches tend to be tight and focused, while those of poems would typically be loose. The thematics of recipes are stable while those of poetry are infinite; the dialogics of plays are per definition at least bilateral (actor/audience) while those of novels are undetermined. Moreover, the importance of each component varies according to the genre. Whereas thematics and tactics are most relevant to recipes, dialogics and dialectics are essential criteria in the framing of the genre of theatre.

In 2006, Rastier revised his definition of textual genres, distinguishing 'four hierarchical levels above the text': 'speech' (for instance in legal texts, literary texts or scientific essays); 'generic fields' (theatre, poetry, narrative genres); genres themselves (comedy, romance, crime novels, news, memoirs and travelogues), and sub-genres (such as epistolary novels), although he adds in a note that the issue of sub-genres is quite problematic (p. 1).[7] Without dwelling on Rastier's aim of producing a practical and formal model where carefully differentiated genres each find their own special place, I nevertheless suggest that this proposed differentiation is both interesting and useful precisely because it underlines the difficulty of the task at hand. Here, I work from the assumption that the original Malrieu and Rastier framework still provides an efficient analytical tool – especially when considered in the light of Allen's cognitive perspective, because it emphasizes the idea of expectations associated with particular genres.

As mentioned earlier, Allen's model (founded on Fauconnier and Turner's theories) aligns genres with mental spaces. When the components of mental spaces are not naturally compatible, it is possible to speak of input spaces. For example, one can say that the idea of 'a dog' (mental space 1) is not naturally compatible with that of 'classroom' (input space/mental space 2). In the context of applying this theory to the question of genre within Rastier's frame-

---

7   See also Françoise Canon-Roger and Christine Chollier, *Des genres aux textes: Essais de sémantique interprétative en littérature de langue anglaise*, Vol. XIII, n. 3, (Artois: Presses université, 2008), pp. 9–30.

work, I suggest that input spaces appear at the generic level, when a generic component (as defined in Malrieu and Rastier's model) intervenes in an unexpected (and somewhat 'shocking') way in a given genre. As such, one could say that the dialectics of recipes (mental space 1) would be ill-suited to the intrusion of a tactic implying retroactivity (mental space 2). The former of these two examples gives rise to the need for cognitive processing of a linguistic nature; the second to cultural processes, such as disambiguation. In the following, as I apply these ideas to the analysis of extracts from *Victor Hugo, My Love*, I suggest that these two processes are not always clearly distinguishable, and secondly (I will return to this later) that the impact of the cultural dimension constitutes the most crucial part of the interpretation of the text. The examples will illustrate each of the generic components in Rastier and Malrieu's classification. They will also illustrate how subtly components can work together by combining in occasionally unexpected ways: these new combinations (input spaces in Allen's terminology) generate new generic areas.

Victor Hugo, My Love as 'generic cocktail': Linguistic and cultural interpretations

As far as the thematics of *Victor Hugo, My Love* are concerned, love and commitment remain central to the drama, the letters, the poetry and to the political speeches found throughout the text. As for the dialectical organization of the text, which covers the period between 1833 and 1884, some scenes are chronologically close (as is made clear by the dates of the letters), while others are further apart. At both tactical and dialogical levels, however, the generic organization of the text is characterized by instability and heterogeneity. The tactical component in the form it takes here is not typical of epistolary works. Because the predominant genre of *Victor Hugo, My Love* is theatrical, Sogno found it necessary to rearrange the chronological order of the original letters in the interests of creating narrative tension.[8] The rearrangement of the chrono-

---

8   This came out during an interview I made with Sogno, undertaken on October 30, 2014 in Monaco. The interview was the starting point of a collaboration between Anthea Sogno and myself. The discussion centered around the possibility of her play being translated and adapted for a Norwegian audience.

logical order of the letters illustrates how the mental space of drama intrudes into the mental space of epistolary correspondence in a disruptive but meaningful way.

Still, it is on the level of dialogue that generic mélange is most obvious in the play. The scenes in the play are mainly composed of exchanges between a first and second-person speaker – 'je' and 'tu' or 'vous' (the latter two being less and more formal versions of 'you', designating the other protagonist). While the audience is aware that there are only two actors on stage (Juliette and Victor), the way in which the spectator (or reader of the text) becomes a 'third protagonist' is worth noting. There are a number of moments when the audience is directly interpellated in the intimate and bilateral communication on stage; for instance, when the dialogue includes the reading of letters and poems. Juliette's voice here mingles with Victor's, as in the tragic twelfth scene, which unfolds after Victor and Juliette have each lost their respective daughters. Passages from the poems 'We live, we talk' and 'Claire P.' (both from Victor Hugo's 1856 *The Contemplation*) are both declaimed on stage, with Hugo reciting excerpts from the first, and Juliette taking over, reading lines from the second:

> *Victor:*
> *en lui passant un voile de deuil sur les épaules:*
> On est flot dans la foule, âme dans la tempête…
> Tout vient et passe; on est en deuil, on est en fête;
> On arrive, on recule, on lutte avec effort…
> Puis, le vaste et profond silence de la mort!
>
> *Juliette:*
> Le parfum des fleurs est faux, l'aurore est fausse,
> L'oiseau qui chante au bois ment, et le cygne ment,
> L'étoile n'est pas vraie au fond du firmament,
> Le ciel n'est pas le ciel et là-haut, rien ne brille,
> Puisque, lorsque je crie à ma fille: 'Ma fille,
> Je suis là. Lève-toi!' Quelqu'un le lui défend;
> Et que je ne puis pas réveiller mon enfant![9] (Scene 12)

---

9 '*Victor:/covering her shoulders with a mourning veil:/*We're a flood in the crowd, soul in the tempest/Everything comes and goes by; we are in mourning, we're celebrating;/We arrive, we move back, we struggle with efforts…/Then, the vast and deep silence of death!/*Juliette:/*The scent of flowers is false, dawn is false,/The bird in the wood lies, and the swan lies,/The star is not true in the firmament,/The sky is not the sky and up there, nothing shines,/Because, when I cry to my daughter: "Daughter,/I'm

It is difficult to say with certainty whom Victor and Juliette are addressing, and who is speaking in the case of Juliette, demonstrating the necessity of an exceptional cognitive process on the part of the addressee, if the full referential impact of the scene is to be grasped. The Spanish scholar Elvira Arnoux's argument that stylistic isotopy may be interrupted by the introduction of a different genre is relevant here.[10] Whereas in a theatrical scene, the dialogical components are normally easily to identify, here we come across components that we do not normally associate with the theatre such as poems and letters. These components require non-linguistic knowledge in order to be fully understood. I suggest that this knowledge is cultural – a point I will more fully explore with reference to cognitive and pragmatic theory.

Building on the model that was introduced before, input spaces require a cognitive adjustment because they bring about an isotopic rupture. In the light of cognitive theories, it can be argued that disambiguation is a central process in the treatment of this rupture.[11] This step is part of the interpretative treatment of an utterance that is required in order to obtain a message that makes sense. I suggest that this method can be successfully applied to genre studies even if it has its roots in the cognitive study of statements.

According to Moeschler and Reboul, disambiguation involves two processes: a linguistic, but pragmatic, identification of references by the addressee on the one hand, and a non-linguistic, cultural processing on the other. Both processes are seen to address the need to complete the information that is given in the original message. Moeschler and Reboul discuss disambiguation in relation to the following examples (pp. 151, 173):

(a) Mary to John: Where is the cat?
(b) George Sand is sitting on the left-hand shelf. Bound in leather.

---

here. Arise!" Someone forbids her to do so;/And I cannot wake my child!' The translation of Victor's speech is taken from <http://blogs.transparent.com/french/victor-hugo-on-vit-on-parle-we-live-we-talk/> [accessed 1 October 2012].

10   Elvira Arnoux and Maite Alvarado, 'La escritura en la lectura. Apuntes y subrayado como huellas de representaciones de textos', in *Propuesta de intervención pedagógica para la comprensión y producción de textos académicos*, ed. by María Cristina Martínez S. (Sede, Colombia: Universidad del Valle, 2002), pp. 207–26. http://catedraunesco.univalle.edu.co/pdf/2008/Propuestaintrvencion1.pdf [Accessed 19 January 2015].

11   Jacques Moeschler and Anne Reboul, eds., *Dictionnaire encyclopédique de pragmatique* (Éditions du Seuil, 1994), pp. 105–77.

In order to understand example (a), the addressee – John – will have to identify the reference to the cat, which is not given in the text. The message can be processed or disambiguated if John shares with Mary the pragmatic knowledge of which cat she is talking about. In text (b) – as in text (a) – a thematic disambiguation is required to understand the message: what does 'George Sand' refer to? The theme of the text – George Sand – appears in a surprising context whereby it is suggested that one is actually talking about an object, obviously a book. In order for the new and unexpected thematic intrusion to be cognitively processed, the addressee needs to know that George Sand is a writer. Then it will become clear that the true referent has been referred to indirectly, by means of the use of a figure of speech, a synecdoche. This disambiguation is a decoding process involving several steps, where it becomes apparent that George Sand refers to a famous French novelist and that her name is used to denote a book she has authored. Here decoding is indeed enabled by cultural knowledge, and it is thanks to this knowledge that the exchange can be understood: a book by George Sand is sitting on the left hand shelf, and it is bound in leather.

I want to take this a stage further and to apply this method of analysis to the field of generic studies by suggesting that the shock caused by the intrusion of one genre into another (involving the idea of input spaces mentioned previously) requires a similar form of disambiguation. I shall illustrate this with reference to an example which occurs at the end of Scene 11, which is marked by the passionate, even oppressive presence of Juliette directly addressing Victor. Here, the latter seems to sever the dialogical connection between them, by giving a reply that does not require a direct addressee, namely a recital of his celebrated poem, 'Tomorrow, at Dawn' (from *The Contemplations*):

> *Juliette:*
> Oh! Je voudrais t'envelopper de mon amour pour que la douleur ne puisse pas passer au travers! (Devinant que Victor préfère rester seul, elle l'embrasse et sort.)[12]

---

12 'Juliette:/Oh! I would like to wrap you in my love so that pain cannot come through! (Guessing that Victor prefers to stay alone, she kisses him and leaves.)'

Victor:
Demain, dès l'aube, à l'heure où blanchit la campagne,
Je partirai. Vois-tu, je sais que tu m'attends.
J'irai par la forêt, j'irai par la montagne.
Je ne puis demeurer loin de toi plus longtemps.
[…]¹³

Again, here, even if the poem appears to represent Victor's reply to Juliette, it is not easy to identify whom Victor is actually talking to (i.e. to identify the dialogic parameter in Rastier's generic description). I would argue in this case that cultural disambiguation, as a cognitive process, is a vital element in dealing with this dialogic ambiguity. Hugo's poem is one of the most well-known in French literary history and is very often cited in contexts of mourning: most French spectators would understand the reference to Hugo the poet and to the content of the text, both of which would make it possible for them to make sense of the poem's intrusion into the play. The extreme grief Hugo suffered after the death of his daughter represents a rupture in the generic fabric of the play – this rupture is achieved by the insertion of a monologue (the poem) at the end of a dialogue with Juliette. In other words, one can easily speak of a generic intrusion of the poetic genre into the theatrical genre, and to justify this intrusion by the fact that at the end of a dialogue between two clearly identified protagonists, the poem is suddenly addressed to an addressee who is both undefined and silent. By dint of this cultural disambiguation, the audience can consider itself interpellated as Victor's true addressee in this moment. The poetic message can also be considered as a form of flirtation with the audience, now united by its shared familiarity with the poem.

The same dialogical mechanism is used in scene 13 (32), where Hugo's most celebrated speech about democracy and education occurs in the midst of a romantic conversation with Juliette:

---

13 '*Victor:*/At dawn tomorrow, when the plains grow bright,/I'll go. You wait for me: I know you do./I'll cross the woods, I'll cross the mountain-height./No longer can I keep away from you./[…]' The translation of Victor's speech is from <http://muse.jhu.edu/journals/ncf/summary/v031/31.1greenberg.html> [Accessed 1 December 2014].

> *Victor:*
> Messieurs, marquez chacune de vos journées parlementaires par une mesure utile et populaire. Dites à tous ces malheureux et égarés: nous ne sommes pas vos vainqueurs, nous sommes vos frères!
>
> *Juliette:*
> Je me dépêche mon amour car je veux être à midi sonnant à la porte de l'Assemblée afin d'être bien placée. Je voudrais déjà être au grand moment, je sens déjà l'émotion me gagner et qui ne cessera de croître jusqu'au moment où tu descendras de la tribune. [...][14]

Whereas Victor is clearly addressing deputies at the French parliament ('Messieurs', he says), Juliette replies to Victor's speech by expressing her feelings for him ('mon amour'). Again, this is an instance of generic leakage, where language from one genre (poetry) appears unexpectedly in another (theatre). The effect is surprising and suggestive, the spectators' understanding of the implications of this unexpected intrusion depends on their prior knowledge of specific elements of Hugo's life and career.

Conclusion

I have shown that *Victor Hugo, My Love* consists of a generic mélange despite the fact that it was written to be performed on stage and therefore poses as a piece that ought to correspond to traditional conceptions of a drama. In order to argue this, I have discussed the notion of genre within a cognitive framework where it can be assimilated to an idea of mental spaces. I show that this theoretical framework can be used to explain what goes on in the process of intrusion of one generic form into another, among other things in terms of an unavoidable cognitive 'shock' that necessitates a certain type of processing. In order to elaborate on this notion of genre I have drawn on Rastier and Malrieu's descriptive model. The descriptive categories that they provide were used to identify certain forms of generic collisions and to invoke the strategies of cog-

---

14 '*Victor:*/Gentlemen, may each of your parliamentary days be marked by a useful and popular measure. Tell all those who are unhappy and lost: we are not your betters, we are your brothers!/ *Juliette:*/I hurry my love because I want to be ringing the doorbell of the Assembly at noon in order to find a good place. I wish I were there already, I already feel the emotions take over. They will only grow stronger until you come down from the rostrum. [...]'

nitive processing which they necessitate. In the case of the play *Victor Hugo, mon amour*, I put forward two forms of processing: linguistic and cultural, pointing out the fact that they are not systematically differentiated. Having examined the mostly cultural processing which the generic cocktail of the play necessitates, two consequences emerge. By dint of its nod to its audience, *Victor Hugo, mon amour*'s success is perhaps due to its capacity to produce a climate of dialogic communication not only between the protagonists but also between these protagonists and their spectators-listeners. On the other hand, the play excludes audiences who do not possess these cultural references. An understanding of this fact would obviously be crucial to any attempted translation of the piece. Non-French audiences who are less familiar with Victor Hugo's works might not feel part of such a triangular communication. The translator of the play could in view of this choose to privilege the thematic content of the text and avoid input spaces demanding cultural processing. A potential translator would also be well advised to conceive his or her task as a process of interpretation and creation where genre is envisaged as a path, not a goal.

Bibliography

Allen, Martina, 'Against "hybridity" in genre studies: Blending as an alternative approach to generic experimentation'. *Trespassing Journal: An Online Journal of Trespassing Art, Science, and Philosophy*, 2 (2013), pp. 3–21 <http://trespassingjournal.com/Issue2/TPJ_I2_Allen_Article.pdf> [accessed 2 June 2014].

Arnoux, Elvira and Maite Alvarado, 'La escritura en la lectura. Apuntes y subrayado como huellas de representaciones de textos', in *Propuesta de intervención pedagógica para la comprensión y producción de textos académicos*, ed. by María Cristina Martínez S. (Sede, Colombia: Universidad del Valle, 2002), pp. 207–26 http://catedraunesco.univalle.edu.co/pdf/2008/Propuestaintrvencion1.pdf [accessed 19 January 2015].

Canon-Roger, Françoise and Christine Chollier, *Des genres aux textes: Essais de sémantique interprétative en littérature de langue anglaise*, Vol. XIII, n. 3 (Artois: Presses université, 2008).

Fauconnier, Gilles and Mark Turner, *The Way we Think: Conceptual Blending and the Mind's Hidden Complexities* (NY: Basic Books, 2003).

Malrieu, Denise and François Rastier, 'Genres et variations morphosyntaxiques'. *Traitement automatique des langues*, 42.2 (2001), 548–77 <http://www.revue-texto.net/Inedits/Malrieu_Rastier/Malrieu-Rastier_Genres.html> [accessed 22 January 2013].

Moeschler, Jacques, and Anne Reboul, eds., *Dictionnaire encyclopédique de pragmatique* (Éditions du Seuil, 1994).

Rastier, François, 'La traduction: Interprétation et genèse du sens'. *Texto!* <http://www.revue-texto.net/Lettre/Rastier_Traduction.pdf> [accessed 23 January 2013].

Sogno, Anthéa, *Victor Hugo, mon amour ou 'Aimer c'est plus que vivre'* <http://www.victor-hugo-mon-amour.fr/boutique-victor-hugo-mon-amour> [accessed 1 October 2012].

4   Wole Soyinka's 'armoury of creativity': Cultural mélange from *Opera Wonyosi* to 'Guerrilla Theatre'

Christiane Fioupou

Just after the Civil War (1967–1970), Nigeria saw the emergence of the oil boom: in its wake, institutionalized corruption and irresponsibility, financial and industrial scandals, galloping criminality, religious hypocrisy, police and army brutality, iniquitous decrees, and other abuses became rife in the country, then under military rule. To use the now classic and even clichéd phrase, the oil-boom had turned to oil-doom. It is in this context of excess and arrogant materialism that Wole Soyinka – playwright, director, actor, musician, singer, poet, novelist, essayist, and human rights activist – set out to write and stage *Opera Wonyosi*.[1]

In response to Ulli Beier's suggestion that 'different situations require a different response from the writer', Soyinka replied that 'the armoury of creativity that is at your disposal is so vast that one would be a fool not to use whatever corresponds to the theme one wishes to use at the moment'.[2] Nigeria itself is a highly populated, multilingual, and multicultural country: for historical and colonial reasons, English is its official language, but there are over three hundred other languages, the three most widely spoken being Hausa, Igbo and Yoruba – not to mention the *lingua franca*, Pidgin English. True to his own requirement, Soyinka drew upon Nigerian sources and beyond, extending his

---

1   Wole Soyinka, *Opera Wonyosi* (London: Rex Collings, 1981). All further references, given parenthetically by page number in the text, are to this edition.
2   Ulli Beier, 'Wole Soyinka on "Identity", 1992', *Conversations with Wole Soyinka*, ed. by Biodun Jeyifo (Jackson: University Press of Mississippi, 2001), pp. 167–81 (p. 174).

creative arsenal by borrowing also from European theatre: *Opera Wonyosi*, premiered in December 1977, is adapted from Bertolt Brecht's *The Threepenny Opera* (1928), itself a reinterpretation of John Gay's *The Beggar's Opera*, created two centuries before in 1728. Conceived or situated in different historical and geographical contexts – Nigeria and the Central African Republic, Germany and Britain, the twentieth and eighteenth centuries – the three plays are scathing satires of inequity and corruption at all levels of society. The aim of this chapter is to identify Soyinka's *Opera Wonyosi* as a multifaceted, intertextual, complex and fecund theatrical and musical mélange. The conclusion briefly focuses on some of its avatars and their reception as 'Guerrilla' or 'Shotgun' theatre. As I have just finished translating *Opera Wonyosi* into French, I shall occasionally allude to some of the challenges with which I was confronted when translating an already composite work into yet another language.

A motley title

When *Opera Wonyosi* opens, Dee-jay, the Master of Ceremonies, tells the audience that the play could be called 'the Beggars' Opera' (because 'that's what the whole nation is doing – begging for a slice of the action'), the 'Way-Out Opera', or the 'Trafficking Opera' (p. 1). But as it evolves, we understand that the Opera will not be worth, as in the original German title, '*Dreigroschen*' – 'three pennies' or 'quatre sous' in their English or French translations – but *Wonyosi*, a type of imported lace costing more than five hundred dollars a yard.[3] This outrageously expensive material was so fashionable at the time that it had become a status symbol in 'the right circles' (p. 38). When *Opera Wonyosi* had its premiere on 16 December 1977 at the University of Ife, the audience was immediately invited to grasp the ironic and satirical stance of the play in the English-Yoruba bilingual pun contained in its motley title: pronounced with the appro-

---

3 The original title in German is *Die Dreigroschenoper*. For the English version, see Bertolt Brecht, *The Threepenny Opera*, English book by Desmond Vesey, English Lyrics by Eric Bentley & Foreword by Lotte Lenya (New York: Grove Press, [1949] 1960) and, for the French version, *L'Opéra de quat'sous*, trans. by Jean-Claude Hémery (Paris: L'Arche, [1955] 1974). All further references, given parenthetically by page number in the text, are to this edition. For Brecht's source, see John Gay, *The Beggar's Opera*, in *Eighteenth Century Plays* (London: Everyman's Library, [1728] 1964), pp. 108–59.

priate tones, transcribed in the programme, *Òpèrá Wónyòsi* can be freely translated as 'the dupe buys the "Wonyosi" cloth'.⁴ Apparently, the play was initially called 'The Wonyosopera' with an explanatory note on the play script acknowledging the intertexts: 'Also known as *The Beggar's Opera*, *The Threepenny Opera*. In the manner of Bertolt Brecht from a theme by John Gay'.⁵ As we can see, 'Wonyosopera', a portmanteau-word combining 'Wonyosi' and 'Opera', structurally closer to the English title of Brecht's 'Threepenny Opera', already triggered ironical puns on 'sop opera' and 'soap opera' to qualify a ferociously satirical play that has none of the maudlin quality of a TV serial.

London, Lagos, and Bangui, 'to the swelling act/Of the imperial theme'⁶

As he was writing *Opera Wonyosi*, Soyinka remained loyal to the spirit and framework of Gay's and Brecht's plays, but found it difficult in the Nigerian context to keep to Brecht's final twist when the Queen's messenger comes just in time to save the gangster Macheath from the scaffold. But it so happened that the announcement in the Central African Republic of the coming coronation of Jean-Bedel Bokassa, President-for-Life and soon-to-be Emperor, gave the playwright the opportunity to expand the geographical province of his satire on turpitude and power-hungry megalomania and he decided that the play's action would take place not in Lagos but in Bangui, during the preparations for the Emperor's coronation, in the Nigerian expatriate quarter – a microcosm of Nigerian society. In *Opera Wonyosi*, Macheath (alias Mack or Mackie) will thus escape the firing squad by the skin of his teeth thanks to the imperial pardon for 'all common criminals' (p. 82) granted by Emperor Boky. Unlike the Queen who is never seen in Brecht's play, Boky appears as the central boisterous and vicious character in scene 3 and in the last tableau when he

---

4   Yemi Ogunbiyi, 'Òpèrá Wónyòsi: A study of Soyinka's Òpèrá Wónyòsi', *Nigeria Magazine*, 128/129 (1979), 3–14 (p. 3 n. 1). All further references, given parenthetically by page number in the text, are to this edition.
5   Bernth Lindfors, 'Begging questions in Wole Soyinka's Opera Wonyosi', *Research on Wole Soyinka*, ed. by J. Gibbs & B. Lindfors (Trenton NJ: Africa World Press 1993), pp. 149–59 (p. 158 n. 3).
6   *Macbeth* (New York: Norton, 2013), Act 1, Scene 3, ll.128–9. My homage to WS (William Shakespeare), to WS (Wole Soyinka), and to the author of *The Imperial Theme*, the Shakespeare scholar George Wilson Knight, Soyinka's mentor at the University of Leeds.

sweeps onto the stage in his imperial chariot, dressed in full Napoleonic attire, just as Bokassa was. The coronation of the 'real' Bokassa actually took place on 4 December 1977, only twelve days before *Opera Wonyosi* had its première. Soyinka had not waited for Bokassa's fall in order to expose this indecent masquerade, supported or condoned by financial, political and religious international networks. Bokassa was 'abandoned' by France less than two years after his crowning, when he stopped being acceptable after the arrest and slaughter of the school children who had demonstrated against the uniform imposed by the emperor on behalf of his family's lucrative business. Following that event, Soyinka modified some passages of the play before its first publication in 1981, notably tampering with chronology in scene 3 by anticipating the emperor's violence towards these children on the eve of his coronation, adding a few gruesome and bloodcurdling details to the already tragicomic antics of the tyrant, a mixture of history and fiction, a caricature-within-a-caricature.

'Verily, verily is it spoken'… 'Cement Chop Small Man': A linguistic mosaic

Since Soyinka borrowed from multiple linguistic and topical sources, he provided the reader with twenty-three Textual Notes (pp. 85–86) in the published version of *Opera Wonyosi*, which clarify the allusions that are likely to be too culturally specific for a non-Nigerian. They range from brief explanations or definitions of Nigerian issues (the privatisation of marble resources at Igbeti; *Taphy* as the 'authorized' flogging of civilians by soldiers; the Decree on Secret Societies; Attack Trade 'named for the brisk across-the-trade business during the Civil War'; Bar Beach as 'the public execution arena in Lagos' and its degrading 'Show', or the no less obscene decomposition of corpses in public places that prompted the theatrical innovation of carrying a coffin onto the stage to stir public awareness), to translations of words or phrases into English from different national languages, Pidgin English or local slang. As a translator, I have retained most of the notes and added a few extra ones likely to help the Francophone reader or potential director concerning the rituals, music or dance to which I have not already alluded in my introduction to the play.

Except for the two innovative scenes that totally depart from his predecessors' models – scene 3 containing Boky's ravings and that of the trial (scene 8)

– Soyinka keeps to the general plot. In passages from the first two scenes, where Soyinka deliberately borrows from Desmond Vesey's English translation of the *Threepenny Opera*, I have, in my French version, endeavoured to draw whenever possible from the 'canonical' French translation by Jean-Claude Hémery with a view to conveying the Brechtian intertextual references intended by Soyinka.

However, most of the play is steeped in topical allusions in a variety of languages and registers, including standard English interspersed with slang, graphic insults close to Brecht's or Gay's, legal vocabulary during the trial scene – with the actual text from the Decree on Secret Societies (p. 73) – or a few odd words in Pidgin English. Though the play takes place in Bangui, a former French colony whose official language is therefore French, most characters are Nigerian expatriates who left their home country during the Civil War. Accordingly, everyone speaks English in this microcosm of Nigeria; as Anikura (the equivalent of Peachum in Brecht and Gay), King of Beggars-cum-businessman-cum-'richest man in Bangui' puts it: 'we try to retain all the living styles we had at home, down to the naming of streets' (p. 5). And as if to give the play's language a mock-sense of verisimilitude, the blood-lusty crowd – gathered for Mackie's execution, but performing an about-turn when the bandit is saved – burst into repeated cheers, alternating between 'Long live the Emperor!' and 'Vive Vive Vive l'Empereur' (p. 82). Also, as part of the debunking process, Boky's bombastic and delirious speeches are studded with French words such as insults to his men – 'you scum, you *residue de bidet*' (p. 24) – or pseudo-paternal soothing words about children: 'Les pauvres. Mes enfants. Les petits. Oh they break the heart of their loving Papa Emperor' (p. 27); after this the tyrant starts to rehearse his Goon Squad in beating up school boys to the rhythm of 'Putting in the Boot', his obscene misinterpretation of the South African Gumboot Dance.

Though the dialogues in scenes 1, 2, and 7 could be described as a form of Nigerianized *Threepenny Opera*, they are also peppered with eclectic intertextual references, such as, in the same sentence, a biblical phrase juxtaposed with a line adapted from William Congreve's *The Mourning Bride* – 'verily, verily is it spoken, hell hath no fury like an aggrieved father-in-law' (p. 45), unexpectedly uttered by Mackie as he is entering the Playboy Club/whore-house through the window to meet Sukie the prostitute. There is also a quotation from the eighteenth-century from Alexander Pope's 'Moral Essays' on the 'ruling passion' that, ironically, turns out to be the title of a song (p. 57), a callous hymn on gaining power through money, sex and ritual murder, interpreted by Mack and Lucy, one of his 'wives'.

An example of Soyinka's linguistic eclecticism can be found when Anikura lectures on 'the five types of misery most likely to touch people's hearts' (p. 7). His speech is very close to Peachum's, but here Soyinka gives free rein to his biting satire by illustrating the 'Victim of Modern Industry. Collapsed chest' with an original song: 'Big Man Chop Cement; Cement Chop Small Man' (pp. 8–9). This alludes to the cement scandal, called 'the Cement Bonanza' (p. 8), when hundreds of ships overflowing with cement congested Lagos harbour for over a year. By the time they were unloaded by overworked labourers, Nigerian officials and business sharks as well as foreign suppliers had already made considerable profits. The title is in Pidgin English and the lyrics are a mixture of standard and Nigerianized English, with snippets of American jive: 'this cat is right on the ball/Like a sailor in town, high as a kite/[...] Superfly dandy' (p. 9), with a probable reference here to Curtis Mayfield's soundtrack from the 1972 'Blaxploitation' film, *Super Fly*. The gist of these texts in international and popular varieties of English tallies with what is encapsulated in the Pidgin title (in Pidgin English, 'chop' means to eat, to gorge oneself, to be greedy and corrupt)[7] and summarized in the last four lines: 'A man's lungs for clean air is meant/Not for breathing in clouds of cement/And overtime pay comes to mere chicken feed/When the cement tycoon has filled out his greed' (p. 9).

'Blood, blood, glorious blood': Recycling a medley of tunes

Soyinka is faithful to the spirit of Brecht and his sense of theatre, which he 'admire[s] enormously', and which is close, he says, to the form practised in Nigeria by professional touring companies known under the name of the Yoruba Popular Travelling Theatre.[8] Making full use of dialogue, music, song,

---

7   For the translation of Pidgin English into French, see Christiane Fioupou, 'Translating Pidgin English, Rotten English and Ubuesque English into French', *Writing Back in/and Translation*, ed. by Raoul Granqvist (Frankfurt: Peter Lang, 2006), pp. 75–90.

8   Nii Bentsi-Enchill, 'Soyinka on theatre', *West Africa* (22–29 December 1986), p. 2640. The article reports on a gathering organized in Stockholm when Soyinka received the Nobel Prize for Literature in 1986.

dance and all the resources of the theatre, the playwright turns his ferocious satire into true visual, musical and verbal pyrotechnics.

Opera Wonyosi opens and closes with Kurt Weill's classic 'Mack the Knife', with Brecht's lyrics adapted and Nigerianized by Soyinka. Among the fourteen pieces that are sung in the play, it is the only one explicitly referred to both in the stage-directions and in Dee-Jay's words praising Louis Armstrong's interpretation (p. 1). Also, one can easily guess that the lyrics and tune of 'Jenny Leveller' (pp. 46–47) are partially adapted from Brecht and Weill's 'Pirate Jenny', another famous classic sung in German by Lotte Lenya, later performed in English, notably by Nina Simone, Judy Collins and Marianne Faithful, and in France by popular women singers such as Colette Renard or Juliette Gréco.

Similarly, those familiar with 'St Louis Blues' (1914) – a favourite jazz and blues song if only for its interpretations by Bessie Smith, Billie Holiday or Louis Armstrong – can identify Mackie's 'Farewell Song' (pp. 81–2) as a free and ironical recycling of Handy's lyrics. 'I hate to see that evening sun go down/'Cause my baby (s)he has gone left town' becomes in Soyinka's version, just before Mack is to be publicly executed by firing squad: 'I hate to see the morning sun come up/For it reminds me that my hour is up' (p. 81). The original chorus: 'I got the St Louis blues, blue as I can be' is re-appropriated to suit the grotesque coronation and execution scene, using blue at its face value, as it were:

> I've got the imperial blues
> I'm as blue as I can be
> But not as blue as I'll be
> In the face as the bullets hit me
> Or grey or blue-black or whatever niggers are when they quench. (pp. 81–2)

Here 'quench' – one of the very few words in Nigerian Pidgin English used in *Opera Wonyosi*, meaning to 'die' or 'snuff it' ('clamser' in French slang) – has to rhyme with 'cold cold trench', uttered by Mack (and then followed by the chorus, 'la fosse glacée glacée'). Brecht, incidentally, in the 'Ballad in Which Macheath Begs Pardon of All' (p. 93), his own version of the song to Weill's music, had borrowed, adapted, and translated into German some passages from 'La Ballade des pendus' (The Ballad of the Hanged Men') by mediaeval French poet François Villon. In his French translation, Jean-Claude Hémery reverted to some of Villon's original lines, particularly the famous opening and the last line of the first two stanzas ('Mais priez Dieu que tous nous veuille absoudre', p. 85) – to render the Villon intertext conspicuous to the French public. (One may note here an interesting shuttle movement between two European literary sources.)

The British repertoire is also parodied by Soyinka's satirical pen. The familiar English nursery rhyme and folk song 'Who Killed Cock Robin?' ('Who killed Cock Robin?/I, said the Sparrow,/With my bow and arrow,/I killed Cock Robin'), becomes 'Who Killed Neo-Niga?', enabling Soyinka to lambast new forms of exploitation and irresponsibility (pp. 33–34). With the chorus performed by Boky's Goon Squad 'to a parody of drill formations' (p. 33), the text follows the nursery rhyme's question-and-answer pattern and is played out by the Beggars and the various social stock characters, for example the Bigshot:

> BEGGAR. Who killed Neo-Niga?
> BIGSHOT. I, said Sir Bigger
> Puffing on his cigar
> I killed Neo-Niga (p. 33)

In the same vein, Soyinka uses the 'sweet serenade' or refrain from 'The Hippopotamus Song (Mud, Mud, Glorious Mud)', drawn from the English Musical Revue by Flanders and Swann, *At the Drop of a Hat*, which has been very popular in Britain since its creation in 1956:

> Mud, mud, glorious mud
> Nothing quite like it for cooling the blood
> So follow me follow
> Down to the hollow
> And there let us wallow in glorious mud.[9]

---

9 <http://video.search.yahoo.com/video/play?p=hippopotamus+mud+mud+glorious+mud> [accessed 4 November 2013]. In my translation, I have followed the score of this original song and, in my preface to the play, given the full English title of the parodied text for potential Francophone directors to be able to recognize and sing Soyinka's lyrics in French: 'Sang, sang, glorieux sang,/Comme don à Dieu rien de plus exaltant/Faut bannir le gibet/Que j'aille me vautrer/Dans l'jus cramoisi de cet odieux truand' (my translation, in *Opera Wonyosi* [Paris: Présence Africaine, 2014]).

In his version, Soyinka parodies the Hippopotamus lyrics to expose the common practice of public executions: as Mack's impending death is part of the coronation festivities, the bandit will contribute, according to Dee-Jay, to the 'splendour', 'colour' and 'pageantry' of the event by 'bleeding through several holes to the delectation of the populace – men, women and children, the aged and crippled, from all walks of life [...]' (p. 77). Accordingly, Soyinka created a 'Patient, swathed in bandages, on crutches' – followed by a nurse 'with a drip-bottle still attached to his arm' – in whose mouth he put '[a]ctual suggestions in Readers' Letters to Newspapers' (note 21, p. 86): 'Before they shoot them, they should drain their blood and put it in a bloodbank' (p. 78). However, as soon as the patient realizes that for the beauty of the show 'there's got to be blood', he changes his mind, breaking into a song in Dee-Jay's microphone:

> Blood, blood, glorious blood,
> Nothing quite like it for offering to God
> Banish the gallows
> So I can wallow
> In the crimson juice of the criminal sod! (p. 78)

One stanza later, he dies 'happy' (p. 79). This hilarious gory hybrid that fuses a cowardly pseudo-sacrifice – which manipulates man's basest instincts in the name of God or morals – with a jocular popular song is very representative of the play's mood and its cross-cultural mélange.

The music of the other songs, though their titles or themes are related to Brecht's and Gay's, would be difficult to identify were it not for Yemi Ogunbiyi's 1979 seminal article concerning Soyinka's 1977 production. The critic confirms that except for Weill's 'Mack the Knife', Soyinka drew most of his scores from a variety of places and musical sources. For instance, according to Ogunbiyi: 'Polly's "Song of Lost Innocence" brings to mind the lullaby quality of Ella Fitzgerald's voice almost frivolously but evocatively "skating around the notes", as they say in jazz, and venturing in a way which normally we would expect in an instrumentalist' (p. 7).

One important Nigerian source among this international medley of tunes, songs and voices is also provided by Ogunbiyi. According to him, 'The Song of Ngh-ngh-ngh' (pp. 11–12), interpreted by Anikura and his wife to debunk love and marriage, 'captures the unique style of a late popular Nigerian folk singer, Njemanze, whose free and twisty, throat nasalisations, against the background of the tunes of his own Igbo language, were easily adaptable to lyrics and became ravingly popular in the mid-fifties' (Ogunbiyi p. 7).[10]

In this song, each stanza opens with 'Oti o. Ngh-ngh-ngh' – *Oti o* meaning, according to Soyinka's note, 'Never never' – hence a mixture of Yoruba words and their non-verbal equivalent. As we shall see, Soyinka uses Njemanze's music in his later satirical sketches, for his melodies are adaptable to most of the original lyrics in *Opera Wonyosi*, such as the one about the cement scandal (pp. 8–9).

From the singable to the unsingable and unsung songs

For Ogunbiyi, a privileged spectator of *Opera Wonyosi* in 1977, 'there can be no question that the play's strength as effective theatre derives largely from its "singable" songs' (p. 7). Yet, significantly, in the two innovative punchy scenes that also work well in theatrical terms (scenes 3 and 8), little place is given to 'singable songs'. In scene 3, the 'singable songs' are replaced by the 'Lagosian lynch-mob rallying rhythm' (p. 28), led by Inspector Brown, or Boky's histrionic ravings about his friend Idi Amin, or the beating up of schoolchildren. In scene 8, when Anikura, accompanied by his Beggars on a refresher course on how to 'bag' new positions, improvises a court trial to demonstrate that the Army is a secret society, only one song, 'a high point in the *deroulement* of events', the 'Beggars Anthem', is heard (pp. 70–71). Later, when the dates of violent acts are enumerated by Alatako, the Lawyer-Beggar – with the chorus of Beggars answering each time that the culprits are 'Unknown soldiers' – and Dee-Jay is asked to sing 'The Ballad of the Unknown Soldier', he replies:

> DEE-JAY. Gee, I'm sorry, haven't got all the sound effects for that yet. We tried to get the real thing, you know, the sound of smashed windscreens, bones crunching, koboko descending, violated daughters, screaming students, you know, the usual stuff. But the recording machine got smashed.
> ANIKURA. What! Who dared?

---

10 For Israel Nwoba Njemanze, see <http://www.youtube.com/watch?v=oYtKtiRGBrM> [accessed 4 November 2013].

ALL. Unknown soldiers.
(The BEGGARS break into the 'Unknown Soldiers' Dance, full of contortions, limping and groaning.) (p. 74)

This scene appears as a concrete rendering of various attacks cited in the play, notably 'the widely reported details of the burning down of the Kalakuta Republic' (p. 74) in 'Feb. 1977' (p. 72), which refers to the actual violence waged against the commune of the Afrobeat musician Fela Anikulapo Kuti in retaliation for his satirical songs against the Army. Fela's record, 'Unknown Soldier', released in 1979, tells of the army raid that was left unpunished because the official inquiry had only found an 'unknown soldier' to blame. His lyrics, in Pidgin English, could be seen as the musical and angry equivalent of Dee-Jay's list of army abuses quoted above: 'Them dey break, yes/Them dey steal, yes/Them dey loot, yes/Them dey fuck some of the women by force, yes/Them dey rape, yes/Them dey burn, yes (x3)/Them commot one student's eye, yes/Them break some some head (x2)'.[11] And when later in the song Fela says 'Them throw my mama out from window', he is simply reporting what actually happened to his mother (and Soyinka's aunt), Funmilayo Ransome-Kuti, a great Nigerian figure famous for her commitment to women's rights and anti-colonial stance. In *Opera Wonyosi*, the Beggars '*break into "The Unknown Soldiers" Dance*' (p. 74) but do not sing the ballad of the same name. With the benefit of hindsight, we can easily imagine Fela's song reverberating as a substitute for the Beggars' 'unsung song'. In a way, this was corroborated by Soyinka in his 2006 memoirs, where he wrote of the Kalakuta investigation: 'The role of Obasanjo's military regime was laid bare beyond all doubt, and the exercise gave birth to what became a public refrain for all suspected crimes thereafter – *Unknown Soldier*'.[12] We could then venture to say that Soyinka's satirical and parodic theatrical piece and Fela's Afrobeat music with Pidgin English lyrics echo each other here, two complementary artistic expressions attacking the same corrupt and violent military dictatorship.

---

11   Fela Anikulapo Kuti, 'Unknown soldier' (1979), in *Fela: The Complete Works of Fela Anikulapo Kuti* (Wrasse Records, 2010). See also: <http://www.youtube.com/watch?v=GnRfgzXrFTI> and lyrics: <http://www.lyricsmania.com/unknown_soldier_lyrics_fela_kuti.html> [accessed 4 November 2013].
12   Wole Soyinka, *You Must Set Forth at Dawn, Memoirs* (Ibadan: Bookcrafts, 2006), p. 379.

From *Opera Wonyosi* to 'Guerrilla Theatre'

Soyinka was prevented from taking his 1977 production of *Opera Wonyosi* to Lagos, and as a result, he had to conjure up other means of expression from his 'armoury of creativity'. To this end, he formed a group out of the University of Ife company called the Guerrilla Theatre Unit, and wrote 'short, biting and highly popular skits attacking governmental hypocrisy, corruption and sadistic policies'.[13] This form of protest was taken to the streets, markets and other open public places as *agit-prop*, 'Guerrilla' or 'Shotgun' theatre, described by Soyinka as a political weapon that allowed the Theatre Unit, composed of actors, dancers, musicians and singers, to 'aim, shoot, and go'.

It is a well-known fact that being a director as well as a playwright, Soyinka is always ready to breathe new dynamism into his plays and rework them during rehearsals when he feels the urge to adapt them to changing situations. In 1983, the civilian regime of Shehu Shagari had been in power for four years, and Soyinka had become an unrelenting critic of the corruption and violence of the regime. As he was directing *Opera Wonyosi* at the University of Ife, he seized the opportunity to transform the important scene satirizing the military power (scene 8), replacing Colonel Moses by Dr. Mokotan, a civilian advocating the 'Ethical Revolution', yet another smoke-screen presented as a panacea by the Nigerian government.[14] The same year, Soyinka again made use of the 'Ethical Revolution' charade in one of his satirical sketches performed with his Guerrilla Unit. *Etika Revolution* was played at the University of Ife to an audience that had come to listen to President Shagari's speech. The songs from the Shotgun plays, in a mixture of Pidgin and Standard English, became very popular in Nigeria when an LP, *Unlimited Liability Company*, including *Etike Revo Wetin?*, was released and widely played on the radio.[15] The songs soon spread, like so many anthems, not only in Lagos but throughout the country,

---

13   Biodun Jeyifo, *Wole Soyinka: Poetics, Politics and Postcolonialism* (Cambridge: Cambridge University Press, 2004), p. xxviii. The 'Chronology' of Jeyifo's illuminating study gives a very good overview of Soyinka's commitment to the arts and politics.

14   Joachim Fiebach, *Trends in the European Theatre since the 1960s: Towards a Theory of Theatre after Brecht* (Ife: University of Ife Monographs on Literature and Criticism, 1984), pp. 39–40.

15   Wole Soyinka, *Unlimited Liability Company* (Ewuro Productions, 1983). The lyrics are provided on the back jacket of the vinyl. For samples of the record, see <http://www.youtube.com/watch?v=a73wSaXE3VM> [accessed 4 November 2013].

sung by people from all walks of life. The chorus to *Etike Revo Wetin?* ('I love my country I no go lie/Na inside him I go live and die/I love my country I no go lie/Na him and me go yap till I die') seems to have been on everybody's lips.

As the song begins 'with history' and the recent Civil War, it chimes with the themes of *Opera Wonyosi*, but is perhaps more readily accessible to the general public. For instance, the 'Cement Bonanza' of the *Opera* resurfaces in *Etike Revo Wetin?*:

> One time each day na Regatta Day
> A thousand ships in Lagos Bay
> As if to say na naval display
> By all the nations for Seamen's Day
> But me, I think na naval blockade
> By angry nations for debts unpaid.
> Country Seek, go look for foreign aid,
> Dis no to ceremonial parade
> Our budget finish for demurrage fee
> Cement de choke we mouth for sea.

On the record jacket, Soyinka acknowledges that he is indebted to the music of Njemanze, the Igbo singer, who, as we have seen, was also a strong inspiration for *Opera Wonyosi*. In its turn, *Etike Revo Wetin?* has become a source of inspiration and has been re-appropriated by many Nigerian writers ever since.[16] Dan Izevbaye, who has written extensively on Soyinka's more complex or less accessible plays, considers the *Etika Revo Wetin?* side of the record as 'memorable not only for its fuller documentation of the looting of the nation, but also for its revival of a truly popular and enduring musical idiom for satirical use'.[17] For him, the other side, *Unlimited Liability Company*, is likely to last as satire

---

16 One thinks, for instance, of Niyi Osundare's *Songs of the Season*, a selection of poems from his weekly column of political and social issues in the *Sunday Tribune* since 1985, an experiment with what he calls 'verse journalism'. When he reads some of his poems in public, he insists on borrowing the tune of 'I love my country' from Soyinka's LP. Niyi Osundare, *Songs of the Season* (Ibadan: Heinemann Frontline, 1990), pp. 23–4 and pp. 17–8.
17 Dan Izevbaye, 'Assets and liabilities: Unlimited liability company as an artist's investment in the popular cause', *Before Our Very Eyes: Tribute to Wole Soyinka*, ed. by Dapo Adelugba (Ibadan: Spectrum Books, 1987), pp. 170–82 (p. 180). For the reception of the record, see also Dapo Adelugba, 'Yapping: A form of patriotism', in *Before Our Very Eyes*, pp. 183–211.

for it 'is capable of transcending its immediate target, and of being adapted to new situations' (p. 180).

We could say the same of *Opera Wonyosi* which, though it is heavily anchored in Nigeria's topicality, could be easily transposed to a more 'globalized' contemporary world: after all, the wearing of 'Wonyosi' in the play is but a prerequisite to a change in social status, a subterfuge for more power and more money. Polly, Mack's wife, becomes gang leader when her husband is in hiding or in prison, transforms their armed robbers into businessmen who attend board meetings, and, to this end, makes them wear Wonyosi-like lace. Similarly, she becomes a shareholder in a multinational corporation to 'go legitimate like the bigger crooks' (p. 62). In fact, the last words pronounced by Anikura, 'power is delicious', encapsulate the overriding themes in both the play and the Guerrilla sketches: when plutocracy reigns supreme, the most unexpected actions are explained by the power one can gain through money or by the money one can get by being in power.

What is portrayed in Soyinka's *Opera*, as in the works of Gay and Brecht, is that the worlds of business, politics and religion soon forget to set up shop against one another when they learn how to convert their former rivalries into mutual protection schemes. This is how Anikura explains his sudden reconciliation with Mackie, his former enemy and rival, when he is saved from the firing squad by Emperor Boky:

> We men of influence – of power if you like – respect one another. We speak the same language, so we usually work things out. (p. 82)

And the play ends to the tune of 'Mack the Knife' with Boky in his imperial chariot followed by a jarring mélange of sycophants dazzled by the imperial diadem.

Conclusion

This short chapter is not able to do full justice to the vast 'armoury of creativity' on which Soyinka draws. The challenge of translating *Opera Wonyosi* has enabled me, however, to take the measure, once again, of his immense culture and the wealth and variety of his sources of inspiration, and above all, to appreciate the dramatic genius that has shaped and fused them into an original and exciting work: a work that, while it addresses the historical moment and the specificity of Nigerian and African regimes, transcends that topicality. *Opera Wonyosi* is a theatrically powerful indictment of corruption that has universal significance – and its avatars that took to the streets in the form of Guerrilla Theatre attest to the generative force of their original.

Bibliography

Adelugba, Dapo, 'Yapping: A form of patriotism', in *Before Our Very Eyes: Tribute to Wole Soyinka*, ed. by Dapo Adelugba (Ibadan: Spectrum Books, 1987), pp. 183–211.

Anikulapo-Kuti, Fela, *Fela: The Complete Works of Fela Anikulapo Kuti* (Wrasse Records, 2010).

Beier, Ulli, 'Wole Soyinka on "identity", 1992', *Conversations with Wole Soyinka*, ed. by Biodun Jeyifo (Jackson: University Press of Mississippi, 2001), pp. 167–81.

Bentsi-Enchill, Nii, 'Soyinka on theatre', *West Africa* (22–29 December 1986), p. 2640.

Brecht, Bertolt, *L'Opéra de quat'sous*, trans. by Jean-Claude Hémery (Paris: L'Arche, [1955] 1974).

Brecht, Bertolt, *The Threepenny Opera*, trans. by Eric Bentley (New York: Grove Press, [1949] 1960).

Fiebach, Joachim, *Trends in the European Theatre since the 1960s: Towards a Theory of Theatre after Brecht* (Ife: University of Ife Monographs on Literature and Criticism, 1984).

Fioupou, Christiane, 'Translating Pidgin English, Rotten English and Ubuesque English into French', in *Writing Back in/and Translation*, ed. by Raoul Granqvist (Frankfurt: Peter Lang, 2006), pp. 75–90.

Gay, John, *Eighteenth Century Plays* (London: Everyman's Library, 1964).

Izevbaye, Dan, 'Assets and liabilities: Unlimited Liability Company as an artist's investment in the popular cause', in *Before Our Very Eyes: Tribute to Wole Soyinka*, ed. by Dapo Adelugba (Ibadan: Spectrum Books, 1987).

Jeyifo, Biodun, *Wole Soyinka: Poetics, Politics and Postcolonialism* (Cambridge: Cambridge University Press, 2004).

Lindfors, Bernth, 'Begging questions in Wole Soyinka's Opera Wonyosi', in *Research on Wole Soyinka*, ed. by J. Gibbs, and B. Lindfors (Trenton, NJ: Africa World Press, 1993), pp. 149–59.

Ogunbiyi, Yemi, 'Òpèrá Wónyòsi: A study of Soyinka's Òpèrá Wónyòsi', *Nigeria Magazine*, 128/129 (1979), 3–14.

Osundare, Niyi, *Songs of the Season* (Ibadan: Heinemann Frontline, 1990).

Shakespeare, William, *Macbeth* (New York: Norton Critical Edition, 2013).
Soyinka, Wole, *Opera Wonyosi* (London: Rex Collings, 1981).
Soyinka, Wole, *Unlimited Liability Company* (Ewuro Productions, 1983).
Soyinka, Wole, *You Must Set Forth at Dawn, Memoirs* (Ibadan: Bookcrafts, 2006).
Soyinka, Wole, *Opera Wonyosi*, trans. by Christiane Fioupou (Paris: Présence Africaine, 2014).

5 A 'jazzy literature': Cultural hybridity and multilingualism in Mongo Beti's *Trop de soleil tue l'amour*

Inger Hesjevoll Schmidt-Melbye

Trop de soleil tue l'amour (1999), written by the Cameroonian Francophone author Mongo Beti (1932–2001), displays an interesting cultural mélange. One of the characters from the novel describes Cameroonian society as '[un] vrai patchwork d'ethnies et de cultures, tour de Babel linguistique de surcroît'.[1] With over 230 different languages and linguistic and cultural traces left by no less than three European superpowers, Germany, France and Great Britain, Cameroon is in fact one of the most multilingual countries in the world.[2] The creolized language 'Camfranglais' is an illustration of the linguistic diversity that characterizes everyday Cameroonian life. Beti is one of the many African authors who received their education in Europe and profited from their knowledge of colonial languages. That being said, Beti was for all of his life a politically involved author who protested against all kinds of injustice. We can therefore hardly speak of Beti's literary writing without mentioning that his relationship to the culture and language of the former colonizers in his native country remained complex and problematic during his whole authorship.

The novel in question, built around a crime plot, illustrates modern Cameroonian society in the wake of colonization. It touches on a number of

---

1 A 'true patchwork of ethnicities and cultures, and even more so, a linguistic tower of Babel' [my translation]. In Mongo Beti, *Trop de soleil tue l'amour* (Paris: Editions Julliard, 1999), p. 99. All further references are to this edition and are given parenthetically by page number after quotations in the text.
2 In 1993, Carole de Féral noted 239 different languages in Cameroon. Ten years later, Ambroise Queffélec estimated the number at 248. In John Kristian Sanaker, Karin Holter, and Ingse Skattum, *La francophonie – une introduction critique* (Oslo: Unipub, 2006), p. 208.

serious topics such as corruption, torture, alcoholism, sexual abuse, dictatorship, nepotism and espionage. But the solemnity is mediated through a cynical tone, gallows humour and irony, and Beti's literary characters are all somewhat stereotyped. Throughout the novel enigmas appear in the form of strangers and unexplained events. Zam, the protagonist, is a journalist who regularly drowns his sorrows in alcohol and risks his life investigating political injustice. Together with his beloved Bébète, with whom he has a complicated relationship, he unmasks a plot against him. Although the thematics of the novel is clearly an interesting object of study in and of itself, I will be focusing on Beti's narrative style, which is characterized by linguistic creativity and literary innovation. I have chosen as my starting point the following question posed by the Italian Africanist Itala Vivan, which in my opinion is relevant both to studies of hybridity and multiculturalism in general, and to Beti's ideological and aesthetic position in particular:

> If hybridity used to be not only negative but an absolute monstrosity, if [...] at present we acknowledge that hybrid is beautiful and hybrid is also good, for it is part of the morality of anti-racism, *what is the aesthetics of all this?*[3] [my emphasis]

According to Vivan, hybridity in art has become more and more accepted, even praised, and multicultural authors can be said to have contributed politically to this development. But as she puts it: *What is the aesthetics of all this?* Is there always an ideological motivation to the use of linguistic techniques such as code-switching and various forms of self-translation as well as a literary style characterized by a mix of several cultures' aesthetic conventions? Could this *métissage* benefit from a less political interpretative scope? I will try to sketch some answers to these questions by looking at passages from *Trop de soleil tue l'amour*, passages that demonstrate a few of the many strategies Beti uses to incorporate elements from different cultural contexts.[4] I will argue that rather

---

3 Itala Vivan, 'African Thresholds: Hybridity through the Looking-Glass', in *Seuils/Thresholds*, special issue of *Anglophonia: French Journal of English Studies*, ed. by Christiane Fioupou (Toulouse: PUM, 2000), pp. 91–101 (p. 97).
4 For each original citation in French, I offer an English equivalent. I have tried to translate as literally as possible, and to imitate the different language registers used by Beti, but I have had to find a balance between this and representing the meaning of the textual fragments.

than Bakhtinian hybridity-as-fusion, we are dealing with a juxtaposition of elements (a patchwork) where elements join together in an interplay reminiscent of that found in improvised music.

A constant play with French language and culture

Beti's European formation becomes visible in passages where he alludes to writers and aesthetic works from the French canon, or when he employs non-standard forms of the French language such as Old French. But the novel is first and foremost marked by an extensive use of slang or vulgar language, applied in a particularly creative way, such as when one of the characters tell another: 'tu n'es qu'un minable mac merdique qui veut me soutirer du fric'[5] (p. 103). The rhythm created by the alliteration, the assonance and the end rhyme in French makes the statement sound musical and childish despite its vulgar content. In fact, the novel in question contains children's language as well, although employed by grown characters in patronizing ways, as when Eddie asks Zam 'Tu as bobo?'[6] (p. 42), or when the narrator alludes to Zam's dysfunctional relationship: '[Bébète] se tenait avec obstination auprès de Zam comme un toutou apeuré'[7] (p. 57). Beti even makes use of outdated French slang expressions like 'nib de nib'[8] (pp. 76, 165).

Beti also lets his characters play with French words to emphasize certain aspects of the story. The unpleasant Frenchman Georges Lamotte, who exploits young girls, has probably not been given his name accidently – among other things, the word *motte* can refer to the female genitalia. Moreover, as 'motte de beurre' means a piece of butter, Lamotte's surname can be said to invoke an unpleasant or greasy side to his character. Thus, when Eddie repeats 'Lamotte, Lamotte, Lamotte-de-beurre. Oui…', the reader can possibly tie the pun to the neocolonial presence in Cameroon, here represented by Lamotte (p. 181). Moreover, Beti creates a meta-level comment on the use of the French language among Cameroonians. In the following passages, it is explicitly indicated that a certain word or expression belongs to a variety of the French language

---

5 'you're nothing but a pathetic shitty pimp who wants to squeeze out my dough'.
6 'Have you got a boo-boo?'
7 '[Bébète] held stubbornly on to Zam like a scared doggie'.
8 'nothing, nix'.

used in the Cameroonian society where the story takes place: 'un axiome local selon lequel la bouche qui mange ne parle pas', and 'Et avec lui, un peu c'est souvent beaucoup, et même *très beaucoup* comme nous disons ici'[9] (pp. 198, 155). This explicit linguistic awareness reminds the reader of the fact that even though Beti writes fluently in French, his identity as well as his aesthetic expression is far from culturally homogenous.

Literary crossroads and code-switching

Beti's literary style is furthermore marked by an interesting mix of European writing conventions and African oral elements, which involves for instance an extensive use of repetition. When a character reports having insisted on something by repeating it, the repetition seems more or less natural even to non-African readers: 'Il peut beaucoup t'aider, beaucoup, beaucoup, beaucoup. Tu as compris, *j'ai dit* beaucoup, beaucoup, beaucoup. Pourquoi tu ne comprends pas ça, ouais! Salut'[10] (p. 167; my emphasis). At other times, however, this stylistic device attracts more attention when appearing directly in a European language, without any explicit reference to the repetition: 'C'est ça la fonction publique, papa. C'est tranquille, tranquille, tranquille'[11] (p. 178). Another feature of the African oral tradition is the creative use of metaphors and rhetorical figures, often connected to fauna and flora. In the following example, Beti describes the hostility that Zam displays towards his best friend at a certain point in the story by using a simile involving the braying of a donkey – at the same time exploiting the similarity between the French verbs *brailler* and *braire*: 'Zam lui braillait aussi fort qu'un âne qui brait'[12] (p. 227). Beti also uses code-switching between French and his mother tongue Éwondo, examples of which are imported directly and remain untranslated in the French text. The interjections 'Aka' or 'Ékyé' are particularly recurrent throughout the novel, each comprising several possible significations, depending on the context. By doing this, Beti accentuates the geographic location of the novel.

---

9 'a local idiom saying: the mouth that eats doesn't talk'; 'And when it comes to him, a little means often *beaucoup* [a lot], or even *très beaucoup* [more than a lot], as we say here'.
10 'He can help you a lot, a lot, a lot, a lot. Do you understand, *I said* a lot, a lot, a lot. Why don't you understand that, huh! Bye!' [my emphasis].
11 'The public sector is like that, papa. It's relaxed, relaxed, relaxed'.
12 'Zam bawled at him as strongly as a donkey that brays'.

From time to time, footnotes are employed to explain or to translate linguistic or cultural elements supposedly unknown to French readers, i.e. '–Yë mabissi!' translated into French as 'Rien à foutre!'[13] (p. 14). Furthermore, many other languages make a brief 'guest appearance'. As readers, we are taken aback when words in Spanish, Italian and Latin are interspersed among the French of the novel. At times these words appear with no particular marking, while at other times they are written in italics or even accompanied by a meta-comment: 'Il procédait [...] par des incursions oratoires qui retentissaient comme autant de pronunciamientos', 'Bon sang, mais bien sûr qu'elle avait une double vie *cosi fan tutte*', and 'Il y a la méthode, le *modus operandi* comme on dit en latin'[14] (pp. 196, 175, 55). Although several of these textual examples are established international expressions, they add more color to an already colorful linguistic landscape. The reader's attention is furthermore drawn by references to surprising cultural contexts such as Haiti and Chile, and Beti even lets one of his characters make up a language from Siberia.

However, it is the English language that occupies the second most important position in the novel. In some dialogues, the use of English seems more or less natural, as when the character in question uses a fixed expression: 'Tu es [...] en quelque sorte *the right man at the right place*, tu comprends ça ?'[15] (p. 121). In other passages, however, only one English word is inserted in the French phrase, for no apparent reason other than putting multilingualism on display: 'Because, moi, je veux savoir' and 'Je m'en vais. Bye-bye'[16] (pp. 113, 140). According to the Cameroonian specialist in African literature, Paul Bandia, the elements borrowed from the English language in *Trop de soleil tue l'amour* 'contribute [...] to the heteronomy of the text by undercutting the dominance of the French'.[17] In this light, the apparently accidental use of English words can be said to have both political and aesthetic significance.

---

13   'I don't give a shit!'
14   'He proceeded [...] with oratorical incursions which resounded like pronunciamientos'; 'Goddamit, but of course she led a double life, *cosi fan tutte*'; 'It's the method, the *modus operandi* as they say in Latin'.
15   'You're [...] in a way *the right man at the right place*, do you understand that?'
16   'Because I, I want to know'; 'I'm off. Bye-bye'.
17   Paul F. Bandia, *Translation as Reparation: Writing and Translation in Postcolonial Africa* (Manchester: St. Jerome Publishing, 2008), p. 158.

For the Cameroonian people, obviously, English is just as much a colonial language as French. Still, it seems to me that the English words and expressions are given a more 'respectful' treatment in the novel than the French ones. In other words, while the French language is put to work in many varied ways, the English language is less 'tampered with'. This is actually rather logical, considering that Beti had a more profound knowledge of French, but also that he probably had a less ambivalent relationship to English. The French colonial administration in Africa was known to impose more extreme assimilation politics than their British counterpart, and there is thus reason to think that for many Cameroonians, there are fewer complications and sensitive associations tied to the English elements than to the French. However, I believe that it is also possible to see the incorporation of elements from different languages in the French phrases as a way of breaking down traditional hierarchies. In contrast to many other African Francophone authors, Beti does not 'violently' subvert the French written language.

A trifle with the narrative framework

Beti adopts an ironical approach to his own work and demonstrates, by virtue of his daring literary style, that the traditional conventions associated with the novel as a genre can be stretched quite far to make certain points. On several occasions, for instance, he makes fun of his own characters. One example of this is when Ébénezer, a fraud and a pimp, is introduced in this particularly shrewd way: 'l'homme à l'éternelle saharienne de bonne coupe, appelé Ébénezer, un prénom comme on n'en fait plus [...]'[18] (p. 203). A few pages later, Beti repeats this negative assessment of the name, and in so doing simultaneously alludes to the naming tradition in African discourse. The subtle insertion of meta-comments reveals Beti's play with different aesthetic traditions: 'Sitôt dépouillé de son éternelle saharienne de bonne coupe, le sieur Ébénezer, un prénom comme on n'en fait plus, même chez nous [...]'[19] (p. 209). Names traditionally occupy an important place in the oral tradition in several African

---

18 'this man with the perpetual safari jacket with a nice cut, who was called Ébénezer, a first name never used nowadays [...]'.
19 'As soon as he was disposed of his perpetual safari jacket with a nice cut, mister Ébénezer, a first name never used nowadays, even here [...]'.

cultures, and they can be employed either to praise a person or to mock him. By insisting on the archaic character of the name 'Ébénezer', the narrator's comment could therefore be seen as simultaneously humoristic and political. That is, the remark 'même chez nous' could be interpreted as a subtle and ironic comeback from a colonized and traditionally mistreated country, insinuating that Cameroon is undergoing a process of modernization which surpasses even that of France.

In other passages, the ridiculing is even more obvious, as when ironic remarks are placed in footnotes. Once again, Ébénezer is viewed in an unfavorable light, this time when he talks about an alleged encounter between the Cameroonian president and Margaret Thatcher. The following comment appears in the footnote presented by the presumed authorial voice: 'Chronologie approximative, sinon carrément douteuse, Margaret Thatcher ayant abandonné le pouvoir en 1990. Mais qu'attendre d'autre de l'homme à la saharienne de bonne coupe?'[20] (p. 194). Some pages later, this happens again: Ébénezer makes another, and this time much more serious, mistake when he talks about a contemporary political development and states that it is happening 'cinq mille ans après Toutankhamon'[21] (p. 200). The reader is then informed that 'Ce type est decidément brouillé avec la chronologie'.[22]

These interventions in the novel lead us to problematize the narrator's position. Does he situate himself within or without the fictional framework? In my opinion, Beti's play with narrative levels corresponds to the Bakhtinian idea of opposing authority, and his exploitation of narrative techniques can be seen not only as a political contribution intended to weaken the continuing presence of imperial powers in post-colonial African countries, but also as a parody of the narrator's superior and omniscient position which was for a long time so dominant in the European literary tradition. Once more, we observe that Beti's authorship is both politically defiant and aesthetically sophisticated.

---

20 'Approximative chronology, if not straight out dubious, considering that Margaret Thatcher had abandoned power in 1990. But what else could you expect from this man with the perpetual safari jacket with a nice cut?'
21 'five thousand years after Tutankhamun'.
22 'That guy is clearly confused when it comes to chronology'.

A 'jazzy literature'

As we have seen, Beti's narrative style consists of a constant play with all kinds of linguistic, literary and cultural references, as well as letting his writing in a European language be influenced by the African oral tradition. We shall now see that the novel also contains a significant number of references to musical phenomena, especially jazz and blues. Zam is a passionate jazz fan, and he namedrops a lot, showcasing his knowledge of jazz artists and songs: 'j'allais oublier Ella scatant dans un *Take the A train* étourdissant'[23] (p. 8). However, the jazz and blues references are not randomly scattered in order to make the text seem more international and 'educated'. There are several occasions when these elements are truly *appropriated* by the characters, as when, towards the end of the novel, Eddie adapts the song lyrics of 'Back O'Town Blues' to Zam's situation by replacing the pronoun 'I' with 'she': 'comme un vrai bluesman qui pleure sans retenue: – *But she was'nt* [sic] *satisfied, she had to run around.* Tu entends ça? jamais contente!'[24] (pp. 158–59). I suggest that the prominent position given to musical elements in the novel could be understood as another possible way of breaking down hierarchies, this time between the genres of literature and music.

Beti's jazzy cultural mélange could be interpreted in terms of the Bakhtinian idea of *intentional hybrids* that 'shock, change, challenge, revitalize or disrupt through deliberate, intended fusions of unlike social languages and cultures'.[25] However, rather than thinking in terms of Bakhtin's *fusions*, I believe that the different languages and varied linguistic contexts in Beti's novel ought to be characterized as separate pieces that are merely placed next to each other. Just like the clearly demarcated fabrics in a patchwork, these pieces give the impression of not really being stitched together. Moreover, while it is true that Beti can be said to cast an auto-reflexive light upon translation, interpretation and multilingualism, he actually abstains, in most cases, from translation, and

---

23 'I almost forgot Ella scatting in an astonishing *Take the A train*'.
24 'like a true bluesman who cries, unrestrained: *But she was'nt* [sic] *satisfied, she had to run around.* Do you hear that? Never happy!'
25 Pnina Werbner, 'Introduction: The dialectics of cultural hybridity', in *Debating Cultural Hybridity: Multi-Cultural Identities and the Politics of Anti-Racism*, ed. by Pnina Werbner and Tariq Modood (London: Zed, 1997), pp. 1–26 (p. 5). The wording is Werbner's.

appears rather to indicate that not all words or expressions *can* be translated. In other words, even if Beti can be said to blur the boundaries between cultures, I think we can state that it is a more a question of juxtaposing them than of *fusing* them, because each language and culture gets to keep its distinctive qualities. This brings to mind the Greek post-colonialist Nikos Papastergiadis' reading of Bakhtin:

> [T]he 'doubleness' of the hybrid voices is composed *not* through the *integration* of differences but via a series of dialogical counterpoints, each *set against the other*, allowing the language to be both the same and different.[26] [my emphasis]

If we follow the idea of a jazzy literature, Beti's narrative style can be seen as an allegory of the improvisation of a jazz band, where the attention is drawn towards one instrument at a time, giving each of them the opportunity to 'shine'.

Conclusion

Beti's literary production thematizes differences between cultures and the tragic results of conflicts and miscommunication, which are presented through a fascinating mix of languages, discourses and various perspectives on art and on human life. Beti writes in a style that could serve to remind us of the infinite possibilities residing in cultural encounters. Even though his hybrid narrative form seems to be triggered initially by political injustice, I suggest that it is possible to put aside this aspect and concentrate on finding out what happens to a literary text when different languages and cultures meet. I think that writers like Beti, whether we prefer to call them cross-cultural, inter-cultural or something else, offer a kind of aesthetic experience that calls into question our traditional perception of art. By offering such a great number of facets and perspectives, Beti can be said rather to adhere to the African oral tradition or to postmodern ideas of literature in the Occident, where the principle of dialogue

---

26 Nikos Papastergiadis, 'Tracing hybridity in theory', in *Debating Cultural Hybridity: Multi-Cultural Identities and the Politics of Anti-Racism*, pp. 257–81 (p. 267).

is valorized, than to older, classical Western works, where the author was seen as the sole creator of the text. It is interesting to note that one of the characters in the novel is described as 'une espèce de sergent Garcia africain'[27] (p. 119). Sergent Garcia is a French artist who defines his own style as 'salsamuffin', a true mix of different musical genres. I therefore interpret 'une espèce de sergent Garcia africain' as an allusion to an Africanization of something that is already hybridized, a possible metaphor of the cultural mélange in the novel as a whole.

I propose that by means of Beti's refreshing literary attitude, he invites us to draw inspiration from new contexts, and to oppose the general human inclination to categorize and exclude. I suggest that the aesthetics to be found in such a 'patchwork of cultures' precisely resides in the mixing of conventions. In my opinion, this approach offers more of a challenge to the reader than if the author had presented a more harmonious fusion of cultures, for with the classic metaphor of a melting pot would have been more appropriate. Beti instead tears apart our comfort zones, the reader's familiar sphere, and forces us, if not to fully take in the quality of each cultural context, at least to notice their existence. Throughout *Trop de soleil tue l'amour*, Beti never once conceals the complicated issues of life, nor does he simplify the complexity of a multicultural community. However, despite his sharp political involvement, he manages, in *Trop de soleil tue l'amour*, to *depict* the multicultural modern world more than *judging* its state.

The novel's mixing of cultures could either lead to a feeling of 'unhomeliness' as described by Freud and the postcolonial theorist Homi Bhabha, or it could create the sensation of possible new homes, filled with yet unexplored ideas. We can become more involved in political questions or we can simply appreciate the hybrid style and enjoy the musical and multicolored literary language, without forgetting that the undertones remain blue in a story such as *Trop de soleil tue l'amour*. I will leave the final words to one of Beti's own characters: 'Il n'y a rien à comprendre dans la vie. Il y a le feeling, un point c'est tout. Le feeling, tu sais ce que c'est? C'est comme dans le blues'[28] (pp. 41–2).

---

27 'a kind of an African sergent Garcia'.
28 'There is nothing to understand in life. It's all about the feeling, that's it. The feeling, you know what that is? It's like the blues'.

Bibliography

Bandia, Paul F., *Translation as Reparation: Writing and Translation in Postcolonial Africa* (Manchester: St. Jerome Publishing, 2008).

Beti, Mongo, *Trop de soleil tue l'amour* (Paris: Editions Julliard, 1999).

Papastergiadis, Nikos, 'Tracing hybridity in theory', in *Debating Cultural Hybridity: Multi-Cultural Identities and the Politics of Anti-Racism*, ed. by Pnina Werbner and Tariq Modood (London: Zed, 1997), pp. 257–81.

Sanaker, John Kristian, Karin Holter, and Ingse Skattum, *La francophonie – une introduction critique* (Oslo: Unipub, 2006).

Vivan, Itala, 'African thresholds: Hybridity through the looking-glass', in *Seuils/Thresholds*, special issue of *Anglophonia: French Journal of English Studies*, ed. by Christiane Fioupou (Toulouse: PUM, 2000), pp. 91–101.

Werbner, Pnina, 'Introduction: The dialectics of cultural hybridity', in *Debating Cultural Hybridity: Multi-Cultural Identities and the Politics of Anti-Racism*, ed. by Pnina Werbner and Tariq Modood (London: Zed, 1997), pp. 1–26.

6 Franglais as an example of cultural mélange

Sophie Vauclin

In the American poet Marianne Moore's poem 'Marriage', the speaker describes a woman named Eve who was 'able to write simultaneously/in three languages – /English, German and French/ and talk in the meantime'.[1] The ability to speak and write in different languages has often been prized, but it is interesting that although Eve can 'write simultaneously [...] in English, German and French', the three languages in the poem remain separate and integral – they are not mixed. In reality, of course, there has always been crossover between languages, but with the process of globalization, researchers have become more and more interested in evaluating the degree to which words, phrases and grammatical structures migrate from one language to another. In this study I focus on the integration of five English words in the French language, adopting a sociolinguistic approach in an attempt to see *not* how the words are used productively by speakers and writers of the language (this would be the common approach), but how they are received by readers and listeners – using *receivers' understanding* of the given words as a measure of their degree of integration into the French language.

According to the French dictionary *Le Petit Robert*, a language is a system of expression and communication common to a social group (a linguistic community). The notion of a unified linguistic community is, however, one which

---

1 Marianne Moore, *Becoming Marianne Moore: The Early Poems, 1907–1924*, ed. by Robin G. Schulze (Berkeley: The University of California Press, 2002), pp. 115–16.

is becoming more and more out of synch with emerging realities: we are living in an increasingly intercultural society and changes in our vocabulary, among other things, reflect this. The use of anglicisms in French (or speaking *Franglais*, a term invented by the journalist André Rigaud in 1955) is, as is well known, a politically sensitive issue, but today it is becoming increasingly clear that linguistic change has to be seen on a more global scale, since population movement, migration and global communication have never been more prolific.[2] In looking more closely at the extent to which these five English words are adopted by French speakers, I want to explore the idea that the French may be witnessing the emergence of a multicultural language – their language.

The study

I began my investigation by devising and sending questionnaires to French-speaking respondents whose level of proficiency in English was known to be a result of their encounters with the language within the French school system, rather than of, for example, extended stays in Anglophone countries.[3] In the questionnaire, respondents were asked to try to explain the meanings of a selection of English loanwords taken from Titiou Lecoq's *Les Morues*, published in 2011.[4] This novel was chosen because it is contemporary: the goal of my research is to understand and evaluate some *recent* adoptions into French of words that were originally English. The fact that this book appeared in 2011 ensured that I would have a current or up-to-date lexical base to work from. Not all of the books published in 2011 are necessarily sources of freshly borrowed English words, however; thus it was necessary to find a text that featured a number of fictional oral dialogues, since spontaneous oral dialogues – which are models for fictional dialogues – are a great source of borrowed words and code-switching. Lecoq's text was chosen because the author represents this kind of orality in a convincing manner. It was very impor-

---

2   See, for example, Peter Grigg, 'Toubon or not Toubon: The influence of the English language in contemporary France', *English Studies*, 78:4 (1997), 368–84.
3   This knowledge was obtained on the basis that all of the respondents were directly or indirectly acquainted in some way with the researcher.
4   *The Sluts* [this and all subsequent translations are mine] (Vauvert: Au diable Vauvert, 2011).

tant as well that the words chosen made me react; that I, as a French speaker, had to stop and think in order to be able to process their meaning, since this indicated a certain level of unfamiliarity or freshness in a given word, as well as pointing to potential problems as regards the issue of the word's integration into the language. A number of questions were then developed: Are the French able to understand certain words? Do the French understand these words correctly (in regards to their original meaning)? Has the original meaning of some of the words changed since their adoption into French and, if so, in what way? Can these words be said to belong to the French vocabulary today?

The questionnaire

One hundred questionnaires, anonymously completed, form the corpus for this study. The questionnaires began with general questions regarding age and gender. For the sake of convenience, I present the results for age (which proved to be the most significant variable) in a table below.

Table 1 Ages of respondents

12 to 19 years (N=13)
20 to 29 years (N=14)
30 to 39 years (N=16)
40 to 49 years (N=22)
50 to 59 years (N=12)
60 to 69 years (N=16)
70 and over (N=7)

Among the one hundred respondents thirty-three were men and sixty-seven women. The respondents were asked to pass judgment on their own level of proficiency in English, and the majority responded that their level was either *faible* [poor], or *moyen* [mediocre].

The main body of the questionnaire consisted of a list of sentences extracted from the novel, each containing a recent English loan word or expression that the respondents were asked to define or explain, without using any aids such as dictionaries.

Selection of words

As a reference point I have used *Le Petit Robert*, on the grounds that any word included in this dictionary has to be approved by a committee of lexicographers who track down neologisms, hybrid forms, and loan words using written sources in the French language (including books, newspapers, and the internet).[5] Of the words selected for this study, one is included in *Le Petit Robert* while the others are not, which brings out interesting contrasts and complexities.

The following are the words selected from *Les Morues*, in their immediate contexts:

1. Il avait toujours eu le teint pâlot du **nerd**[6] (p. 140)
2. Des fleuves de **slime** devaient dégouliner sous la rue de Valois[7] (p. 126)
3. Il fallait bien appeler cela la **coolitude**[8] (p. 201)
4. C'est de la politique de la **lose**[9] (p. 192)
5. T'es carrément un **no-life**[10] (p. 65)

Of these, only *nerd* has an entry in *Le Petit Robert*; *slime*, *coolitude*, *lose* and *no-life* have not. In the following, I deal with these in turn.

Nerd

Nerd was selected because its inclusion in the dictionary shows that it is officially viewed as an integral part of the French vocabulary. The dictionary entry states that the word was accepted in 1995, that it is of Anglophone origin, and that it can be defined it as follows: 'Personne passionnée de sciences et de techniques, notamment d'informatique, qui y consacre la majeure partie de son temps, jusqu'à l'asociabilité'.[11]

---

5 *Le Nouveau Petit Robert* (Paris: Dictionnaires Le Robert, 1993).
6 'He had always had the pale complexion of a **nerd**'. Here and in what follows, the emphasis is mine.
7 'Rivers of **slime** were dripping below the Rue de Valois'.
8 'It had to be called **coolness**'.
9 'It's a **losing** politics'.
10 'You're a downright **no-life**'.
11 'Someone passionate about science and technology, especially computers, and who devotes most of his time to it, to the point of becoming an asocial person'.

Initially, one might be tempted to think that the fact that the word has an entry in Le Petit Robert means that the majority of respondents in this study should recognize it. The definition shows that *nerd* has been part of the French language for nearly twenty years: it was first accepted into the dictionary in 1995. From a historical perspective, it is, however, still a relatively new word and one therefore wonders if it is really understood as belonging to the language. This is what my questionnaire seeks to find out.

The table below shows a variety of responses. People aged 50 and over simply do not understand the word *nerd*, and this is clear either from a lack of definition/explanation of the given word or expression by respondents in this age group, or because they have provided an incorrect definition/explanation. Hence, for these respondents, *nerd* would probably not be regarded as a word 'belonging to the French language'.

Table 2 Understanding of *nerd* in relation to age

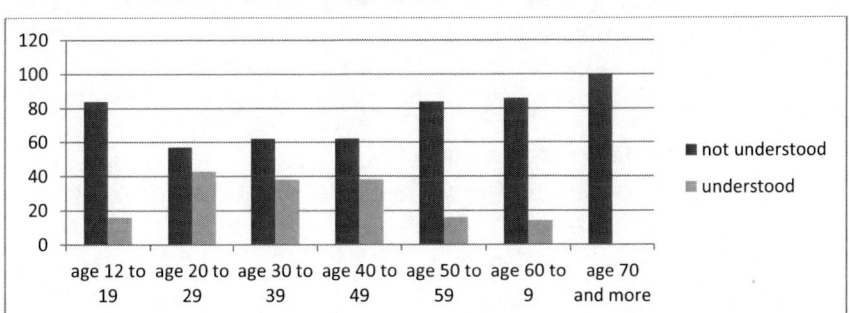

Perhaps more surprisingly, many young people under the age of 19 (who are still in high school) do not appear to recognise the word either. One would think that *nerd* is a word that belongs to the world of young adults – roughly speaking, to the world in which Titiou Lecoq's novel is set. Lecoq's book dramatizes the lives of a group of young and trendy people living in Paris – people like the author herself, in fact – who are *bobos*, an acronym derived from the English 'bourgeois bohemian', and understood to refer to a person of means, young and cultivated, who seeks authentic values and a life of creativity. The blurb on the back cover describes it thus: 'C'est l'histoire des Morues, trois filles et un garçon, trentenaires féministes pris dans leurs turpitudes amoureuses et professionnelles. […] le roman de comment on s'aime et on se désire, en France, à l'ère de l'internet. C'est le roman d'une époque, la nôtre'.[12] The interesting question raised by these findings is, of course, whether the language used in the book can truly be said to be a cultural mélange between English and French: is it a true representation of French as used by *all* the French, or is it characteristic only of the language of the trendy thirty-somethings in Paris? The present study certainly confirms that this is indeed the relevant age-range – the word is clearly best understood by people between 20 and 40 years old, who generally explain or define *nerd* by recourse to the word *geek* (also an English loanword in French). Both words are connected to a fairly recent social phenomenon, i.e. the information culture of computers and the Internet. The reason for the lack of currency of this word among the youngest age group could in fact be that this kind of way of spending one's time – with eyes glued to a computer screen – is now so established and everyday that it will no longer earn you a derogatory label, and hence *nerd* is no longer a relevant word. The explanation for the lack of knowledge of the word among people over 50 is, of course, different. It was only during the 1990s that the Internet became popular and accessible to all. At this time, the current fifty-somethings would already have been past the point of maximum influentability by a new craze, and hence the word would not have stuck for them.

Gender is not a significant factor for the understanding of *nerd*, as table 3 shows.

Table 3   Understanding of *nerd* in relation to gender

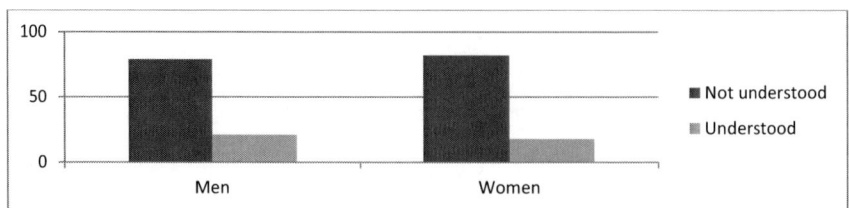

---

12 'This is the story of The Sluts, three girls and a boy, feminists in their thirties, trapped in their own (and others') romantic and professional turpitudes [...] a story about the ways in which we love and desire each other, in France, in the era of the Internet. It is the story of an epoch: ours'.

78% of men and 81% of women do not know the word: age is therefore the primary factor in understanding what *nerd* means. This is also the case for the remaining words, and thus the issue of gender will not be focused on in the following.

Slime

Unlike the term *nerd*, *slime* does not have an entry in *Le Petit Robert*, but nevertheless appears in Lecoq's novel: 'Madame la ministre lui tendit sa main molle. Elle ne prenait même pas la peine de tenter de noyer discrètement le poisson. Ema serra sa main en **slime**. Tandis qu'elle la raccompagnait à la porte, Ema pensa que c'était ça le mystère des arcanes du pouvoir. Des fleuves de **slime** devaient dégouliner sous la rue de Valois'[13] (p. 126).

In Titiou Lecoq's text the word *slime* is used more or less in the same way as the original English word, to denote a viscous substance. The vast majority of my French respondents do not understand this term. Overall, only 13% knew its meaning. Respondents who did understand the word gave definitions using the French equivalents of phrases such as *viscous greenish deposit*, *something viscous*, *gelatinous liquid*, and *thick sticky mud*. Interestingly, two of the respondents, a twenty-year old man and a thirty-two year old woman, mentioned the film *SOS fantômes* [*Ghostbusters*] from 1984, which depicts rivers of green slime in the sewers of New York – slime which then turns into monsters. This illustrates how foreign words, especially English words, travel with popular culture. Nevertheless, even if the word is used in a recent French novel, it probably cannot really be said to be a part of the French language. In using it, the writer mainly addresses people of her own age group – ones likely to be familiar with the movie.

---

13 'The minister held out her limp hand [...] Ema squeezed her **slimey** hand. While she showed her to the door, Ema thought that that must be the mystery of the corridors of power. Rivers of **slime** were dripping below the Rue de Valois'.

Table 4 Understanding of *slime* in relation to age

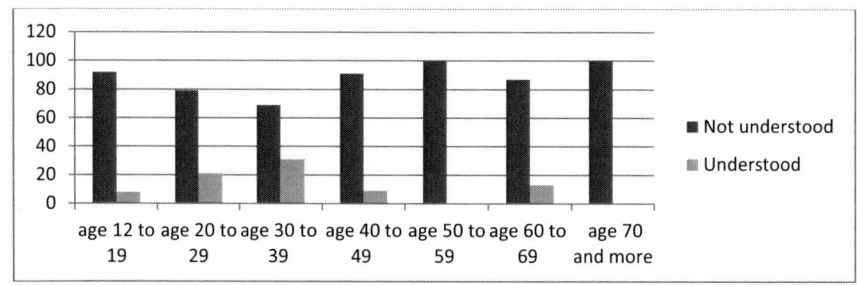

The respondents who understood *slime* comprise a small group of people (31%) in their thirties who belong to the same generation as the author. In the previous and subsequent generations (20 to 29 years, and 40 to 49), the word is less well understood or not understood at all (20% and less than 10%, respectively).

Looking at *nerd* and *slime* together, an interesting pattern emerges. In both cases, we see that the youngest age group do not understand well a word that is generally understood by all 20–40-year-olds. This might suggest that at least some English loan words are so strongly connected to a given, limited, sociohistorical context that they fall into *and* out of use within a relatively short period. In other words, loan words, which are normally thought of as permanent facts of the receiving culture, may in fact come and go.

Coolitude, la lose and *no-life*

We turn now to the last three words of the study, which, despite the fact that they objectively share the same status as *slime* in not having been entered into *Le Petit Robert*, are nevertheless significantly better known to French speakers than the latter.

Table 5 Understanding of *coolitude, la lose, no-life,* and *slime*

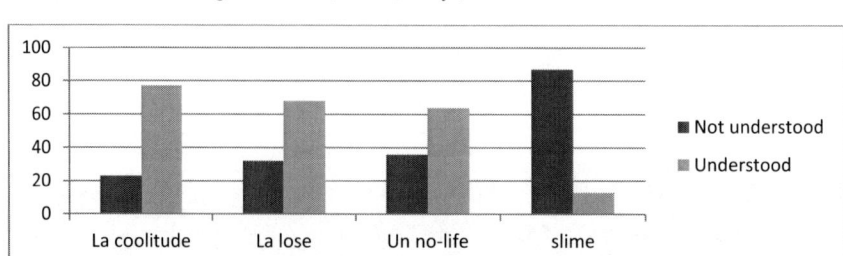

77% of the respondents report that they know and understand the word *coolitude*. 25% used the adjective *cool* (which does figure in the French dictionary) to explain the meaning of *coolitude* and 39% use the word *attitude* in their responses. Since *coolitude* is a portmanteau term combining the words *cool* and *attitude*, this is a predictable result. Words used to translate *coolitude* were the French equivalents to *zen, peace, nonchalance, wellness, relaxation,* and *serenity,* and adjectives like *relaxed, casual,* and *calm*. Two people proposed translations that reveal perhaps some knowledge of *coolitude*, since they suggest the possible (negative) results of embracing this particular attitude: a man of 61 years proposed *loneliness*, a woman of 66 years *carelessness*. A 78 year old man did the same but with a positive slant in suggesting *the opposite of loneliness*.

Table 6 provides a breakdown of the numbers for *coolitude* with regard to age.

Table 6 Understanding of *coolitude* in relation to age

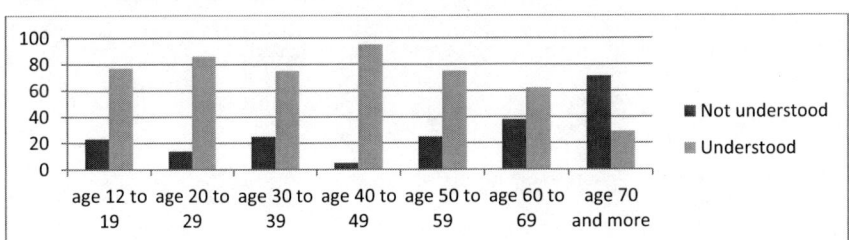

Here, we do not observe the same pattern we saw with *nerd* and *slime*. Although the respondents' understanding of the word does peak somewhat in the age group of 40–49, there is still a decent level of understanding of the word both among the younger and the older respondents. The word *cool*, which we may safely assume forms some kind of template for the understanding of *coolitude*, appeared, according to *Le Petit Robert*, as a loan word in the early 1970s. Those aged 70 today would have been around 25 at that time, and the results then suggest that they were already too old for this new word to be perceived as relevant by them and their peers. For others, *cool* has become a commonplace item of French, urban vocabulary, making the leap to *coolitude* a relatively straightforward one.

The expression *la lose* is associated in Titiou Lecoq's novel with the political world. *(La) lose* as such does not appear in Le Petit Robert, but *loser* does, and thus again there is an 'ancestor loan word' which functions as a template for the understanding of the term under scrutiny. Contrary to *cool*, however, *loser* has only been listed since 1980, which suggests that time since entry into a much-used dictionary is not a, or the only, criterion determining the level of knowledge of a word within a general populace (since both words – *coolitude* and *lose* – seem to be equally widely understood amongst the members of the group of respondents as a whole). Lecoq's neologism, using the English root *lose*, denotes, however, not a person, but rather some kind of state of affairs: 'Mais comment lui expliquer les préceptes, que certains comme Antoine appelaient politique de **la lose**, qui régissaient sa vie?'[14] (p. 192).

As with *coolitude*, we see that everyone apart from the very oldest generations, report that they understand the expression *la lose*:

Table 7 Understanding of *la lose* in relation to age

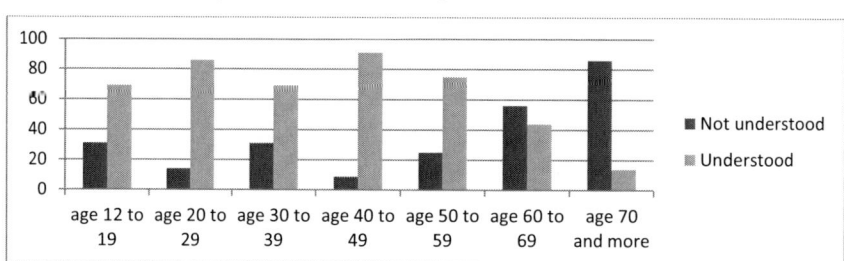

The respondents' respective interpretations of the expression (below) are all in line with *Le Petit Robert*'s definition of *loser* as a person who is a failure. Other sources of understanding of the expression may be the use of the expression in dramatic titles such as *Les rois de la lose*,[15] and article titles such as 'Katie Holmes, 2012 l'année de la lose',[16] which has led to the emergence of definitions of the expression in various online dictionaries such as Reverso,[17] Wik-

---

14 'But how to explain to him the principles that governed his life, which some people like Antoine would call a **losing** politics?'
15 *The kings of la lose*, <http://www.lesroisdelalose.com/Les_Rois_de_la_Lose/Accueil.html> [accessed 19 October 2014].
16 Perrine Stenger, 'Katie Homes, 2012 year of la lose', <http://www.voici.fr/news-people/actu-people/la-piece-de-katie-holmes-arretee-faute-de-spectateurs-475436> [accessed 19 October 2014].
17 <http://dictionnaire.reverso.net/francais-definition/spirale%20de%20la%20lose> [accessed 19 October 2014].

tionary,[18] and Sensagent.[19] As far as the present respondents' definitions go, 60% of them have translated *la lose* using a representative from the lexical field of *loss*, either in the form of a noun or an adjective (capable of describing the political world Lecoq refers to). The remaining translations are also negative or pejorative (using French equivalents of the words *rubbish, lousy, failure,* and *bad luck*). In other words, we may conclude that *la lose* is relatively well understood by French speakers.

The expression *no-life* is used by Titiou Lecoq to describe one of the characters in the novel: 'De toute façon, tu ne fais rien de ta vie. T'es carrément un **no-life**. Tu pourrais te rendre utile pour une fois' (p. 65). As regards understanding in relation to age, the pattern that we saw in the case of *coolitude* and *la lose* is in many ways continued here; however, the cut-off line for understanding of *no-life* goes at 50 (while that for *coolitude* and *la lose*, as we saw, goes significantly later).

Table 8 Understanding of *no-life* in relation to age

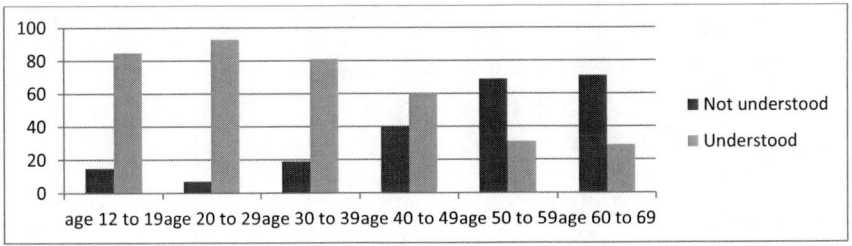

It is not easy to provide an answer to why this difference should exist, other than to point to the fact that unlike *coolitude* and *la lose*, there is, in the case of *no-life*, no ancestor loan word in *Le Petit Robert*, suggesting perhaps, that *life* is a word that has entered French at a later stage (and is thus less well integrated into the language). The various translations of the expression offered by those who understand it suggest likely sources for that understanding.

---

18 <http://fr.wiktionary.org/wiki/lose> [accessed 19 October 2014].
19 <http://dictionnaire.sensagent.com/lose/fr-fr/> [accessed 19 October 2014].

Table 9 Translations of *no-life*

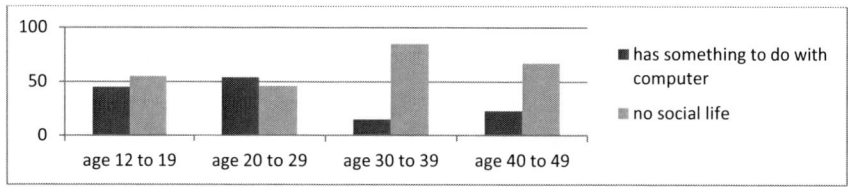

Here, we notice that teenagers and young adults translate the word *no-life* in terms of being addicted to computer games or computers (12 to 19 years: 45% and 20 to 29 years: 54%). Respondents between 30 and 50 years, on the other hand, understand the term, but do not generally associate it with the world of computing. The majority within this group understand a *no-life* to be a person with no social life, full stop. This, of course, reflects social realities – the youngest age group were born into a world of computers, the older not. Common definitions and uses of *no-life* (alternatively *no life*, without the hyphen) on the Internet vacillate between the more specific and the more general definitions chosen by the respondents. While the French Wikipedia's definition focuses on cyberaddiction, as does, interestingly, a video by *francetvéducation*, which presents an interview with 'a teenage *no-life*',[20] other sources, e.g. the online French television channel *Nolife*, use the term in its more general sense. These kinds of use testify to an increasing integration and acceptance of this expression, especially in its more specific meaning, but also as a more general term.

Discussion and conclusions

To sum up, of the five words investigated here, some show drastically different, other quite similar patterns. *Nerd*, despite having been listed in *Le Petit Robert* since 1995, shows a relatively low level of integration, while *slime*, not listed in the dictionary at all, is the least well understood. *Coolitude*, *la lose* and *no-life* are all significantly better understood than *nerd* and *slime*, despite the fact that none of them are listed in the dictionary in and of themselves. This

---

20 <http://education.francetv.fr/videos/cyberdependance-confessions-d-un-ado-no-life-v108784> [accessed 19 October 2014].

indicates that a word's inclusion into *Le Petit Robert* is not a reliable indicator of a loan word's level of integration into the French language. *Nerd* being listed and yet being one of the least well understood words in this study suggests two things: one, that the process of inclusion into the dictionary involves attention to trends, rather than the monitoring of stable frequencies of use/levels of understanding within the population; and secondly, that the main role of dictionaries is to record and conserve, rather than influence new generations of language speakers. What does influence speakers, the study suggests, are relevant socio-cultural developments and popular culture. The development and spread of computer and Internet culture, for example, plays a great role in determining the extent to which, and how, the public perceives loans such as *nerd* and *no-life*. Furthermore, French websites that use Anglophone loans as part of their self-labelling (e.g. the TV station *Nolife* mentioned earlier) and/or in their catchphrases or elsewhere will be making a significant contribution to making such loans known to the general public, as will indeed cultural artefacts such as *Les Morues*.

As far as the current results can in any way tell us anything of the future of French as a *langue mélangée*, the most important and interesting result is perhaps how the fates of *nerd* and *slime*, which both seem to be currently going out of fashion, remind us that the inventory of a language is never fixed: linguistic and indeed cultural mélange is a dynamic, even potentially reversible, process. While this might put some language purists temporarily at ease, it still remains the case, however, that for every loan word that loses currency, probably at least five new ones will be *gaining* currency. With the advent of the Internet, language use and linguistic absorption have become much less controllable activities, and no amount of language policy is probably ever going to be able to stem the influx of high-frequency *lingua franca* words into the vocabularies of the world's languages, as long as users find it practical and desirable to adopt them. Experience from a number of languages shows, however, that the use of loan words is a highly context-bound activity: they are most often the hallmark of oral and informal communication, and of texts that draw on such oral and informal use. In other words, there are contexts where such fresh loans as those exemplified here, are not accepted and hence not (or only rarely) used – such as political and academic discourse. Mélange is thus not only dynamic, but also often partial and context-bound. This means that the core of a given national language is always likely to be preserved at some level or other, and together with solid language policies in place, such a core is also likely to persist in the longer term.

Bibliography

Anon, 'Les Rois de la Lose', <http://www.lesroisdelalose.com/Les_Rois_de_la_ Lose/Accueil.html> [accessed 19 October 2014].

'Cyberdépendance: confessions d'un ado "no-life"', FranceTvÉducation, <http://education.francetv.fr/videos/cyberdependance-confessions-d-un-ado-no-life-v108784> [accessed 19 October 2014].

Grigg, Peter, 'Toubon or not Toubon: The influence of the English language in contemporary France', *English Studies*, 78:4 (1997), 368–84.

Le Nouveau Petit Robert (Paris: Dictionnaires Le Robert, 1993).

Le Wiktionnaire: An Online French Dictionary, <http://fr.wiktionary.org/wiki/lose> [accessed 19 October 2014].

Lecoq, Titiou, *Les Morues* (Vauvert: Au diable Vauvert, 2011).

Moore, Marianne, *Becoming Marianne Moore: The Early Poems, 1907–1924*, ed. by Robin G. Schulze (Berkeley: The University of California Press, 2002).

Reverso: An Online French Dictionary, <http://dictionnaire.reverso.net/francais-definition/spirale%20de%20la%20lose> [accessed 19 October 2014].

Sensagent: An Online French Dictionary, <http://dictionnaire.sensagent.com/lose/fr-fr/> [accessed 19 October 2014].

Stenger, Perrine, 'Katie Homes, 2012 l'année de la lose', <http://www.voici.fr/news-people/actu-people/la-piece-de-katie-holmes-arretee-faute-de-spectateurs-475436> [accessed 19 October 2014].

7 The mélange of multimodality: Picture books in translation

Riitta Oittinen

The interplay of verbal, visual and even aural resources play an important role in communication in the modern world. Written text (visual verbal), illustration (visual nonverbal) and speech (aural verbal) are all important modes of communication, which we interact with on a daily basis. This applies to translation studies and translation as well, because increasing numbers of text being translated include multimodal elements, such as sounds and images. As demonstrated by Mary Snell-Hornby, it is only recently that translation studies has accepted multimodality as a resource of translation.[1] The development most likely began when Katharina Reiss, in 1971, decided to add an audiomedial text type to her typology.[2] Afterwards, the text type was renamed as multimedial, covering texts with visual and/or aural elements, in other words nonverbal communication. Later on, Reiss drew the conclusion that all texts, whatever their type, carry multimedial and nonverbal meanings, which are thus parts of the texts to be translated.

Today the kaleidoscope of translations covers areas such as picture books, films, comics, opera libretti, TV programmes, subtitling and the translation of manuals as well as technical documents. Interpreters, too, need to pay attention to the body language of the person who is being interpreted in order to tease

---

1 Mary Snell-Hornby, *The Turns of Translation Studies: New Paradigms or Shifting Viewpoints?* (Amsterdam: John Benjamins, 2006), pp. 84–5.
2 Katharina Reiss, *Möglichkeiten und Grenzen der Übersetzungskritik* (München: Max Hueber Verlag, 1971).

out a fuller sense of what is being said. Nevertheless, the focus in translation studies is still primarily on verbal language. Although relatively little attention has been paid to the contribution made by nonverbal visual and aural elements in translation, in the last decade or so these areas have attracted the interest of scholars such as Klaus Kaindl (2004), Jehan Zitawi (2004), Jürgen Schopp (2005), Yves Gambier and Henrik Gottlieb (2007), Margherita Ippolito (2008), and Sari Kokkola (forthcoming), just to mention a few.[3]

In what follows, I look into the verbal, the visual and the aural (picture books read aloud) within the context of picture book translation.[4] I show that when the different modes mix into a multimodal mélange, this sometimes entails cultural mélange, and it often becomes impossible to separate out any details from the whole, without this whole being altered.[5] As an example I use the Finnish book creator Mauri Kunnas's humoristic version of the Finnish national epic *The Kalevala,* along with humoristic versions of Akseli Gallen-Kallela's traditional visual depictions of *The Kalevala.*

---

3 Klaus Kaindl, 'Multimodality in the translation of humour in comics', in *Perspectives on Multimodality,* ed. by Charles Ventola and Martin Kaltenbacher (Amsterdam: John Benjamins, 2004), pp. 173–92; Jehan Zitawi, *The Translation of Disney Comics in the Arab World: A Pragmatic Perspective* (Manchester: The University of Manchester, School of Modern Languages, 2004); Jürgen Schopp, 'Gut zum Druck?' *Typographie und Layout im Übersetzungsprozess.* Acta Universitatis Tamperensis 1117 (Tampere: University of Tampere, 2005); Yves Gambier and Henrik Gottlieb, *(Multi)Media Translation: Concepts, Practices and Research* (Amsterdam: John Benjamins, 2007); Margherita Ippolito, 'The relationship between text and illustrations: Translating Beatrix Potter's Little Books into Italian', in *Who's Story? Translating the Verbal and the Visual in Literature for Young Readers,* ed. by Maria González Davies and Riitta Oittinen (Newcastle: Cambridge Scholars, 2008), pp. 85–96; Sari Kokkola, 'The role of sound in subtitling narrative fiction films' (forthcoming).
4 Picture books may also include other stimuli that have an influence on how the books are understood: there may be smells or different activities for the child, such as flip-a-flap-books or draw-it-yourself-books, where the pages are empty except for the written text, allowing the child to illustrate the story her/himself. There may also be stimuli for the tactile sense, such as using different materials that the child can touch, or there may be other kinds of stimuli for the child, such as pushbuttons that make different sounds. This article, however, only concentrates on the verbal, the visual and the aural (reading aloud).
5 A special thank you to Anne Ketola for helping me to open up and define 'mélange' and 'mix of modes'.

The relationship of the verbal, the visual and the aural in texts

Even on the first encounter the verbal and the visual have a strong impact on the definition of a text – both the original and that of the translator. Further, picture books, for example, are often read aloud, which, giving them an aural aspect, makes them a very special kind of book. Apart from their aural aspects, films include side materials, trailers, posters, and DVD covers.[6] Illustrated texts are interpreted in a certain context: time, place, culture, ideology, audience, and genre are all factors in the interpretation; on the other hand, the reader's interpretation is strongly influenced by the co-text, which include the elements of the actual text to be read, the material network of meanings consisting of the information given by the different modes.[7] In the case of picture books or other texts containing visual elements, the actual pictures themselves are only one element of a visual totality which also includes the print itself, the size and shape of letters, the headings, composition, and picture sequence as well as the elements of the typography and layout and the visual design as a whole.[8] The cover picture, too, has a pre-influence on understanding a book: a cover might, for instance, show the main characters and their surroundings, as well as suggesting an atmosphere. Moreover, a cover often contains intertextual elements and cultural markers, such as the separate covers for children and adults of J.K. Rowling's *Harry Potter* series, as well as the covers of Disney's *Cinderella* which depict a character who is the spitting image of the original in the film.[9] In this way it is made possible for the reader (and viewer) to

---

6 The narratologist Gérard Genette discusses texts in several of his writings and uses categories such as paratexts, peritexts and epitexts. Paratexts are divided into peritexts (the concrete parts of the text: paper, cover, headings) and epitexts (book/film reviews, diaries, letters). According to Genette, a work of art is a combination of the peritext and the actual story; a text is a part of a work of art excluding anything paratextual. Gérard Genette, *Palimpsest: Literature in the Second Degree*, trans. by Channa Newman and Claude Daubinsky (Lincoln: University of Nebraska Press, 1997), pp. 24–6.
7 Riitta Oittinen, *Translating for Children* (New York and London: Garland Publishing, 2000), pp. 92–129.
8 Riitta Oittinen, 'From Thumbelina to Winnie-the-Pooh: Pictures, words and sounds in translation', in *Le verbal, le visual, le traducteur/The Verbal, the Visual, the Translator*, ed. by Riitta Oittinen and Klaus Kaindl (Montréal: META, 53.1 [2008]), pp. 76–89 (pp. 77–9).
9 For *Cinderella* see also Maria González Davies 'Fairy tale retellings as translation: Developing verbal and visual intercultural competence', in *Who's Story? Translating the Verbal and the Visual in Literature for Young Readers*, ed. by Maria González Davies and Riitta Oittinen (Newcastle: Cambridge Scholars Publishing, 2008), pp. 115–29.

recognize the character and expect a similar story. In each instance, the cover is part of the artwork.[10]

In other words, the notion of text in such instances is not easy to define, but may refer to the verbal only or to the verbal-visual-aural mix of originals or translations (iconotexts such as picture books and films). 'Text' may also refer to the whole intertextual world of texts that translators have exploited when creating their translations.[11] In other words, every time a book is illustrated, a song or poem performed or an audiovisual text subtitled or dubbed, a change occurs in the visual and aural aspects and thus in the whole situation in which the texts are understood. These changes are multiplied and made more complicated, because besides translating, audiences and cultures inevitably change, too. All this creates circumstances where the details are part of an entity and cannot be separated from it, or the whole context of understanding.

The Russian philosopher Mikhail Bakhtin would describe this situation as multivoiced dialogics: a reading experience consists not only of the texts as they are, but also of the voices of different illustrators and sound designers, as well as writers in contexts such as the past, present and future. Indeed, human sounds, pictures and words are never created in a vacuum, but always occur in specific circumstances. Bakhtin also makes a distinction between 'the given' and 'the created': '"The given" is the "material," the resources, with which we speak and act'.[12] Speaking of translation, this would be taken as meaning the medley of sounds, illustrations and words presented in a source text. Still, no text is simply a 'product' of what is given: every process of understanding and interpreting the text creates something that did not exist before (p. 166). Hence, in translating complex modes such as texts containing images and written texts read aloud with words (seen on paper), the voices of composers, illustrators, writers, translators, and readers are melded together into new meanings. In

---

10   See Kaisu Rättyä, 'Kirjan kansikuva peritekstinä' ['Book cover as a peritext'], in *Tutkiva katse kuvakirjaan* [*A Scholarly Look at Picture Books*], ed. by Kaisu Rättyä and Raija Raussi (Helsinki: BTJ Kirjastopalvelu Oy and Suomen Nuorisokirjallisuuden Instituutti 2001), pp. 177–93.
11   Riitta Oittinen, 'From Thumbelina to Winnie-the-Pooh: Pictures, words and sounds in translation', pp. 76–89.
12   Mikhail Bakhtin, *Problems of Dostoyevsky's Poetics*, trans. by Caryl Emerson (Minneapolis: University of Minnesota, 1987), p. 166. All further references to this edition are given parenthetically by page number after quotations in the text.

other words, any changes in the set of conditions, such as a sound or an illustration, transform the situation of understanding into something new.[13]

This situation could also be depicted as multimodality, where texts employ different modes such as spoken language, written language and illustration, all having an influence on each other, stimulating the different senses of the eye (written verbal text, illustration) and the ear (spoken verbal text). For all that, in one way or the other, these modes are incommensurable and need the amplification of all the other voices.[14] For example, pictures may represent aspects that are impossible to fully depict verbally (see also the illustration on p. 103).[15] According to the principles of multimodality, the verbal, the visual and the aural when separate, carry a different meaning from when they are together: in a new context, such as in picture book translation, the different constituents of texts are mingled within a new story, a new work of art, and a new mix.

The above may be described through Hans-Georg Gadamer as well: translating is a hermeneutic process and understanding is not decoding, but stepping into the hermeneutic circle and contributing to the multitude of voices. In other words, understanding is like a process of mélange: 'the merging of various horizons, those of the different readers and those of the different writers [and, those of the illustrators, often living in different cultures]'.[16] In the case of an illustrated text, it may be depicted as a polyphonic form of art: it is an art form with many different voices to be heard and seen. During the translation process, translators enter the hermeneutic circle of understanding the texts they translate, and start with an initial understanding of the entity, reading the text first with curiosity and wonder. Moving further from the first

---

13   Mikhail Bakhtin, *The Dialogic Imagination*, trans. by Caryl Emerson and Michael Holquist (Austin: University of Texas Press, 1981), p. 30.
14   See also Kai Mikkonen, *Kuva ja sana. Kuvan ja sanan vuorovaikutus kirjallisuudessa, kuvataiteessa ja ikonoteksteissä* [*Word and Image. The Interaction of Word and Image in Literature, Pictorial Arts and Iconotexts*] (Helsinki: Gaudeamus, 2005).
15   Jay Lemke, 'Travels in hypermodality', *Visual Communication*, 1 (2002), 299–325 (p. 303). My thanks to Anne Aaltonen for bringing this to my attention.
16   Riitta Oittinen, *Translating for Children* (London and New York: Garland Publishing, 2000), p. 19; Hans-Georg Gadamer, *Truth and Method* (*Wahrheit und Methode*) trans. by Garrett Barden and John Cumming (New York: Crossroad, 1985) pp. 271, 273.

meeting with the text, they start pondering on the entity and solving the smaller problems. In other words, translation may be described as moving between parts and entities, from the big picture towards smaller items and the other way around.[17] The original story as well as the forthcoming translation have purposes, which have an influence on the way the translator interprets the parts of the entity. This reading is also influenced by the translator's individual situation and her/his relation to the present reality, such as culture and society, which are all part of the situation of hermeneutic understanding or dialogics or mélange.

The illustrations in a picture book produce an effect on the reading (by the child her/himself, looking (at the pictures and written text), listening (to the adult reading a book aloud)), and on the whole experience, through conformity and deviation: in one way or another, illustrations take stories into new mixes of modes. This happens through, e.g., focal points: the illustrator may stress certain scenes or certain characteristics of the persons in the story. This happens in the first picture in *Voices in the Park* (1998)[18] by Anthony Browne: at first the reader pays attention to the big house with windows like eyes and a door like a mouth. Yet the verbal text gives the looker another focal point: 'It was time to take Victoria, our pedigree Labrador, and Charles, our son, for a walk'. This makes the reader pay attention to a detail at the bottom of the picture depicting a gorilla lady, boy and dog. The house does not appear in the story later. David Lewis studies the relationship of the verbal and the visual using the case of a picture book as an example.[19] Texts are interanimated, according to Lewis, through the interaction of the verbal and the visual; they are also flexible through the changes of interanimation from page to page due to the activity of the author, illustrator and reader. Moreover, texts are complex and diverse, because they contain diverse words and images and their combinations are both thematically and formally complex (p. 37).

---

17 Mary Snell-Hornby, *The Turns of Translation Studies: New Paradigms or Shifting viewpoints?* (Amsterdam: John Benjamins, 2006), p. 69. All further references are to this edition and are given parenthetically by page number after quotations in the text.
18 Anthony Browne, *Voices in the Park* (London: Doubleday, 1998), np.
19 See David Lewis, *Reading Contemporary Picturebooks: Picturing Text* (London and New York: Routledge, 2001), pp. 36–7. All further references are to this edition and are given parenthetically by page number after quotations in the text.

The relationship of words and images has also been described as echoing: words and images stand in a dialogue and respond to each other. For example, in audiovisual texts or, e.g., texts for the theatre, images have, by virtue of echoing, different meanings and tasks and they may take different roles.

In audiovisual texts, picture books, and the like, the three semiotic modes of verbal, visual and aural are always present. In other words, picture books, for example, may be depicted as iconotexts that include the three different modes (understanding the aural, reading aloud, as a mode, too) and they thus share many features with comics and animated films: they are all based on a series of images and have a serial character. Instead of frames, however, picture books involve the turning of pages. Picture books, because they are read aloud, may also be described as a dramatic experience, which approximates theatre and film.

Conventions and nonverbal communication

As readers of illustrations, we need to be aware of several conventions, such as understanding black and white pictures indicating colour. In fact, when we look at a picture of a landscape in black and white, we can, through our imaginations, add depth and colour to the picture. Illustrations also show what the scenery, the characters and their situations look (or sound) like – or they may simply be intended to entertain and decorate the story. They add and omit and make the readers of the book pay special attention to certain parts of the story.[20] Having seen something, a human being tries to figure out what the entity is like and how the pieces fit the bigger picture.

John Spink argues that the nonverbal visual aspect of a text has four functions: an illustrated text may be more based on pictures than on words, or the other way around; there may be collaboration between the verbal and the visual, or the visual may tell quite a different story than the verbal.[21] The collaboration between the verbal and the visual could be looked at in terms of an

---

20 Riitta Oittinen, *Translating for Children*, pp. 32, 101.
21 This description is taken from Juha Herkman, *Sarjakuvan kieli ja mieli* [*The Language and Understanding of Comics*] (Tampere: Vastapaino, 1998), p. 59. See also John Spink, *Children as Readers: A Study* (London: Clive Bingley, Library Association Publishing Limited, 1990).

indexical relationship between the modes: according to Charles Peirce, in texts there are words, icons and indexes; the word is an artificial sign based on an agreement; the icon is a picture, while 'index' points to the nature of the relationship of the two.[22] Using picture books as an example, a picture (showing, e.g., a fox) can be viewed as an icon that refers to something in the real world (a real fox); a word in a picture book (read aloud or silently) can be viewed as a symbol based on an agreement. In addition, there is an indexical relationship between the two: the verbal (spoken or written words) refers to the visual (illustrations) and vice versa. In texts the visual can be understood as the reason for the verbal, and the verbal can be interpreted as the reason for the visual. Of course, the indexical relationship varies from text to text and page to page, which is fundamental in understanding texts, such as comics and audiovisual texts and their narration.[23]

In what follows, this interplay between the verbal and the visual – as well as the aural when a book is read aloud – is demonstrated by reference to an extract from one of Riitta Oittinen's illustrated stories about a wolf, a bear and a fox, which begins 'Olipa kerran susi, karhu ja kettu' ['Once upon a time there was a wolf, a bear, and a fox'].[24] The verbal text is written in two different languages, Finnish and English. At this point we recognize that the story is a fairytale – written for the purpose of being read aloud – as it begins with the words 'once upon a time'. We also know that the story is about three animals or more, but we have no knowledge of what the characters are like and how they relate to each other. However, if we look at the illustration, we get a lot of additional information. By placing the characters in a setting, pictures make the reader believe in the story.

---

22   Charles S. Peirce, *Collected Papers by Charles Sanders Peirce* (Cambridge and London: Harvard University Press, 1932), II, p. 229.
23   Riitta Oittinen, *Kuvakirja kääntäjän kädessä* [*Picture Book in Translator's Hands*] (Helsinki: Lasten keskus, 2004).
24   Riitta Oittinen, *Olipa kerran Susi, Karhu ja Kettu* [*Once upon a Time there was a Wolf, a Bear and a Fox*] (forthcoming).

Figure 1 Oittinen, 'The Wolf, the Bear and the Fox'

The picture shows the Wolf, the Bear and the Fox on board a ship named Martta. The friends are travelling and looking out of the round windows, and they seem very comfortable together. They are probably good friends, and it is probably going to be a nice adventure. It is night time and the skies are black and dotted by stars. There is also a lighthouse in the horizon. All this obviates the need for verbal explanations such as 'there is a ship on its way', 'it is night time' and 'there are stars in the sky'.

If we take a better look at the picture, however, we may start wondering who is actually in charge of the ship, as the zebra standing at the steering wheel has closed his eyes and seems to be asleep. And so are the other dancing, dining, and swimming zebras, too. The only characters that are awake are the three friends. After turning one more page of the book, the reader of the written story learns more: the friends are on Martta as they could not sleep because of a small, snoring worm that had come for a visit. The mood in the picture is soothing and silent, so the reader feels at ease and assured that nothing bad is going to happen.

It is interesting to look into the relationship of the verbal, the visual and the aural from the angle of visual grammar advocated by Günther Kress and Theo van Leeuwen.[25] They apply semiotics as well as M.A.K. Halliday's grammar to reading images, and base their idea on pictures displaying the same kinds of regularities and liabilities as words. Kress and Leeuwen look at visual communication from a sosiosemiotic angle: like words, pictures mirror ideology, power, status, and culture. The visual language, too, aims at a certain target, and visual entities have structures and tasks. For example, the characters shown in pictures have a certain role and a certain status, created by the author and the illustrator. In other words, authors and illustrators make choices, which all have an influence on how the given entity is understood. This is about meanings and action: in pictures, somebody is doing something and aiming for a certain purpose. How well we understand the entities depends on how much we share and how similar our backgrounds are. Using Kress and Leeuwen's terminology, books and films may be described as multimodal texts using 'more than one semiotic code' (p. 183).[26]

The multimodal and cultural mélange of Mauri Kunnas and *The Canine Kalevala*

Mauri Kunnas is one of the best known and most productive picture book creators in Finland. His books, comics, and animated films have been translated into 26 languages.[27] Kunnas tells stories about dogs, elves, space, the wild west, vampires, ghosts and Father Christmas/Santa Claus, as well as the European epic tradition, such as King Arthur and his knights.[28] Kunnas' heroes are dogs, and his style is colourful and rich in humoristic detail, which he combines with everyday realism depicting life in the Finnish countryside in the

---

25   Günther Kress and Theo van Leeuwen, *Reading Images: The Grammar of Visual Design* (Oxford and New York: Routledge, 1996). All further references are to this edition and are given parenthetically by page number after quotations in the text.
26   See also Kress and van Leeuwen as they are described in David Lewis (2001), pp. 145–67.
27   Statistics by *Suomalaisen Kirjallisuuden Seura* 2014.
28   For more on Kunnas in translation see Oittinen (2004), pp. 32–143. See also Melissa Garavini's *La traduzione della letteratura per l'infanzia dal finlandese all'italiano: l'esempio degli albi illustrati di Mauri Kunnas* (doctoral thesis, University of Turku, 2014).

nineteenth century: while his books are full of action and humour, they also include poetic depictions of nature. Kunnas has closely examined not only old Finnish traditions, but also landscapes, tools, and household utensils, which makes his books believable despite their fantastic nature.

Kunnas' picture book *Koirien Kalevala* (1992), translated into Swedish by Lars Huldén (*Hundarnas Kalevala* [*The dogs' Kalevala*], 1994) and into English by Tim Steffa (*The Canine Kalevala*, 1992), is interesting for its intertextuality, which plays out on several levels. The story is based on the Finnish national epic *The Kalevala* and the book also includes illustrations that constitute humorous versions of Akseli Gallen-Kallela's paintings, which are used as illustrations of the original national epic. The translations of Mauri Kunnas' picture books are examples of what happens when texts are translated from Finnish into Swedish and English, when there is a multimodal mix.

Kunnas' story begins with the second poem of the original *Kalevala*, which depicts the creation of the world. From there on, the book closely follows the stories of the epic. Even though a great deal has been left out, the main themes and elements are there. Väinämöinen, the central hero in the book, is a great man, whom Joukahainen wants to fight with. It is Väinämöinen, however, who wins the battle and sings Joukahainen into a swamp. Joukahainen is not released before he promises his sister to Väinämöinen. Joukahainen gives Aino, the fair maiden, to Väinämöinen to be his wife, but Väinämöinen himself believes that Aino is just a house-help for him. Then the story goes on with several fantastic adventures.

What is significantly different between the two works, the original *The Kalevala* and Kunnas' retelling of it, is the mood of the stories: the poetic and often tragic atmosphere of the original has been replaced by humour, laughter, and irony. This change has a strong influence on the characters in the story. For example, Väinämöinen, the great hero in the original, becomes a tiny, crying dog desperately trying to catch Aino, who is transformed from a fair maiden into a big lady not at all interested in the poor Väinämöinen.

The characters are also characterized by their visual appearance. While Kunnas' book contains a lot of verbal text, the storytelling mainly relies on the visual information. On the one hand, the pictures give more depth to the stories told; on the other hand, the pictures provide the settings for the stories and place them in their historical context. The illustration both confirms and deviates from what is said in the verbal text. Through deviation, the illustrator creates humour, even irony. For example, the time of the written story often contradicts that shown in the pictures: while the story is visually placed in the 19th century, the written text may contain very modern phrases and details. The pictures themselves sometimes include modern objects that certainly were not found in the nineteenth-century Finnish countryside. For example, in a scene where Väinämöinen goes swimming, he leaves his false teeth lying on a stone. The detail also underlines the great age difference between the two, Väinämöinen and the young maiden Aino.

The humour in Kunnas's *The Kalevala*, is often created by changing the point of view. Yet the visual jokes function only if the reader recognizes the original paintings behind the canine versions. This is the case with a picture in which the epic's blacksmith Seppo Ilmarinen and his horse plough a field of vipers. In Gallen-Kallela's original, the vipers are mean and the reader feels strongly for the great brave hero. In Kunnas' canine version, the setting is turned upside down: the reader feels sympathy for the poor vipers, who are in great pain.

When it comes to translating *The Canine Kalevala*, the problems caused by textual or nonverbal visual intertextuality and culturally specific details are numerous and difficult to solve. First of all, the translator should consider carefully whether the target-language readers have the ability to deal with the culturally specific information given visually and verbally; how well they know the original stories of *The Kalevala,* and to what extent they are able to recognize Gallen-Kallela's paintings behind Kunnas' canine versions. This is mainly an issue of cultural mélange: how to create a funny story in the target language so that the reader finds it believable.

To give one pertinent example, old Finnish vocabulary has caused many and great problems for the translators. In one scene, Lemminkäinen takes up his skis, 'the long lyly and the short kalhu'. In both translations, while the translators have not rendered the names of the skis, both of them verbally depict what the skis look like. What they look like is evident from the illustration as well. Yet the readers of the translations may feel confused, as they do not know whether the look of the skis and the way of skiing is part of folklore and old Finnish traditions, or whether the funny character Lemminkäinen has a funny way of skiing, too. In the latter case, the scene mainly characterizes Lemminkäinen.[29]

The different solutions chosen in the two translations are due to several reasons, especially cultural differences. The landscapes are not very different from what life used to be in Sweden. (The Swedish-language version is also directed to the Swedish-speaking population in Finland.) In other words, the pictures and stories are more easily understood by a Swedish speaker than an English speaker.

The cultural differences are many and varied between the original and its translations. For example, in the scene where Kunnas depicts Lemminkäinen's mother with her dead and reborn son, Kunnas' illustration shows a rake with long pegs (tines), and the Swedish translator mentions the same thing ('en räfsa [a rake] med långa tinnar [with long tines]'). The English translator, on the other hand, solves the problem differently, referring to 'a long-handled rake'. The English-language version is, however, logical: Lemminkäinen's mother has raked the bottom of the deep river of the dead, *Tuonelan virta*, and found the bits and pieces of her dear son. To be able to do this, the rake certainly needs to be long-handled. Yet Kunnas' picture shows a quite ordinary rake, again part of the old everyday life, when hay was made by man-power.[30] The result is cultural mélange. In another scene, Aino is gathering a bunch of twigs and making a *vihta*: a leafy whisk, which is a tied bunch of birch twigs, used in the Finnish *sauna*. The Swedish-language reader probably realizes that Aino is making a *vihta*, but the English-language reader most likely does not know how the twigs would be used and what a Finnish *sauna* is like. Moreover, the Swedish translation gives a clear reference to the use of the bunch of twigs, while the English translation does not state what Aino is going to do with the *vihta*. To understand the scene, previous knowledge of the tradition is required: if the reader does not recognize the background, s/he misses a lot of information.

Even though it is clear that all the three books (original + two translations) are 'about' the original Finnish *Kalevala*, it is also clear that Kunnas's Finnish-language version stands closest to the original story of *The Kalevala*.

---

29   See also Riitta Oittinen, 'Translating culture: Children's literature in translation', *Literatuur zonder leeftijd*, 67 (2005), 45–56.
30   Unfortunately copyright restrictions mean that the pictures cannot be reproduced here.

This is especially evident in the relationship of the verbal and the visual and with regard to intertextuality. While the translators have mainly translated a witty and humorous picture book, the original digs deeper: it is a rewritten *Kalevala* for Finnish child readers (and grown-ups, too). This is especially evident in the illustrations based on Akseli Gallen-Kallela's originals, recognized by Finnish readers. It is very much the case with *Lemminkäisen äiti*, *Lemminkäinen's mother*, which is said to be Gallen-Kallela's homage to his own mother. The artist himself has said: 'An artist's work is often hard. Painting that canvas, I deliberately tried to make mother take on an expression of pain by talking about things so sombre and gloomy that even she, with her strong nerves, finally bursts into tears'.[31] The picture is full of symbolism and strong feelings, and it is often mentioned as representing the very core of being Finnish. Kunnas' interpretation of the painting could also be depicted in a pantagruelian way as being happy, gay and benevolent. Kunnas's version is full of the defeat of fear and carnivalistic laughter, which is almost therapeutic. By making fun, even mocking, the solemn painting and bringing it to the present day, Kunnas makes it easier for the reader and viewer to ponder on the grief the mother feels as she sits at the side of her dead son. By carnivalizing the original, we are allowed to uncrown the original artist and get closer to the picture.[32]

As regards the two translations, the further removed the cultures and languages are from Finland, the more difficult it is for the readers to recognize the originals behind the canine versions. Lars Huldén, the translator of the Swedish version, has been able to tell the reader more, because his readers will probably recognize at least geographical and historical similarities. The English translator Tim Steffa has been in a different position, because – due to a lack of space, perhaps – he has not been sufficiently able to explain things to his target readers, which has made him rely more heavily on the pictures. This situation could very well be described as cultural mélange due to the fact that

---

31 Akseli Gallen-Kallela, Lemminkäinen's Mother. Tempera, 1897, 85 x 118 cm. Finnish National Gallery Ateneum. See http://www.korundi.fi/news/KAUDEN-KLASSIKKO-11102013%E2%80%931 622014,-Gallen-Kallelan-Lemminkaisen-aiti/irhnbeai/4c1b3a33-26bb-4c53-ba10-6b32fea94e03 [accessed 15 April 2015]. See also http://www.gallen-kallela.fi/gallen-kallela-150-vuotta/ [accessed 15 April 2015].
32 See Riitta Oittinen, 'The verbal and the visual: On the carnivalism and dialogics of translating for children', in *Translating for Children: A Reader*, ed. by Gillian Lathey (Clevedon: Multilingual Matters, 2006), pp. 84–97.

the original illustrations are being kept while the translated verbal text loses its cultural specificity.

The audiences of the two translations are in very different positions. The Swedish-language readers – Swedes living in Sweden and especially the Swedish-speaking minority living in Finland – are, to a certain extent, familiar with the stories and illustrations. By contrast, the average English-language reader does not know the original stories, nor can s/he recognize the original illustrations. The culturally and geographically different situations have caused the translators to use different strategies. While the translator of the English version has had to expand and explain and domesticate, the Swedish-language translator has been more able to rely on foreignization, trusting that his audience will recognize at least some of the verbal and the visual hints.

Conclusion

The translators' own life-long experience and all the texts s/he knows are always present in the act of translation. Translators are also readers, situated in time, place and culture, and anything they have read or experienced has an influence on how they translate. While the Swedish translator manages to preserve the link to the original *Kalevala*, the English translator has lost the text's intertextuality almost completely. Due to geographical and cultural closeness to Finland, the Swedish version is quite close to the original. All in all, verbally, visually, and aurally, the different versions depict and form different cultural mélanges.

Bibliography

Bakhtin, Mikhail M., *The Dialogic Imagination*, trans. by Caryl Emerson and Michael Holquist (Austin: University of Texas Press, 1981).

Bakhtin, Mikhail M., *Problems of Dostoyevsky's Poetics*, trans. by Caryl Emerson (Minneapolis: University of Minnesota, 1987).

Browne, Anthony, *Voices in the Park* (London: Doubleday, 1998).

Davies, Maria González, 'Fairy tale retellings as translation: Developing verbal and visual intercultural competence', in *Who's Story? Translating the Verbal and the Visual in Literature for Young Readers*, ed. by Maria González Davies and Riitta Oittinen (Newcastle: Cambridge Scholars Publishing, 2008), pp. 115–29.

Gadamer, Hans-Georg, *Truth and Method*, trans. by Garrett Barden and John Cumming (New York: Crossroad, 1985).

Gambier, Yves and Henrik Gottlieb, *(Multi)Media Translation: Concepts, Practices and Research* (Amsterdam: John Benjamins, 2007).

Garavini, Melissa, *La traduzione della letteratura per l'infanzia dal finlandese all'italiano: l'esempio degli albi illustrati di Mauri Kunnas* (doctoral thesis, University of Turku, 2014).

Genette, Gérard, *Palimpsests. Literature in the Second Degree*, trans. by Channa Newman and Claude Daubinsky (Lincoln: University of Nebraska Press, 1997).

Herkman, Juha, *Sarjakuvan kieli ja mieli* (Tampere: Vastapaino, 1998).

Ippolito, Margherita, 'The relationship between text and illustrations: Translating Beatrix Potter's *Little Books* into Italian', in *Who's Story? Translating the Verbal and the Visual in Literature for Young Readers*, ed. by Maria González Davies and Riitta Oittinen (Newcastle: Cambridge Scholars Publishing, 2008), pp. 85–96.

Kaindl, Klaus, 'Multimodality in the translation of humour in comics', in *Perspectives on Multimodality*, ed. by Charles Ventola and Martin Kaltenbacher (Amsterdam: John Benjamins, 2004), pp. 173–92.

Kokkola, Sari, *The Role of Sound in Subtitling Narrative Fiction Films* (forthcoming)

Kress, Günther and Theo van Leeuwen, *Reading Images: The Grammar of Visual Design* (Oxford and New York: Routledge, 1996).

Lemke, Jay, 'Travels in hypermodality', *Visual Communication*, 1 (2002), 299–325.

Lewis, David, *Reading Contemporary Picturebooks: Picturing Text* (London and New York: Routledge, 2001).

Mikkonen, Kai, *Kuva ja sana. Kuvan ja sanan vuorovaikutus kirjallisuudessa, kuvataiteessa ja ikonoteksteissä* (Helsinki: Gaudeamus, 2005).

Oittinen, Riitta, *Translating for Children* (New York and London: Garland Publishing, 2000).

Oittinen, Riitta, *Kuvakirja kääntäjän kädessä* (Helsinki: Lasten keskus, 2004).

Oittinen, Riitta, 'Translating Culture: Children's literature in translation', *Literatuur zonder leeftijd*, 67 (2005), 45–56.

Oittinen, Riitta, 'The verbal and the visual: On the carnivalism and dialogics of translating for children', in *Translating for Children: A Reader*, ed. by Gillian Lathey (Clevedon: Multilingual Matters, 2006), pp. 84–97.

Oittinen, Riitta, 'From Thumbelina to Winnie-the-Pooh: Pictures, words and sounds in translation', *META*, 53.1 (2008), 76–89.

Oittinen, Riitta, *Olipa kerran Susi, Karhu ja Kettu* (forthcoming).

Peirce, Charles S., *Collected Papers by Charles Sanders Peirce* (Cambridge: Harvard University Press, 1932).

Reiss, Katharina, *Möglichkeiten und Grenzen der Übersetzungskritik* (München: Max Hueber Verlag, 1971).

Rättyä, Kaisu, 'Kirjan kansikuva peritekstinä', in *Tutkiva katse kuvakirjaan*, ed. by Kaisu Rättyä and Raija Raussi (Helsinki: BTJ Kirjastopalvelu Oy and Suomen Nuorisokirjallisuuden Instituutti, 2001), pp. 177–93.

Schopp, Jürgen, *'Gut zum Druck?' Typographie und Layout im Übersetzungsprozess* (Tampere: Acta Universitatis Tamperensis, 2005).

Snell-Hornby, Mary, *The Turns of Translation Studies: New Paradigms or Shifting Viewpoints?* (Amsterdam: John Benjamins, 2006).

Spink, John, *Children as Readers: A Study* (London: Clive Bingley, Library Association Publishing Limited, 1990).

Zitawi, Jehan, *The Translation of Disney Comics in the Arab World: A Pragmatic Perspective* (Manchester: The University of Manchester, School of Modern Languages, 2004).

PART II
Textual-Musical Practices

8 Travelling nationalisms? US hip hop and the French connection

Priscilla Ringrose

Since the early 1980s, France's hip hop movement has been the privileged cultural vehicle of the second and third generation of black and *beur* immigrants of France's suburbs. With reference to James Lull's theory of cultural interactions, this chapter examines the re-territorialisation of US hip hop culture in France in the 1980s and 90s.[1] Tracing the beginnings of the US and French movements, it focuses in particular on the concept of hip hop nationalism, examining the ways in which it evolved in the US and was subsequently renegotiated in the French socio-cultural environment. According to Jeffrey Louis Decker, hip hop nationalism is '"an imagined community" that is based less on its realization through state formation than on a collective challenge to the consensus logic of the US nationalism'.[2] Decker identifies two alternative strategies of US nationalistic-type rap.[3] The first draws on 1960s-inspired black militancy with an Islamic thrust; the second on Afrocentric themes.[4] In this chapter, I examine the extent to which these strategies were transculturated and/or indigenized in the French context.

---

1 James Lull, *Media, Communication, Culture: A Global Approach* (Cambridge: Polity, 1995). Future references are given in parenthesis and by page number in the text, and are to this edition.
2 Jeffrey Louis Decker, 'The state of rap: Time and place in hip hop nationalism', in *Microphone Fiends: Youth Music, Youth Culture*, ed. by Andrew Ross and Tricia Rose (New York: Routledge, 1994), pp. 99–121 (p. 100).
3 'Rap' refers to the musical component of the wider term 'hip hop', which includes other art forms, such as break-dancing and graffiti art.
4 Decker, pp. 99–100.

Transculturation

Androutsopoulos and Scholz, following James Lull, view the appropriation of rap in the European context as 'the emergence of a new cultural territory' involving three separate phases moving from de to re-territorialisation.[5] The first phase, deterritorialization, is the process by which cultural effects are uprooted from their source context; the second, cultural melding and mediation, consists of three forms of cultural interactions: transculturation, hybridization and indigenization. According to Lull, transculturation, facilitated by the mass media and culture industries, refers to 'a process in which cultural forms literally move through time and space, where they interact with other cultural forms, influence each other, and produce new forms' (p. 153). The second, hybridization, refers to the contact and mixture of new and familiar cultural forms that lead to the formation of 'cultural hybrids' (p. 155). Finally, the third form, indigenization, means that 'imported cultural forms take on local features' (pp. 155–56). Indigenization, in the view of Androutsopoulos and Scholz, does not necessarily mean a complete rejection of the original model, but rather indicates 'a symbolic struggle for cultural autonomy', where imitation is eschewed in favour of innovation (p. 468).

To what extent can the US notion of hip hop nationalism be understood as undergoing transculturation, hybridisation and/or indigenization when reterritorialised into the French context? Did French hip hop of the 1980s and 1990s produce indigenised forms of militant and/or Afrocentric rap?

Beginnings of US and French hip hop culture

The origins of rap-style lyrics can be traced back to New York City's borough of Manhattan. It was there that the Last Poets, a group of young black militant musicians, laid the groundwork for the emergence of hip hop with their 'politically-charged raps, syncopated rhythms and dedication to raising African-American consciousness.'[6] During their late 1960s and early 1970s, the

---

5 Jannis Androutsopoulos and Arno Scholz, 'Spaghetti funk: Appropriations of hip-hop culture and rap music in Europe', *Popular Music and Society*, 26.4 (2003), 463–79 (p. 467). Future references are given in parenthesis and by page number in the text, and are to this edition.
6 *Factbites* <http://www.factbites.com/topics/Opiate-(album)> [accessed 6 September 2013].

Last Poets connected with the more militant factions of the Student Non-Violent Coordinating Committee, one of the principal organs of the Civil Rights Movement, but also found a natural ally in the revolutionary politics of the Black Panther party. The 'hard-hitting proto-rap lyrics' of their first album (1970), written in the Black Panther spirit, called on blacks to rise up against the white establishment, while taunting them for not resisting the system that had oppressed them for so long: 'Niggers are scared of revolution/but niggers shouldn't be scared of revolution/because revolution is nothing but change, and all niggers do is change'.[7]

Hip hop proper, in the form of dancing, rapping and deejaying, was born in the mid-1970s in Manhattan's neighbouring borough of the Bronx. The first major hip-hop DJ, Kool Herc, introduced the huge sound systems of his native Jamaica to the inner-city block parties that presaged the rise of rap. Using two turntables, he merged percussive fragments from older records with popular dance songs to create a continuous flow of music, adding the spoken interjections which would become the hallmark of rap.[8]

Rap first gained a national audience with the release of the Sugarhill Gang's 'Rapper's Delight' (1979). It was the first commercially successful rap hit and gave its name to this new brand of music, which would soon be injected with an Afrocentric flavour. The first association to be set up under a hip hop banner, Afrika Bambaataa's Universal Zulu Nation promoted an eclectic mix of Biblical and Koranic beliefs, an anti-violent ethos, a commitment to racial harmony, and an Afrocentric ideology, heavily invested with Pharaonic symbols.[9] Following a trip to Africa, Bambaataa (born Kevin Donovan) renamed himself after Bhambatha, a Zulu leader, who, in the early 1900s, led a rebellion against the settler government of the South African British colony of Natal.[10] From the 1980s, when hip hop began to go global, Zulu nationalism was exported to the UK, Australia, Japan and France.

---

7 *Downtown Music Gallery* <http://www.dtmgallery.com/Main/news/20030606.htm> [accessed 2 August 2013].
8 'Hip hop', in *Encyclopædia Britannica Online Academic Edition* <http://www.britannica.com/EBchecked/topic/266545/hip-hop> [accessed 14 July 2013].
9 Olivier Cachin, *L'offensive Rap* (Paris: Gallimard, 1996), pp. 16–21.
10 Paul S. Thompson, 'Bhambatha and the Zula Rebellion 1906', *Journal of Natal and Zulu History*, 26 (2008), 32–59 (p. 32).

According to Tony Mitchell, hip hop's origins have been subject to revisionist histories which cloud over its beginnings in a utopian mist of an all-embracing, racially diverse and heterogeneous culture.[11] The mythology surrounding the beginnings of old school rap has its parallels in the history of French hip-hop, where Afrika Bambaataa is credited with a major founding role. In 1982, Bernard Zekri, a Frenchman of Algerian origin and pioneering rap producer in the United States, organised a French tour of US deejays, rappers, breakdancers and graffiti writers, headed by Bambaataa. In their 1995 track 'Tout n'est pas si facile' ['Not Everything is that Easy'], French rapsters NTM look back nostalgically at those early days of French hip hop:

> 1983, il y a plus de dix ans déjà
> Le Hip Hop en France faisait ses premiers pas
> Il n'y avait pas de règle, pas de loi
> Non surtout pas de contrat [...]
> Peace, Unity, Love and Having Fun
> Le Hip Hop n'a jamais eu besoin de gun[12]

Since those 'good old days', France has become the world's second-largest hip-hop market and the fifth largest global music market, with an unusually high proportion of local product.[13] As Lull points out, 'many cultural crossings are made possible by the mass media and culture industries' (p. 153). In the French context, the rise of rap was facilitated by the flourishing of commercial radio stations and the activities of a number of key rap promoters, such as Parisian DJ Sidney, who by 1982, was hosting the *Rapper Dapper Snapper* radio show and, in 1984, began presenting the *HIP HOP* show on one of the biggest French TV networks, TF1. In 1990, the first French rap compilation, 'Rapattitude' was released, featuring such rising French stars as Supreme NTM, Tonton David, EJM, Dee Nasty and Assassin.

---

11   Tony Mitchell, *Popular Music and Local Identity: Rock, Pop and Rap in Europe and Oceania* (London: Leicester University Press, 1996), p. 27.
12   '1983, more than ten years ago/French hip hop took its first steps/No rules, no law then/And no contracts no way [...]/Peace, Unity, Love and Having Fun/Hip hop never needed the gun'. Joey Starr and Kool Shen, *Suprême NTM: l'intégrale* (Paris: Scali, 2007), p. 139. This and all subsequent lyric translations are mine unless otherwise indicated.
13   Keith Negus, *Producing Pop: Culture and Conflict in the Popular Music Industry* (London: Edward Arnold, 1994), pp. 159–60.

While rap hit the French airwaves, on French soil it took root in the *banlieues*, the deprived areas of dilapidated high-rise government housing estates which encircle most large French cities and house a significant proportion of France's blacks and *beurs*. The rise of rap coincided with France's 'crisis of integration', fuelled by the race riots of the early 80s in the suburbs of Lyon.

The Universal Zulu Nation established its first French chapter in 1984, in the wake of France's second set of major *banlieues* riots. The youth generation living in these suburban ghettos identified with the African-American experience and with life in America's inner cities. For them, the Zulu Nation provided a means of expressing their sense of social alienation and of acquiring a sense of belonging to a wider community, the international hip hop nation. Bambaataa himself appointed the leadership of the French chapter, grandiosely titled 'Kings and Queens'.[14] The fate of the Universal Zulu Nation in France would represent a test case for the transculturation of Bambaataa's particular brand of Afrocentric hip hop nationalism.

US hip hop nationalism: Militant-Islamic style

As Decker points out, the strategies of hip hop nationalism take two major forms: Afrocentric revivalism, promoting Ancient Egypt as the birthplace of African and world civilisation, and as the common link between diverse black communities; and sixties-inspired black American militancy with an Islamic thrust (pp. 99–121).

The second strategy is typified by bands such as Public Enemy, who imbued rap with a radical black political ideology with a flavour of social consciousness. Their 1988 album, *It Takes a Nation of Millions to Hold Us Back*, revived the messages of the Black Panther Party and Malcolm X and endorsed the teachings of Louis Farrakhan. As their lead artist, Chuck D explained:

> I'm not romanticising the sixties. [...] but to understand me and the direction of the Rap group I was later to form, Public Enemy, one needs to understand the environment and realities that the majority of the guys in the Public

---

14 Manuel Boucher, *Rap, expression des lascars* (Paris: Union Peuple et Culture, 1998), p. 485.

Enemy Camp, including myself, grew up facing. We were all born between 1958 and 1961 [...] My influences were the Black Panther Party, the NOI, Muhammad and Malcolm X.[15]

While some of Public Enemy's influences, such as the Black Panther Party, eschewed religion, others, such as Malcolm X and Louis Farrakhan, were strongly influenced by Black Islam. Malcolm X joined the Nation of Islam (NOI) movement in the late 1940s, taking on board its blend of traditional Islam and Black Nationalist ideals. He was succeeded as leader of NOI's New York Temple by Louis Farrakhan, another of Public Enemy's heroes. Farrakhan, who in 1978 went on to form his own NOI sect, objecting to the parent organization's move towards orthodox Islam and attempts to distance itself from radical Black Nationalism. While Farrakhan preached the need to encourage blacks to develop their own resources, he also attracted controversy with his anti-Semitic and anti-white views.

In 'Bring the Noise' (1988), Public Enemy explicitly endorsed Farrakhan's status as spiritual teacher: 'Farrakhan's a prophet and I think you ought to listen to/What he can say to you, what you ought to do'. This created a trend for following the NOI amongst a new wave of Black-Power inspired rappers. Other Public Enemy's tracks such as 'Black Steel in the Hour of Chaos' and 'Don't Believe the Hype' (both 1988) made a wider appeal to black pride, moving hip-hop towards an 'explicitly self-aware, pro-black consciousness that became the culture's signature throughout the next decade'.[16]

For some US hip hop artists, pro-black consciousness took on a more mystical form, inspired by the Five Percenters, an esoteric new religious movement whose most prominent followers amongst hip hop artists were Staten Island's Wu-Tang Clan. By the late 1990s, the Clan, whose name (Wisdom Universe Truth Allah, Nation, God) defers to their Five Percenters allegiance, joined a growing community of hip hop stars, such as Rakim, Brand Nubian, Busta Rhymes and Nas who had already publicly aligned themselves with the movement.

---

15   Chuck D with Yusuf Jah, *Fight the Power: Rap, Race, and Reality* (New York: Delacorte, 1997), p. 27.
16   'Public Enemy', *Hip Online* <http://www.hiponline.com/2858/public-enemy.html> [accessed 3 June 2013].

Founded in 1963 by Clarence 13X (Clarence Smith), a former NOI member, The Five Percenters movement use the figure five to allude to the 'enlightened' élite of the movement's members who have been transformed into 'Supreme Beings', and refer to God as 'the Original Blackman' and the Earth as the 'Original Blackwoman'.[17] While preaching black pride and self-sufficiency, the Five Percenters' doctrine has a much looser relation to Islam than its parent NOI movement, while promoting the anti-white ethos associated with some of its factions. In the video for the track 'Wake Up' from the 1990 *One for all* album, Brand Nubian portrayed the Original Blackman as a divine being and white people as devils, earning them a MTV ban.

US hip hop nationalism: Afrocentric style

The Afrocentric brand of US hip hop nationalism has a generally more tolerant and looser religious framework than its militant Islamic-inspired variety. The lyrics of Jungle Brother's 1989 track 'Acknowledge Your Own History' is typical of Afrocentrism's affirmation of the antecedence of African civilization:

> Christopher chose to explore
> Discovered America! Yeah, sure
> He thought the planet was square
> Travelled through many places, we already been there
> We left tracks, backtrack black
> First civilization, you know where that was found at
> Looking for the true black days of glory
> That's history, that's his history

Hip hop stars who adopt an Afrocentric position often take on a new name, building on the African tradition where 'one's name is supposed to capture the essence of one's being'.[18] Hip hop star Dana Owens, for example, is known as Queen Latifah (Arabic for 'delicate'). As Robin Roberts notes, in the video for the 'Ladies First' track from the 1989 album *All Hail the Queen*, Queen Latifah positions herself in 'neo-nationalistic' mode as 'a leader of African-American

---

17   Ted Swedenburg, 'Snipers and the panic over five percent Islamic hip hop', MERIP (2002) <http://www.merip.org/mero/mero111002> [accessed 3 June 2013].
18   Angela Davis, *Women, Culture, and Politics* (New York: Random, 1989), p. 100.

male and female rappers'.[19] The video subverts the bifurcation between Afrocentric and militant-Islamic style hip hop nationalisms, with intersecting segments featuring prominent historic female African-Americans figures, images of the anti-apartheid struggle, and Queen Latifah as a military strategist removing giant white chess pieces, then performing a black power salute (p. 250). While these images may suggest the diasporic breadth of hip hop nationalism, the community of women that her video evokes, is representative of what Tony Mitchell branded as US hip hop's Americocentrism which 'manifests itself in local, even parochial, tropes such as the family, 'homies' or the 'hood' (neighbourhood), while black (or, for that matter brown) cultures outside of the US are rarely, if ever, acknowledged' (p. 25).

Hip Hop nationalism: The French case

While accusations of parochialism can generally be levelled against the US hip hop community, they do not hold true for Afrika Bambaataa who has proclaimed France his second home.[20] France, however, proved to be a difficult sowing ground for his brand of Afrocentrism, despite his enormous personal popularity.[21] The failure of the Zulu Nation's French chapter, according to Manuel Boucher, can be attributed to its increasingly prescriptive and elitist ethos, rather than to the French hip hop community's rejection of its universalist values (pp. 59–61). By 1987, membership fell dramatically and most hip hop groups and artists no longer claimed Zulu affiliation.[22]

While Bambaataa's brand of Afrocentric hip hop nationalism did not take root, French artists, such as the super group IAM, whose members have French Malagasy/Réunion, Spanish, and Italian roots, have drawn on Afrocentric themes. The group's members ascribe to their acronym a 'mosaic of meanings',[23] invoking US, French and Pharaonic associations – the civil rights slogan 'I AM A MAN', their home town of Marseille 'Invasion arrivée de Mars'

---

19 Robin Roberts, '"Ladies First": Queen Latifah's Afrocentric feminist music video', *African American Review*, 28.2 (1994), 245–57 (p. 246).
20 Boucher, p. 58.
21 André J.M. Prévos, 'Postcolonial popular music in France', in *Global Noise: Rap and Hip Hop Outside the USA*, ed. by Tony Mitchell (Middletown, CT: Wesleyan UP, 2002), p. 42.
22 Emmett George Price, *Hip Hop Culture* (Santa Barbara CA: ABC-CLIO, 2006), p. 93.
23 Delphine Sloan, *IAM de A à Z* (Paris: MusicBook, 2003), p. 5.

['Invasion from Mars'] (Marseille) and 'Imperial Afro/Asiatic Man'. Echoing the tendency within Afrocentric style hip hop to take on new names, four of the group's members have adopted Pharaonic pseudonyms – Akhenaton, Khéops, Imhotep and Kephren.

At the same time, in Androutsopoulos and Scholz's words, IAM has asserted its own 'symbolic struggle for cultural autonomy' (p. 468) by inventing its own brand of Afrocentrism. The band envisions a 'pan-Mediterranean black Islamic' imagined community spanning the 'peoples of the South', based on an elaboration of the continental drift theory which figures the Rhône and the Nile – Southern France and Egypt – joined together as one.[24] While according to Ted Swedenburg, this strategy enables IAM's to connect its members' 'polyethnic' home town of Marseilles with the African motherland (p. 71), it also enables them to engage their spiritual allegiance, intensified from 1993 with band member Akhenaton's official conversion to Islam. Finally, it allows them to circumvent the more uncomfortable associations with the African continent. For while US hip hop's relation to Africa is for the most mired in the distant past, for many French hip hop artists, whose personal history is tied up with more recent immigration, North Africa connotes censorship, religious fundamentalism and poverty.

In their 1993 track 'Contrat de Conscience' ['Contract of Conscience'], IAM allude to the coming of Pharaoh as the answer to Western decadence, in a move interpreted by André J.M. Prévos as a form of 'Pharaonic messianism' (p. 49): 'Qu'entre le pharaon/En cette fin de 20ième siècle'.[25] The track invokes French hip hop's more Eurocentric take on the excesses of Western/white civilization by evoking the rise and continued lure of fascism in Germany ('En Allemagne comme dans les années 30/Les nazis s'organisent et attaquent en bande') and the racial inequalities of post-colonial France ('Quelqu'un comme moi ne peut voyager en 1ère classe?').[26]

Other IAM tracks, such as 'Tam-tam de l'Afrique' ['Tam-tam from Africa'] (1991) take on a more conventional US-style Afrocentric flavour. Here Africa is revered as 'mythic' territory, and mourned as the birthplace of the slave trade:

---

24 Ted Swedenburg, 'Islamic hip-hop versus islamophobia', in Mitchell, p. 71.
25 'May the Pharaoh return/At this end of the 20th century'.
26 'In Germany, just as in the 30s/the Nazis get organised and attack in gangs'; 'Why can't someone like me travel first class/maybe, its true I don't have the social profile?'

> Au fond des cales où on les entassait
> Dans leurs esprits les images défilaient
> Larmes au goût salé, larmes ensanglantées [...]
> Mais sans jamais tuer l'espoir qui les nourrissait
> Qu'un jour, ils retrouveraient ces rivages féeriques
> D'où s'élèvent à jamais les tam tam de l'Afrique[27]

'Tam-tam de l'Afrique' also draws on 'indigenized' forms of Afrocentrism in the sense that it is also inspired by the anti-colonial rhetoric of the Paris-based Francophone Négritude movement of the 1930s. The track's title evokes the works of négritude's most prominent leaders, Senegal's poet-President Leopold Senghor's 'L'appel du tam-tam'[28] ['The call of the tam-tam'] and Martinique's politician Aimé Césaire's 'Tam-tam' (I and II).[29]

IAM's nationalism combines a less 'orthodox' Afrocentrism with a more orthodox version of Islam. Their members explicitly distance themselves from US-style Black Islam, dismissing what they call the 'home-made religions' of the US, which they distinguish from the more 'authentic' Islam practised in France.[30] IAM's religious agenda can be understood as a relatively more benign strategy 'to widen the space of tolerance for Arabo-Islamic culture in France'.[31] As such, its brand of Islam diverges both from the pluralistic religious ethos of the Zulu nation and from the separatist imperative of Black Nationalism, while combining the anti-racist ideals of the former with the general Islamic flavour of the latter.

But although IAM have dismissed Black Islamic discourse as 'nonsense' and the Five Percenters as heretics, US rappers Timbo King, Dreddy Kruger and Prodigal Sunn of Sunz of Man, all affiliated with Five Percenters Wu Tang Clan,

---

27 'They were crammed at the bottom of a hold/In their spirits the images flashed by/Soiled [salty] tears, bloody tears [...]/But the hope which fed them was never killed:/That one day, they would find the enchanted coasts/From where the never-ending African tom-toms beat'. Translation from 'Middle passages: A shared history of the Trans-Atlantic slave trade' <http://www.yale.edu/glc/mpi/docs.htm> [accessed 3 June 2013].
28   Also known as 'Jardin de France' – see Léopold Sédar Senghor, *Poèmes* (Paris: Le Seuil, 1984), p. 223.
29   Aimé Césaire, *Aimé Césaire: The Collected Poetry* (Berkeley and Los Angeles: University of California Press, 1983), trans. by Clayton Eshleman and Annette Smith, p. 134.
30   David Dufresne, *Yo! Revolution Rap* (Paris: Ramsay, 1991), p. 151.
31   Swedenburg, *Global Noise*, p. 71.

appear on the 'La Saga' track of their *L'école du micro d'argent* [*The School of the Silver Mic*] album (1997), where, as Swedenborg notes, they '[threw] in some recognizably Islamic raps' in English (p. 75).

> 'bout to take it to another chamber
> From Medina to Marseille... Marseille Marseille
> Yo I am Suz of Man from the Royal Fam
> Never ate ham never gave a damn

Equally scathing about black Islamic nationalism are NTM (Nique ta mère [Fuck your Mother]), another of the most commercially successful bands in French hip hop. NTM's Joey Starr and Kool Shen compared Farrakhan to Jean Marie Le Pen in their 1991 'Blanc et noir' ['White and black'] track ('Le Pen, Farrakhan, même combat pour la haine' ['same struggle for hate']), spelling out their differences with US-style black militancy: 'we have other preoccupations than the black race extolled by Farrakhan [...] black American nationalists exist for a reason, but here not. The problems are not the same. All those people who copy the US have a problem of imagination'.[32]

While French hip hop groups like NTM and Ministère A.M.E.R. reject Islamic inspired US style Black Nationalism, their anti-police lyrics and confrontations with the law recall the wider moral panic surrounding the more militant brands of hip hop.[33] NTM's 1995 track 'Qu'est-ce qu'on attend? ['What are we Waiting for?'] included this warning of impending urban war:

> Ça fait déjà des années que tout aurait dû péter [...]
> Mais vous savez que ça va finir mal, tout ça
> La guerre des mondes vous l'avez voulue, la voilà
> Mais qu'est-ce, mais qu'est-ce qu'on attend pour foutre le feu ?
> Mais qu'est-ce qu'on attend pour ne plus suivre les règles du jeu ? [...]
> Dorénavant la rue ne pardonne plus
> Nous n'avons rien à perdre, car nous n'avons jamais rien eu[34]

---

32 Boss of Scandal Strategyz, 'Première interview: Sortie du premier Maxi de NTM Authentik, 1991' (First interview: Release of first NTM Maxi Authentik, 1991) <http://www.bosstrategyz.fr/t3220-5-ITW-NTM.html> [accessed 3 June 2013].
33 John Springhall, *Youth, Popular Culture and Moral Panics: Penny gaffs to Gangsta Rap, 1830–1996* (New York: St. Martin's Press, 1998), p. 10.
34 'Things should have exploded years ago [...]/But you know that this is all going to finish

In a 1995 concert organised by the anti-racist NGO SOS Racisme in protest at National Front victories in local elections, NTM encouraged the audience to shout 'nique la police', in a take on NWA's (Niggaz Wit Attitudes) 1988 'Fuck Da Police' track. Following a high profile trial, their six month sentence was eventually repealed following the intervention of France's Culture Minister Jacques Toubon. In a similar vein, the incendiary lyrics of Ministère A.M.E.R's 1995 track 'Sacrifices de poulet' ['Sacrifices of Chicken' (pigs/police)] earned the group an official condemnation from Minister of the Interior Charles Pasqua:

> Les plus jeunes m'écoutent, dans l'école de la rue, je suis un prof
> Premier cours: lancer de cocktails molotovs sans faire de propagande
> Abdulaï nous demande la plus belle des offrandes
> Le message est passé, je dois sacrifier un poulet[35]

Other Ministère A.M.E.R. tracks witness to French hip hop's particular focus on recent colonial history, as a particular feature of its indigenization. In their 1992 track 'Damnés' ['Damned'] they imbue their uncompromising anti-racist rhetoric with echoes of the cries of Francophone anti-colonial heroes. The opening lines ('Damné, condamné, damné depuis des années l'histoire/les faits me poussent à réaliser que de toutes manières/je suis un damné de la terre'[36]) recall the words of Haitian communist anti-colonialist Jacques Roumain's poem 'Nouveau Sermon Nègre' ['New Black Sermon'] with its rerun of the Internationale anthem ('Arise ye wretched of the earth'), the inspiration for Frantz Fanon's seminal 'The Wretched of the Earth' (1961). A.M.E.R.'s 'The Damned' attacks the evils of greed, discrimination and dispossession perpetuated in colonial and contemporary France:

---

badly/The war of worlds you wanted, is here now/But what, but what are we waiting for to put things up in smoke?/But what are we waiting for before we stop following the rules of the game? [...]/From now on the streets will not forgive/We have nothing to lose, because we never had anything'.
35 'The young listen, in the school of the street, I am the prof/Lesson one: throw Molotov cocktails, no propaganda/Abdulai asks us for the most beautiful of sacrifices/The message is passed on; I have to sacrifice a chicken (pig/policeman)'.
36 'The damned, condemned, damned since the beginning of time/The facts make me realise that in every way I am one of the wretched of the earth'.

> Comme au Monopoly Marianne a des rues en Afrique, des hôtels aux Antilles,
> C'est ça sa contribution au développement de ses colonies [...]
> Territoire ennemi enrichi par nos ancêtres resservis par les traîtres [...]
> Ai-je un droit sur les terres de chez moi nos ancêtres ont-ils eu des droits
> Ou le schéma était-il encore une fois des damnés comme Kunta Kinté, devant vos lois ? [...]
> Héros à la guerre, zéro dans la vie, derniers embauchés
> Premiers renvoyés, prisonniers des pages poussiéreuses de l'histoire
> Appelés en France pour balayer les trottoirs[37]

In a similar vein, Sléo rappers Sly and Jazzyko, who formed Criminal Posse, decry the fate of soldiers from France's former African colonies who fought in the First World War in their 1995 'Monnaie de Singe' ['Monkey Money'] track:

> J'observe ces vieux combattants usés par la guerre
> Par tant de services rendus au nom de la terre mère
> Leur patrie! Quelle patrie? La leur est ici!
> Leur sang a coulé dans la Somme et dans la Marne [...]
> Mais quelle reconnaissance, les médisances sont toujours là
> Pour l'homme de couleur, l'intolérance ne s'arrête pas
> Parce que quand ils ont posé la médaille sur son linge
> L'étalage des menteurs l'a payé en monnaie de singe[38]

But while Sléo's track concerns itself with the injustices perpetuated in contemporary France and in the colonial past, Ministère A.M.E.R.'s lyrics also encompass the history of the slave trade. Their reference to the 'factional' Gambian-born American slave, Kunta Kinté, brought to the screen in the TV adaptation of Alex Haley's *Roots*, invokes a community of black peoples,

---

37 'Like in Monopoly, Marianne [France] has roads in Africa, hotels in the Antilles/That's her contribution to the development of her colonies [...]/Enemy territory enriched by our ancestors used again by the traitors [...]/Do I have rights on the lands of my home did our ancestors have right/Or was the whole scheme damned like for Kunta Kinté before your laws [...]/Heroes in war, zeros in life, last to be employed/First to be sent back, prisoners of the dusty pages of history/Called to France to sweep the streets'.
38 'I observe those old warriors, worn out by war/By so many services given in the name of the motherland [...]/Their homeland! What homeland? Theirs is here!/Their blood shed into the Somme and the Marne [...]/But where is gratitude, the slanders are still here/For the man of colour, intolerance does not stop there/Because as soon as they placed his medal on his clothes/The whole parade of liars paid them in peanuts'.

joining together the damned of France and the US, their protests reverberating across the Black Atlantic.

Conclusion

As hip hop was reterritorialised into the French context in the 1980s and 90s, French artists developed their own take on US Afrocentric hip hop nationalism, inspiring it with a pan-Mediterranean flavour and a hint of négritude. Similarly, while a militant brand of French hip hop emerged in the shadow of Black-Power inspired US hip hop nationalism, the French variety carved out its cultural autonomy by distancing itself from the separatist ideologies of Black Islam, and rejecting the radical heroes of the sixties-inspired Black Power movement in favour of anti-racist protest inspired by the poet-politicians of the anti-colonialist struggle.

Bibliography

Androutsopoulos, Jannis and Arno Scholz, 'Spaghetti funk: Appropriations of hip-hop culture and rap music in Europe', *Popular Music and Society*, 26.4 (2003), 463–79.

Boss of Scandal Strategyz, 'Première interview: Sortie du premier Maxi de NTM Authentik, 1991', <http://www.bosstrategyz.fr/t3220-5-ITW-NTM.html> [accessed 3 June 2013].

Boucher, Manuel, *Rap, expression des lascars* (Paris: Union Peuple et Culture, 1998).

Cachin, Olivier, *L'offensive Rap* (Paris: Gallimard, 1996).

Césaire, Aimé, *Aimé Césaire: The Collected Poetry*, trans. by Clayton Eshleman and Annette Smith (Berkeley and Los Angeles: University of California Press, 1983).

Chuck D, with Yusuf Jah, *Fight the Power: Rap, Race, and Reality* (New York: Delacorte, 1997).

Davis, Angela, *Women, Culture, and Politics* (New York: Random, 1989).

Decker, Jeffrey Louis, 'The state of rap: Time and place in hip hop nationalism', in *Microphone Fiends: Youth Music, Youth Culture*, ed. by Andrew Ross and Tricia Rose (New York: Routledge, 1994), pp. 99–121.

Downtown Music Gallery <http://www.dtmgallery.com/Main/news/20030606.htm> [accessed 2 August 2013].

Dufresne, David, *Yo! Revolution Rap* (Paris: Ramsay, 1991).

Encyclopædia Britannica Online Academic Edition <http://www.britannica.com/EBchecked/topic/266545/hip-hop> [accessed 14 July 2013].
Factbites <http://www.factbites.com/topics/Opiate-(album)> [accessed 6 September 2013].
Hip Online <http://www.hiponline.com/2858/public-enemy.html> [accessed 3 June 2013].
Lull, James, *Media, Communication, Culture: A Global Approach* (Cambridge: Polity, 1995).
'Middle passages: A shared history of the Trans-Atlantic slave trade', <http://www.yale.edu/glc/mpi/docs.htm> [accessed 3 June 2013].
Mitchell, Tony, *Popular Music and Local Identity: Rock, Pop and Rap in Europe and Oceania* (London: Leicester University Press, 1996).
Mitchell, Tony, ed., *Global Noise: Rap and Hip Hop Outside the USA* (Middletown, CT: Wesleyan UP, 2002).
Negus, Keith, *Producing Pop: Culture and Conflict in the Popular Music Industry* (London: Edward Arnold, 1994).
Prévos, André J.M., 'Postcolonial popular music in France', in *Global Noise: Rap and Hip Hop Outside the USA*, pp. 39–56.
Price, Emmett George, *Hip Hop Culture* (Santa Barbara CA: ABC-CLIO, 2006).
Roberts, Robin, '"Ladies First": Queen Latifah's Afrocentric feminist music video', *African American Review*, 28.2 (1994), 245–57.
Senghor, Léopold Sédar, *Poèmes* (Paris: Le Seuil, 1984).
Springhall, John, *Youth, Popular Culture and Moral Panics: Penny gaffs to Gangsta Rap, 1830–1996* (New York: St. Martin's Press, 1998).
Starr, Joey and Kool Shen, *Suprême NTM: l'intégrale* (Paris: Scali, 2007).
Swedenburg, Ted, 'Snipers and the panic over five percent Islamic hip hop', *MERIP* (2002) <http://www.merip.org/mero/mero111002> [accessed 3 June 2013].
Thompson, Paul S., 'Bhambatha and the Zula Rebellion 1906', *Journal of Natal and Zulu History*, 26 (2008), 32–59.

9 The sound of (good) music: Cultural and linguistic hybridity in the Scandinavian popular music soundscape

Henrik Smith-Sivertsen

In this chapter the focus will be on the process that resulted in the Anglophone domination of popular music in Scandinavia. Despite having their own respective languages, Norwegians, Swedes and Danes have for decades largely preferred popular music in English. Scandinavian artists often write lyrics in English, even when exclusively targeting a home audience. As shown below, I consider the process of the Anglophonization of Scandinavian popular music and soundscapes as more or less finished in the mid-1960s and definitely sealed by the mid-1970s.

Hybridity, technology and language

Popular music is almost by definition hybrid, both culturally and linguistically. No matter what differences there might be among the various definitions of the concept, *popular music* generally refers to music transmitted to large audiences, either stored in printed forms or via sound recordings or live performances broadcast by radio, television and (more recently) Internet streaming. As the latter forms of transmission (sound recordings and live performances) have been primary since the mid-twentieth century, popular music in general is directly linked to sound and performance.

The invention of the phonograph not only made it possible to record and reproduce specific performances and voices; it also meant that music performed in foreign languages and styles became accessible despite geographical and cultural distances. The radio also made it possible to transmit sounds to a wide range of audiences across borders and long distances. During the first years of Scandinavian Radio history, recordings were rarely used, primarily due to technical issues. However, from the late 1920s the gramophone was increasingly used in broadcasting. Thereby not only the tunes – which up until then (and sometimes even longer) were primarily performed live by national artists in the original languages or translated into the national language – but also the sound of how it was originally performed became audible.

With the advent of sound pictures it even became possible to watch a music performance 'live'. The fact that the first full time sound film, *The Jazz Singer* (1927), had a musician in the lead role is a perfect symbol of the importance of music films during the following decades. In the film, six songs were performed by the actor, Al Johnson. In the Danish newspaper advertisements for the film (Danish release 26 December, 1929) attention was explicitly directed towards the opportunity to hear him perform his 'adorable songs'.[1] As dubbing was never a main practice in Scandinavia (except in films for children), music films in foreign languages played a major part in the ongoing process of making music in foreign languages popular. Performing their songs in films was vital for the international success of both Bing Crosby and Zarah Leander during the 1930s and 1940s, and Elvis Presley and Cliff Richard during the late 1950s and early 1960s.

The phonograph, radio and film made the exchange of recorded music performances, and thereby also musical styles, possible to a different extent than before. Due to technological improvements at every level, the process whereby popular music was internationalized has continued ever since. The musical mediascape in which we now live is a hybrid and mixed one, and this transformation really began to take off in the 1950s and 1960s, because of the rapid development of new techniques of recording (the multitrack tape) and reproduction (the vinyl record and tapes), new forms of mass distribution (television and transistor radio), as well as general improvements within media tech-

---

1 *Politiken*, 30 December 1929, p. 11.

nologies used in information exchange (e.g. the telefax) and global transport infrastructure.

Throughout the decades the speed of the general information flow has risen dramatically. Thus, when a current international star like Katy Perry posts a new music video on YouTube.com, it is accessible immediately in most countries around the world, resulting in viewing and streaming numbers exemplifying an immediate global reach that would have been unimaginable when it all started in the 1920s.[2] The technological developments of the twentieth century have prepared the ground for the process that has put English at the top within the musical world. All sources, from music charts and radio playlists to articles, debates and other forms of content in contemporary magazines, journals, newspapers and books clearly show that Anglophone popular music gained a prominent position within the Scandinavian mediascape during the twentieth century.[3]

One of the most fascinating aspects of the status of English within Scandinavian popular music and culture, is the general feeling that the omnipresence of English is somehow 'natural'. The triumph of English as the language of popular music in Scandinavia has been so total that we rarely notice how ubiquitous it is anymore. At the time of writing, all five songs in the top 5 of the Danish Streaming Top 20 are performed in English.[4] Two are written and performed by native speakers of English.[5] The other three songs are performed by Scandinavians, only one of whom – Swedish DJ Avicii (#1 with

---

2 On 5 September 2013 she released a new video entitled 'Roar'. Within ten days the viewing numbers were more than 34 million.
3 In this article I often make general references to Danish music charts and radio play lists. In both cases I am on solid empirical ground. Since 2005 I have collected most Danish music charts published from 1953 until the present day. Some have already been published on the <danskehitlister.dk> website and the rest are in the process of being digitized. As for the playlists, I have access to a digital archive of all radio programs aired by the Danish Radio Broadcasting Company (Danmarks Radio (DR)) from 1925 to 1968. A searchable database, this is a groundbreaking tool for historical research as I am able to search directly within individual playlists for specific terms, names and titles. Statistically the results of quantitative searches show almost exemplary correlations when analyzing different aspects over time, and I consider the results of my research into this archive very solid, and the conclusions drawn and used in my historical overviews quite firm.
4 'Streaming Top 20' for week 32, 2012, <hitlisten.nu> [accessed 3 September 2013].
5 'La La La' by Naughty Boy (featuring Sam Smith) was at #2; 'Blurred Lines' by Robin Thicke at #5, Ibid.

'Wake Me Up') – is largely known outside Scandinavia. Both the Norwegian hip-hop duo Envy (#3 with 'Am I Wrong') and Swedish Zara Larsson (#5 with 'Uncover') may be dreaming of achieving international success, but yet they sing primarily in English to a Scandinavian audience.

The fact that two Swedish acts, and one Norwegian, are ranked in a Danish music chart with songs performed in English, perfectly reflects how English is *the* inter-Scandinavian language within popular music. The historical, cultural and linguistic bonds between Denmark, Norway and Sweden are very close, and during the years we have shared many hits in our respective languages.[6] However, English has definitely become the main language when exchanging hits.

Considering the first Danish-language song in the charts, 'Skylder dig ik' noget' ['Don't Owe you Anything'] by the up and coming band L.I.G.A. at #6, one sees very clearly that even when songs are performed in one of the national Scandinavian languages, English words (or better still, sounds) are becoming more and more common. In these lyrics 'Baby' rhymes with 'Crazy', 'Mayday' and 'replay', 'Sugar' with the Danish expression 'i stykker' [broken], and 'trouble', 'shit' and 'fuck' are used unproblematically in otherwise fully Danish sentences. Of the other four Danish songs in the charts, only one, #19 'Uden forsvar' ('Defenceless', by Marie Key), is entirely in Danish.[7] The fact that this is one of the few songs on her latest album with no English words like 'ride', 'shit', 'fuck', 'push' and 'crowd', stresses the point.[8] In Danish contemporary popular music, lyrics are overflowing with English words and expressions. Especially slang words, probably learned from TV-series and movies, Internet surfing and chatting, and most certainly from hip hop, are very popular.

---

6   During the 1950s and 1960s it was relatively normal for Scandinavian singers to perform and record songs in other languages. For instance, Swedish artist Siw Malmkvist had several hits in Danish in the early 1960s with 'Du forstår ingenting' ['You don't Understand a Thing'] from 1961 and 'Læs ikke brevet jeg skrev dig' ['Do not Read the Letter I Wrote You'] from 1962, according to Danish newspaper charts compiled by *Quan* and *B.T.*, and Danish singers like Gitte Hænning and Otto Brandenburg sang several songs in Swedish. Gitte Hænning, *Den komplette popboks 1958–1965* [*The Complete Pop Box 1958–1965*] (EMI 3602212, 2006); Frank Toft-Nielsen, *Otto Brandenburg – spor af en baggårdspuma* [*Otto Brandenburg – Footprints of a Backyard Puma*] (København: Gaffa, 2006).
7   #15 'Chuck Norris' (Kongsted) is an instrumental, #13 'Ocean Of You' by Nik & Jay feat. Søren Huss is in English and Danish, #17 'La' mig rule dig' (Pharfar) contains the words 'tight' and 'wind'.
8   Marie Key, 'De her dage' (Sony Music 8888371-2671, 2012).

Going back ten, twenty or thirty years ago there are similar tendencies. In 1985 the Danish singer-songwriter Sebastian wrote a song called 'Den danske sang' ['The Danish Song']. Like all his songs in the 1980s the lyrics were in Danish – at least up until the chorus:

> Because they don't understand you, if you don't sing in English
> Have a Coke and a smile, if you wanna get out
> And you gonna talk sexy, say nothing important
> Let the DJ lead you all the way to the top
> On the top of the pops is an American heartache
> You can beat it like that, just make another one like it
> They love it, oh

He then changed back to Danish for the second verse. The song is clearly critical of the use of English by Danish musicians. By then Danes had been performing lyrics in English for decades, and even in lyrics that were predominantly written in Danish, English words and expressions often popped up. Just like today.

Above I have briefly touched on some of the historical explanations for the prominent status of English in the Scandinavian (and global) soundscapes. In the following I go back to what I consider the beginning, namely the advent of the radio. I will then move through the decades exemplifying how Anglophone music became as natural to Scandinavians as music in their own languages.

The sound of English: The early days

Through radio the sound of English became accessible to large Scandinavian audiences. Because of the access to recordings and visits by Anglophone musicians the sounds of English were already common within specific milieus. The fact that a number of songs performed by Victor Cornelius in 1925, the first Danish vocal recordings to be classified as jazz, were performed in English, reflects this.[9] Due to the strong emphasis on stylistic elements that

---

9   Erik Wiedemann, *Jazz i Danmark i tyverne, trediverne og fyrrerne: en musikkulturel undersøgelse, vol. 1* [*Jazz in Denmark in the Twenties, Thirties and Forties: A Musical-Cultural Study, vol. 1*] (København: Gyldendal, 1982) pp. 98, 103f.

were almost impossible to reproduce in written forms of dissemination, jazz was transmitted either orally by visiting musicians or phonographically via recordings. In both cases the sound of English was an important part of the jazz sound.

Still, the early Scandinavian reception of jazz and modern American popular music in general was mostly an urban phenomenon.[10] By contrast, the new mass media, the radio, became common property nationwide within a few years, and during the late 1920s and early 1930s Anglophone popular music was broadcast daily.[11]

However, even though an important language within jazz in particular and popular music in general, English still had to share most of the air time with other foreign languages like those of the other Scandinavian countries and German during the 1930s. In Denmark, quite logically, due to historical and geographical reasons, the amount of German-language popular music played on the radio was actually on a par with English, and in cinemas European and cross-Scandinavian films were very popular. The American music- and film industry was definitely growing, but the geographic distance was still a major obstacle. Stylistically American popular music was indeed influential, when it came to new fads, dances and genres, but the music was mainly localized through either translation or local composition. The fact that the earliest occurrence (on 9 May 1925) of the term 'jazz' in the Danish radio playlists was from a German title, 'Horch, die Jazzband spielt', performed by the Danish radio dance orchestra in a program described as 'modern dance music' (*Moderne dansemusik*), exemplifies this perfectly.

World War II changed everything. During the war Norway and Denmark were occupied while Sweden remained neutral. In Denmark and Norway the sound of English became highly politicized, and though neutral, Sweden was definitely more culturally and politically oriented towards England and the USA than towards Germany. At the end of the war German almost vanished as a popular music language in Scandinavia. By contrast, the proportion of

---

10   Ibid, p. 106ff.
11   As most music programs were transmissions of live performances by national musicians and singers, the sound of the 'original' recording was rarely heard until late 1930s, and even until the early 1960s a specific recording by a given artist or group was rarely played more than once or twice a week.

Anglophone music played on Danish radio rose dramatically, compared with the years before the war and the occupation.

'Zing A Little Zong'

A process often described as *Americanization* accelerated after the war, but even though this is a useful term in many respects, I would suggest that *Anglophonization* is more appropriate – at least when it comes to music. Even though many of the tunes and recordings were indeed American, I find it important to note that it was the sound of English, irrespective of its national origin, that seemed to matter most in the long run. English became the language associated with freedom, and since the end of World War II, Anglophone music has been a growing part of the Scandinavian soundscape. Helped by the fact that the German music industry was literally left in ruins after the war, the European market became wide open, and until the mid-1950s no real competition existed within Scandinavia.[12]

When the first Danish music charts were compiled and presented in the weekly magazine *Se & Hør* in late March 1953, eight of ten titles were in English, the last two in Danish. However, by examining this chart closer, some important information is revealed, showing that the cultural import and mixing did not take place as a 1:1 relation. A perfect illustration of this is provided by tracing how the song at the top of the list, 'Zing A Little Zong', became a hit: according to the radio playlists the song was introduced to Danish listeners on 30 October 1952 – in its original American recording by Bing Crosby and Jane Wyman. The song was composed for, and performed in, the movie *Just for You*, released in the USA in September 1952. However, the recording of the song was released a bit earlier, as it entered the Billboard charts of *Records most played by Disk Jockeys* in early August of the same year, about two months prior to its debut on Danish radio.[13]

---

12 Not only was the infrastructure destroyed, but also the manufacturing facilities, as they had been used for weapon production during the war and therefore had been bombed.
13 *Billboard Magazine*, 9 August 1952, p. 30. Such a delay was typical and reflects the impact that geographical distance had at that time. For recordings to be made available, local pressing and distribution were necessary, and before that agreements had to be made. The shipping of the recording itself also took considerable time.

On 23 November 1952 the song was played for the second time on the radio, this time during a live transmission from Danish Radio's own concert hall. In the programme the concert was announced as *Musik for alle* [*Music for Everybody*] with the sub-heading: 'The English radio- and gramophone star, Robert Farnon, directs his own arrangements'.[14] One month later it was broadcast again as a live-transmission, but this time from England. On 26 December 1952 Danes could dance to the tunes of Sidney Lipton and his orchestra, and 'Zing A Little Zong' was played along with other hits of the time.

These two transmissions of live performances of the song by British musicians exemplify how American popular music was often mediated via England. When the British-born singer Tommy Steele toured Scandinavia five years later, he was widely received and celebrated as the first 'real' international rock'n'roll star visiting the region.[15] (Later Cliff Richard served the same role, and in both cases their early presence in Scandinavian countries was crucial to their life-long careers as international stars in the region.) After the live transmissions the tune was not played again until 18 February 1953, when the Danish singer Victor Cornelius performed it live. However, from then on things started to happen. On 21 February Danish singer Raquel Rastenni performed a new live version of the song in the show *Dancing in the Studio* [*Dans i studiet*], but this time in Danish. One week later she opened the same show with the tune, and during March she performed the song twice live in *Dans i studiet*. In the same period the English version (both the recording and live performances) was also played regularly.

Even though the song had already been given considerable playing time on the radio, the film in which it was performed undoubtedly helped in making it a major hit. *Just for You* was released in Denmark on 9 March 1953, and with several possibilities to choose from by then, the Danish record buyers helped

---

14 Translation mine. Farnon was actually a Canadian, but after serving overseas during World War II, he settled down in England.

15 Charlotte Larsen Rørdam, 'Above all it's because he's English: Tommy Steele and the notion of Englishness as mediator of wild rock'n'roll', in *Britain and Denmark: Political, Economic and Cultural Relations in the 19th and 20th Centuries*, ed. by Jørgen Sevaldsen (København: Museum Tusculanum: 2003), pp. 493–511.

the song to the top of the charts. Under the title of each song, all the recorded versions were listed, and by late March 1953 two versions in English (the original and another by American singer Helen O'Connell) as well as three in Danish (one by Raquel Rastenni, and duets by Grethe Sønch/Helge Mass and Aase Werrild/Gustav Winckler) were available in the music stores. At that time the different record labels made their respective stars record the same song, following a logic that the important thing was the song, not a specific performance.[16]

Localization and covering

This model was the general one in the early 1950s. Firstly, the songs were introduced in the original language. Shortly after, especially if a song showed hit potential, a Danish translation was arranged and several recordings made. The key point here is that local versions were still needed to make big sales. For the most part, therefore, the 'originals' were not broadcast in isolation, so to speak, but were 'assisted' by national versions. Often local singers even recorded the songs in English, adding another dimension to the issue of hybridity and mixing.

On the opposite page of the first Danish chart presented in *Se og Hør*,[17] a short notice announced that Danish singer Gustav Winckler would follow up his recent success with his Danish version of 'Blue Tango', another American smash hit from 1952, with two Anglophone titles, 'I'm Yours' (a 1952 hit for Eddie Fisher) and 'Never' (from the 1951 film *Golden Girl*). As was common, he recorded the songs in both Danish and English, thereby reaching that section of his audience who preferred songs performed in their own language, while also hijacking the hits in their original language.

As American stars like Eddie Fisher rarely toured Denmark before the1960s, Danish alternatives provided the only opportunity to hear the songs per-

---

16   Michael Coyle, 'Hijacked hits and antic authenticity: Cover songs, race, and postwar marketing', in *Rock over the Edge: Transformations in Popular Music Culture*, ed. by Roger Beebe, Denise Fulbrook, and Ben Saunders (Durham: Duke University Press, 2002), pp. 133–57 (p. 138); Marc Pendzich, *Von der Coverversion zum Hit-Recycling* (Münster: Lit Verlag, 2004), p. 75.
17   *Look and Listen*, a Danish gossip magazine.

formed live by specific voices from the gramophone and radio, and Winckler definitely played that role in Denmark. In the abovementioned notice he was nicknamed 'the Danish Bing Crosby' – a description very often applied to him in the media after his breakthrough in 1950. He began his career imitating Crosby at local singing contests in Copenhagen, and quickly reached the height of his success after signing with a record label and making his debut on Danish radio in 1950. The cultural semantics here are quite interesting. In many ways Winckler *covered* songs recorded by international singers in the same way that white singers covered songs originally performed and recorded by Afro-American musicians, but in his case Danish audiences' general knowledge of the sources (Bing Crosby, USA, Hollywood, etc.) was an important part of the cultural game. Winckler, and others who performed the same role elsewhere, served an important function as mediators between the national culture and the unreachable stars from the records, radio, movies and magazines.

No understanding necessary

The fact that Winckler had no knowledge of English – apart from what he gleaned from music and film when he started his singing career – and that he never went to the States, did not matter much. As was symbolized by his putting on a cowboy hat for the record covers when recording country-songs in the early 1960s, you do not need to go native in order to play with different cultural identities. In Denmark it did not, and does not, take much to be a real cowboy.

A wonderful example of, and comment on, how the sound of English was becoming the sound of popular music, was the Danish-composed song 'Will You Give Me Love' from the 1955-comedy *Det var på Rundetaarn* [*It was at the Rundetaarn Restaurant*]. In the film, the two lead characters, both musicians (played by the famous Danish actors Dirch Passer [DP, in the transcription that follows] and Ove Sprogøe [OS]), perform the song in a restaurant. They open the song by crooning the following verses in Danish:

Table 1 The opening of 'Will You Give Me Love' with direct translation

Danish lyrics	Direct translation
DP: Mit stakkels hjerte trænger til kærlighed. OS: Du er ikke rigtig klog. OS: Man synger kun refræner på am'rikansk OS: Det er hele verdens sprog	DP: My heart needs love OS: You're crazy OS: Popular music[18] is only sung in American OS: That is the language of the whole world

The message in these verses is quite simply that English is the language of popular music. Their style of singing was in itself a clear parody of American crooning, with heavy overacting in both the phrasing and the gesticulating. When reaching the chorus, OS shifts to English:

> Will you give me love?
> Darling, you'll be mine tonight in heaven
> Here you see the skies
> Life will be so beautiful at seven
> Happiness us somewhere is calling
> Will you give me love?
> Come in my garden
> This is our honeymoon

Most of the sentences are clearly not plain English, and generally the content does not really make much sense, but that was never the intention of the lyricist (Victor Skaarup). Instead, the whole song is a joke playing exactly on the sound/meaning aspect, with singer 2 answering with a homophonic translation between every stanza:

---

18 In Denmark 'refræn' [refrain] was used as a general term for popular music until the mid-1960s.

Table 2 The chorus of 'Will You Give Me Love' with direct translation

Stanza	OS	DP	DP (Translation)
1	Will you give me love?	Vil du gi' mig lov?	Would you let me?
2	Darling, you'll be mine tonight in heaven	I haven	In the garden
3	Here you see the skies	Her'r din sidste skejs	Here's your last penny
4	Life will be so beautiful at seven	For sæven	Damn
5	Happiness us somewhere is calling	Har de næsten sommervejr i Kolding?	Are they having summer weather in Kolding?[19]
6	Will you give me love?	Vil du gi' mig lov?	Would you let me?
7	Come in my garden	Kom ind med garden	Bring in the guardsmen
8	This is our honeymoon	Honningmund	Honey mouth

For a joke to work, it needs to point to something common. In this case the joke only works if the listeners (1) know enough English to recognize that the translation is wrong and (2) recognize that they are implicated in the joke. In 1955, most Danes probably did, and most Scandinavians probably still do.

The last battle

During the remainder of the 1950s English was still the most commonly heard foreign language in Scandinavian radio. However, things started changing, at least for a while. By the mid-1950s the results of a general rebuilding of the local music industries of the European countries were clearly visible in the Danish Scandinavian radio playlists and music charts. German *schlager*, Italian *canzone* and French *chanson* were modernized, and not least the annual Eurovision Song Contest, transmitted on both radio and the new mass medium, television, from 1956 onwards, helped to make sounds and tunes from other areas than the Anglophone make their way to Scandinavia. Besides the transmission of the contest itself, the Eurovision Song Contest became important as a meeting place for music publishers, who gathered at the shifting competition sites. On these occasions new networks were established and songs bought and

---

19   Kolding: A Danish town.

sold. Therefore the late 1950s Scandinavian soundscapes became characterized by a language mix not heard either before or since.

In Denmark, German popular music experienced a considerable revival, not least because of television. In the southern areas of Denmark television signals from Germany were quite strong, and most Danes living and growing up in these regions during the following decades watched and listened to German language broadcasts – which is undoubtedly why German speaking artists such as Freddy (Quinn) and Liselotte Malkowsky experienced some of their biggest successes in Denmark in 1956 and 1957 with 'Heimweh' and 'Das Herz Von St. Pauli', respectively.[20] The fact that 'Heimweh' was actually the German version of Dean Martin's 1955 smash hit 'Memories Are Made of This', perfectly illustrates how English was actually challenged by a German comeback during these years.

At the turn of the decade young German singers like Conny Froboess and Peter Krauss were beloved teenage idols regularly hitting the Danish – and even occasionally the Norwegian and Swedish – charts. As late as in 1962 Froboess had a pan-Scandinavian hit with her 'Zwei kleine Italiener' (which, of course, was the German entry for the Eurovision Song Contest that year). However, by 1962 the temporary German (and pan-linguistic) popular music revival in Scandinavia was on its way out. By late 1962 all the Scandinavian charts were heavily dominated by Anglophone popular music, and during the following years its position was consolidated.

Ground having been prepared by the introduction of rock'n'roll in the second half of the 1950s, English was now generally being considered the language of youth music, even though many actually still favored local Scandinavian and, at least in Denmark, German stars. From my own studies on the

---

20   In a 1977 report on the reception of German and Swedish television in Denmark, 22% were reported to have access to German television. 40% of the respondents who had access to German television watched German shows daily, and 84% of the content watched was described as 'entertainment', with film and music shows forming a major part (Kalle Marosi, *Svensk og tysk TV I Danmark, hvor meget ser danskene på udenlandsk TV?* [København: DR, 1977]). Born in 1973 in this region, I can personally testify to the fact that German television was also a big part of the mediascape *after* 1977. If I remember correctly, I was about 14 when I heard James Bond or John Wayne speak in English for the first time (on a skiing trip to Norway, *Goldfinger* was shown one night). Until then I had seen (and heard) most English and American blockbusters, cartoons etc. in dubbed German versions. Naturally, I also watched a lot of German music shows.

reception of popular music in Denmark in the early 1960s, it is evident that youth and the English language were closely connected in the Denmark of the early 1960s.[21] A broad reading of relevant magazines, newspapers, radio playlists and reports showed how at least adult journalists, serving the young audience with information about music, definitely made this connection in their definitions of this new and ever-growing target group. An analysis of the playlists of the earliest Danish radio show, targeted directly at this group, *Teenagerhjørnet* [*The Teenage Corner*], launched in September 1960, tells the story well. During the first two months (and eight shows) a total of 109 songs were played; of these, seventy-three were in English, sixteen were instrumental, fifteen had German lyrics, two were in Italian and Danish, respectively, and one was in Greek. On the programme broadcast 10 October 1960, all fourteen songs were performed exclusively in English. Whether reflecting the tastes of youth or not, it is clear from these playlists that the notion of youth music was essentially equated with English-language music.

During the following years the number of music shows in Scandinavian radio targeted specifically at teenagers rose dramatically, and in all Scandinavian countries youth and English were closely associated. In both Sweden and Denmark a national chart show targeted directly at teenagers was introduced in the autumn of 1961 and of 1962, respectively.[22] Both shows were based on votes from a live teenage audience, and not only did they prefer songs in English; they also had little choice as almost all songs presented were in English.

Moving into 1964, the Beatles smashed any last doubts both in the charts and on the playlists, and with this, a process that began in the early 1920s with the introduction of jazz, and reinforced after World War II, was finally consolidated. Since then English has indeed been the primary sound of popular music in Scandinavia, and from the mid-1970s it has even been a Scandinavian song language.

---

21 Henrik Smith-Sivertsen, 'Refræner, pop og populærmusikforskning – En kritisk gennemgang af Ekstra Bladets spørgeskemaundersøgelse om populærmusik, august 1961' ['Popular music and popular music research: A critical analysis of Ekstra Bladet's survey on popular music, August 1961'], *Fund og Forskning, Bind 50* (*Findings and Research*, Vol. 50) (København: Det Kongelige Bibliotek, 2011).
22 In Sweden *Tio i topp* [*Top Ten*] was launched in October 1961 and only discontinued in 1974. In Denmark *Ti vi ka' li'* [*Ten (Songs) we Like*] substituted *Teenagerhjørnet* in October 1962. It was discontinued in June 1964.

English as musical sounds

On 6 April 1974, a Saturday night, the final chapter of the story was closed. That night the Swedish group ABBA won the Eurovision Song Contest. Their entry, 'Waterloo', was performed in English, and thereby they became not only the first Scandinavians, but also the first non-Anglophone winners to perform in English. Even though there were no rules restricting the languages in which the songs could be sung from 1956 until 1965,[23] and again since 1973, previous winners had all performed in their own languages: ABBA did not.

The lyrics were partly written by the band's manager and record company owner, Stig 'Stikkan' Anderson. Before initiating the ABBA-project during the early 1970s and thereby (again) trying to gain an international audience for one of his acts, he had been the most productive translator of popular music in Scandinavia for about a decade. Starting from scratch in 1959, he positioned himself as one of the most important music publishers in Scandinavia by buying and selling the rights to international popular music. Providing many of the lyrics for the Swedish versions himself, he had gained a deep knowledge and understanding of the anatomy of hits, and all his experience came in useful when he flipped the coin and began to focus on producing English language compositions for Swedish artists aimed at a worldwide audience.

His first attempt had been one year earlier. With the aid of well-established American songwriters Neil Sedaka and Phil Cody he and the male performers behind the B's in ABBA, Björn Ulvaeus and Benny Andersson, came up with the tune 'Ring Ring'. However, the Swedish jury turned it down, and therefore Abba and Stikkan had to wait another year for their next try. The initial title of 'Waterloo' was 'Honey Pie', but going through his wife's Swedish cookbooks, he failed to find the word mentioned, and therefore concluded that it would be familiar only to Anglophone listeners. As most of the target group, then – both the juries and the public watching the Eurovision Song Contest – could not be presumed to understand this phrase, he therefore decided to try again, and, skimming through a Swedish book of quotes and sayings, he eventually

---

23   Sweden was the first country to even perform at the ESC with a song in another language than their own. In 1965 Ingvar Wixell presented 'Absent Friend'. The following year the rules were changed so that, until 1972, each participant had to perform in an official language of their own country.

came across the expression 'meeting one's Waterloo'.[24] Besides being the place where the final battle between Napoleon and the Seventh Coalition took place, Waterloo had become a metaphor for defeat, and since it was known and used everywhere, it was therefore just as good a choice as the international phrase he had used the year before – the sound of a telephone ringing.

Both 'Ring Ring' and 'Waterloo' are what Stikkan Anderson called 'keywords' [nyckelord].[25] His experience had taught him that building song lyrics around such keywords was often very effective, especially when targeting an international audience; the other lyrics did not matter much. When interviewed on Swedish television just after the victory, he explained all this, directly mentioning the importance of a title understood by 'everybody' when addressing 'Europe and the world'. Interestingly, he consistently used the word 'schlager'. Until the early 1960s, this used to be a pan-Scandinavian umbrella term for popular music, the latter becoming gradually displaced by *pop* during the following years. Afterwards it became increasingly used as a term for a specific genre, often associated directly with Germany or with the practice of translating popular music into the Scandinavian languages. The fact that the term *schlager* itself changed meaning in Scandinavia during the late 1950s and early 1960s, symbolizes exactly how the Anglophone world took over the position of the culturally most important big neighbour to Scandinavia. And the fact that Stikkan Anderson still used it to describe ABBA's music thus points to a big paradox – for in many ways Anderson personified the last Scandinavian bastion fighting the new world order of popular music. He had built his empire on the old premise that, despite the supremacy of Anglophone popular music, many Danes, Swedes and Norwegians still preferred songs in their own languages. Now he used all his connections, money and knowledge to conquer the world with ABBA – through the medium of English.

In Stikkan Anderson's perspective, song words were primarily musical. They were the sounds of music, and when he turned to English, this coincided with the sound of music in Scandinavia finally, and once and for all, doing the same. This worked well, despite the fact that Scandinavians do not necessarily under-

---

24   Oscar Hedlund, *Stikkan – Den börsnoterade refrängsångaren* [*Stikkan – The Stock-Exchange-Listed Crooner*] (Stockholm: Sweden Music Förlags AB., 1983), p. 84.
25   Ibid.

stand English wholesale. They know what it sounds like – and it definitely sounds good, even if it does not always make sense to them. Take the example of Envy's 'Am I Wrong', mentioned at the beginning. Since I wrote the first version of this chapter, Envy have changed their name to Nico & Vinz, and have made the charts worldwide with the tune. It has been a #3 hit on the charts of at least 16 countries. Even in the US it has made it big with a #4 on *Billboard Hot 100* and #1 on both *Adult Top 40* and *Mainstream Top 40*. The song opens with the words 'Am I wrong for thinking out the box from where I stay?', which sound quite good when sung, but only make sense if one really wants them to: I doubt that any native speaker would confuse 'stay' with 'stand', or even construct such a sentence. Another example is the sentence 'If one thing I know, how far would I grow': I actually have no idea what this means, but again, it does not matter as long as people do not understand English perfectly. And most people still do not. They just enjoy the sound of music.

Bibliography

Anon, 'Advertisement for *The Jazz Singer*', *Politiken,* 30 December 1929, p. 11.

Anon, 'Records Most Played by Disk Jockeys', *Billboard Magazine*, 9 August 1952, p. 30.

Coyle, Michael, 'Hijacked hits and antic authenticity: Cover songs, race, and postwar marketing', in *Rock over the Edge: Transformations in Popular Music Culture*, ed. by Roger Beebe, Denise Fulbrook, and Ben Saunders (Durham: Duke University Press, 2002), pp. 133–57.

Hedlund, Oscar, *Stikkan – Den börsnoterade refrängsångaren* (Stockholm: Sweden Music Förlags AB., 1983).

Hænning, Gitte, *Den komplette popboks 1958–1965* [on CD] (EMI 3602212, 2006).

Key, Marie, 'De her dage' [on CD] (Sony Music 8888371-2671, 2012).

Marosi, Kalle, *Svensk og tysk TV I Danmark, hvor meget ser danskene på udenlandsk TV?* (København: DR, 1977).

Pendzich, Marc, *Von der Coverversion zum Hit-Recycling* (Münster: Lit Verlag, 2004).

Rørdam, Charlotte Larsen, 'Above all it's because he's English: Tommy Steele and the notion of Englishness as mediator of wild rock'n'roll', in *Britain and Denmark: Political, Economic and Cultural Relations in the 19th and 20th Centuries*, ed. by Jørgen Sevaldsen (København: Museum Tusculanum: 2003), pp. 493–511.

Smith-Sivertsen, Henrik, 'Refræner, pop og populærmusikforskning – En kritisk gennemgang af *Ekstra Bladets* spørgeskemaundersøgelse om populærmusik, august 1961', *Fund og Forskning*, 50 (København: Det Kongelige Bibliotek, 2011).

Smith-Sivertsen, Henrik, *Danske hitlister 1963–2010* <danskehitlister.dk> [accessed 13 September 2014].

Smith-Sivertsen, Henrik, *LARM Audio Research Archive* <Larm.fm> [accessed 13 September 2014].

'Streaming Top 20', in *Hitlisten.NU – Danmarks officielle hitlister* <hitlisten.nu> [accessed September 2013].

Toft-Nielsen, Frank, *Otto Brandenburg – spor af en baggårdspuma* (København: Gaffa, 2006).

Wiedemann, Erik, *Jazz i Danmark i tyverne, trediverne og fyrrerne: en musikkulturel undersøgelse,* I (København: Gyldendal, 1982).

10 Norwegian-English code-switching in popular music lyrics 1960s – 2000s

Annjo Klungervik Greenall

> Sociologists of pop have been so concerned with these 'other things' – lyrical content, truth and realism – that they have neglected to analyse the ways in which songs are about themselves, about language.[1]

In Norway, as in many other Western, non-Anglophone countries, the growing significance of English in the twentieth and twenty-first centuries has caused a considerable change in the national linguistic balance. From the mid-twentieth century onwards, the majority of the Norwegian population has moved from being essentially unilingual to becoming *de facto* bilingual – not in the sense that English has become a second mother tongue, but in the sense that most Norwegians now have two languages which they interact with daily, either passively (reading and listening) or actively (speaking and writing). Norwegians' involvement with English is not a new phenomenon; it started centuries back because of Norway's role as a seafaring nation, but it was not until 1969 that English began its proper journey towards becoming common currency. This is when English was established as an obligatory subject for all pupils in primary and secondary school,[2] and since then, the language has gained increasing momentum in the Norwegian school system, illustrated by a recent change in the national curriculum, where English is no longer

---

1   Simon Frith, 'Why do songs have words?', *Contemporary Music Review*, 5.1 (1989), 77–96 (p. 91).
2   Aud Marit Simensen, 'Europeiske institusjoners rolle i utviklingen av engelskfaget i norsk skole' ['The role of European institutions in the development of English as a subject in Norwegian schools'], *Didaktisk Tidsskrift*, 20.3 (2011), 157–81 (pp. 158–59).

listed as a foreign language alongside German, French and Spanish, etc., but is given independent subject status.[3] This momentum has obviously been fuelled by an awareness of the increasingly important role played by English as an international *lingua franca*. As the major Anglophone nations have established themselves as political and economic superpowers, so the English language has emerged as a language of power and prestige, having become a ubiquitous presence throughout the world.[4] This has had profound effects on Norwegian culture and language that have been welcomed by some, but also lamented by a number of Norwegian language policy makers and scholars.[5] Such effects are above all visible in popular culture. In Norway, as in the other Scandinavian countries, there is obvious English-language dominance within film, TV, on the Internet, and last but not least, within popular music. A quick browse through Norway's leading hit list *VG-lista topp 20* reveals that in the period 1960–2013, the great majority of artists represented (around 80%) are native English-language artists.[6] Up until the 1980s, most of the Norwegian artists on the list sang in Norwegian; after that, their language of choice was English, with a very clear dominance of English-language lyrics after the mid-1990s.

What *VG-lista* does *not* immediately reveal – since this very often demands looking beyond the mere titles of songs – is the presence of another typical characteristic of the linguistic behaviour of an increasingly bilingual population. What I have in mind is a particular form of linguistic mélange known within sociolinguistics as *code-switching*, defined here as any form of alternation between two or more languages within a stretch of discourse.[7] Some of the earliest examples of code-switching (CS) in Norwegian song lyrics are found in the mid-1960s, although unsurprisingly, we do not find very many examples of CS until the 1990s, with steadily growing numbers up until today. The

---

3   *Regjeringen.no* <https://www.regjeringen.no/nb/dokumenter/rundskriv-f-003-06/id109627/> [accessed 22 January 2015].
4   Alastair Pennycook, *The Cultural Politics of English as an International Language* (New York: Longman, 1994), p. 13ff.
5   Witoslaw Awedyk, 'Attitudes of Norwegians towards the growing influence of English', *Folia Scandinavica*, 10 (2009), 143–53.
6   *VG-lista – Topp 20* <http://lista.vg.no/> [accessed 1 August 2013].
7   For a discussion of alternative definitions of code-switching, see Penelope Gardner-Chloros, *Code-switching* (Cambridge: Cambridge University Press, 2009), pp. 12–13.

focus of this chapter is, however, not so much on the quantitative aspects of this development as its qualitative aspects, since it is reasonable to assume that differences in the depth of integration of the English language into Norwegian society from the 1960s until today will have influenced not only the amount of CS used, but also the types of CS used, and their potential functions, and this is something that it is just as interesting to look into. Thus, this chapter constitutes an attempt at charting some of these different types and functions, relating the changes found to general changes in appropriative patterns in regard to English in the Norwegian popular music field as a whole. I start, however, by taking a brief look at some existing studies on CS with English in popular music lyrics elsewhere in the world.

Types and functions of CS in song lyrics

Research on CS with English in song lyrics is most prolific where it reports on developments within non-postcolonial Asian countries such as Japan and Korea.[8] Here, the growing impact of Anglophone cultures and language has led to the emergence of entirely new, increasingly internationally recognized genres such as J-Pop and K-Pop, where code-switching is one of the defining features. Studies from other continents include that of Bentahila and Davies, who looked at code-switching, mainly between Arabic and French, in *rai* music in Algeria and Morocco, although the use of English as an internationalizing feature was also shown to be emerging.[9] Quite a few studies concern themselves with rap music originating in different countries, a genre where languages are mixed in order to connect with local subcultures and to larger, international networks.[10]

---

8   E.g. Alastair Pennycook, 'Global Englishes, Rip Slyme, and performativity', *Journal of Sociolinguistics*, 7.4 (2003), 513–33; Jamie Shinee Lee, 'Linguistic hybridization in K-Pop: Discourse of self-assertion and resistance', *World Englishes*, 23.3 (2004), 429–50; Andrew J. Moody, 'English in Japanese popular culture and J-Pop music', *World Englishes*, 25.2 (2006), 209–22.
9   Abdelali Bentahila and Eirlys A. Davies, 'Language mixing in rai music: Localisation or globalisation?', *Language and Communication*, 22 (2002), 187–207.
10 E.g. Bent Preisler, 'Functions and forms of English in a European EFL country', in *Standard English: The Widening Debate*, ed. by Tony Bex and Richard J. Watts (London: Routledge, 1999), pp. 239–67; Mela Sarkar and Lise Winer, 'Multilingual codeswitching in Quebec rap: Poetry, pragmatics

Obviously, each situation of cultural and linguistic contact has unique features that will inform the theories and models that emerge, tailor-making them to that situation. Still, there are always useful features to be extracted. Many of the studies mentioned here approach code-switching from a discourse or conversation analytical and/or sociolinguistic angle. Typically, in the examples studied, the artist's native language constitutes the matrix into which foreign elements are inserted (this is also the case in my examples). The inserted elements are then classified, and their discourse function is discussed: how does the element contribute to structuring the lyrics and the music? The sociolinguistic function(s) of the elements is/are also considered: what does the artist in question achieve, in a broader sense, by employing the given type of CS in the way that he or she does? As there is no great degree of agreement regarding labels used for the same or similar types and functions of CS in lyrics, and as there is no space here to fully discuss these terminological inconsistencies, I shall here simply adopt, from some selected studies, a few categories that seem useful for my purposes.

Moody offers a classificatory scheme of types of insertional element.[11] His categories are *musical fillers* (such as 'yeah', 'oh', 'baby', etc.), *single words and phrases* (e.g. 'kiss', 'my love'), and *clauses and sentences*. Considering the common occurrence of inserting elements at even higher discourse levels, I opt to expand Moody's model with another category, viz. *verses and/or choruses*. Moody's final category is *code ambiguation*, which may or may not turn out to be specific to the Japanese pop lyrics he is studying. It is a label for the phenomenon of using words that can have meaning in both languages, and so far at least, I have not discovered any examples of this in my material.

Bentahila and Davies contribute two useful discourse analytical categories, *insertional style* and *organizational style* CS.[12] The former refers to cases where single words or clauses in another language are used relatively sparingly, and in places that are not structurally prominent. The latter refers to CS that is

---

and performativity', *International Journal of Multilingualism*, 3(3) (2006), 173–92; Sirpa Leppänen, 'Youth language in media contexts: Insights into the functions of English in Finland', *World Englishes*, 26.2 (2007), 149–69; Edward Larkey, 'Just for fun? Language choice in German popular music', *Popular Music and Society*, 24.3 (2008), 1–20.

11 Andrew J. Moody, 'English in Japanese popular culture and J-Pop music', pp. 209–22.
12 Abdelali Bentahila and Eirlys A. Davies, 'Language mixing in rai music', pp. 187–207.

somehow significant to the organization of the lyrics, such as when shorter or longer elements are inserted in hook lines, in choruses, and/or when they are repeated. As will be seen later, the latter is the dominant form in my cases.

CS also performs a number of sociolinguistic functions. Some of these functions are more obviously relevant in one or a few sociocultural contexts, but many may also occur across several, relatively different contexts. The majority of functions identified in the literature are interrelated and not always easily separable from each other; still, the labels chosen seem to succeed in designating at least a distinguishable conceptual focus. The first and perhaps most basic sociolinguistic function of CS with English is connected to the much-discussed symbolic value of the language, projecting, as it typically does, associations to modernity, chic and sophistication,[13] and, in non-Western countries, Westernization.[14] This is the foundation for the *identity-building function* of CS. At a simple level, by using English insertions, the given artist forges an identity for him or herself as someone who embodies or at least condones such values and ideas. Pennycook[15] suggests (and Leppänen[16] implies) that identity building through CS with English takes place at three levels: at the level of national identity, at the global level (through the use of a global language), and at the level where subcultural (e.g. rap) identities are made. This ability of CS with English to work both locally, globally, and glocally, connects with an issue discussed by Larkey, revolving around how using CS allows the artist to connect with multiple audiences. According to Larkey, '[t]his layering of lyric languages is an effective way of addressing several audiences at once, and serves to authenticate and legitimate the addressor to each different audience.'[17] This could usefully be termed the *connection-building function* of CS with English, which would then be broader than, and encompass Bentahila and Davies' *internationalization*, which pertains exclusively to the global level, to the use of English as 'a key to the international scene.'[18]

---

13   Jamie Shinee Lee, 'Linguistic hybridization in K-Pop', pp. 429–50.
14   Penelope Gardner-Chloros, *Code-switching*, p. 67; cf. also the notion of metaphorical CS in Jan-Peter Blom and John J. Gumperz, 'Social meaning in linguistic structures: Code-switching in Norway', in *Directions in Sociolinguistics: The Ethnography of Communication*, ed. by John J. Gumperz and Dell Hymes (New York: Holt, Rinehart and Winston, 1972), pp. 407–34 (in Gardner-Chloros, p. 59).
15   Alastair Pennycook, 'Global Englishes, Rip Slyme, and performativity', p. 516.
16   Sirpa Leppänen, 'Youth language in media contexts', pp. 149–69.
17   Larkey, p. 10.
18   Bentahila and Davies, p. 190.

One function of CS with English which perhaps does not seem immediately relevant to Scandinavian society is *censorship-avoidance*, noted by Lee,[19] in an article on linguistic hybridization in K-pop. Repressive currents in South Korean society necessitate the hiding of explicit sexual content in English insertions, placing it safely out of reach of older generations whose lack of proficiency in English prevent them from understanding the real message. Censorship-avoidance may be part of the more general function of *resistance*, also discussed by Lee. South Korean youth, who are experiencing a considerable degree of control by parents and society at large, are, through the use of CS with English, able to 'challenge dominant representations of authority, to resist mainstream norms and values, and to reject older generations' conservatism'.[20]

Norwegian song lyrics 1960s to 2000s: From diegetic to extra-diegetic use of CS

As mentioned, some of the earliest occurrences of Norwegian-English CS in song lyrics date back to the mid-1960s, a time when airwaves were thick with English-language music, although the language had yet to become common property among Norwegians. Two of the earliest examples include Norwegian radio personality, singer and composer Otto Nielsen's '**He is dead but he won't lie down**',[21] written by Nielsen and performed in his radio show *Søndagsposten* in 1966;[22] and 'Bli' de poesi tå slekt' ['Can that Kind of Thing Make Poetry'],[23] written by Birger Jørstad and performed by Nielsen in the same programme. The former borrowed the title and the melody of an American song written by Hoagy Carmichael and Johnny Mercer for the Western movie *Timberjack* (1954), but the remaining Norwegian lyrics (apart from some repetitions of the English words in the title) are in Norwegian, and the song is re-written as a critical commentary on the neo-Nazi tendencies in Western Germany at the

---

19 Lee, p. 437ff.
20 Lee, p. 429.
21 Henceforth, I use bold for English (and other non-Norwegian) insertions.
22 *Wikipedia* <http://no.wikipedia.org/wiki/He_Is_Dead,_But_He_Won%27t_Lie_Down> [accessed 2 August 2013].
23 This and all subsequent translations are mine.

time. The second of the two songs, 'Bli' de poesi tå slekt' is written as a lament for the 'loss of poetry' in popular song lyrics. Here, too, only one line is in English: '**Where have all the flowers gone**'.[24]

This kind of example is not easily accounted for by the terminology introduced in the previous section. On the level of discourse, things are simple enough; both cases are obviously examples of insertional style CS. As far as the sociolinguistic functions are concerned, however, these do somehow not seem to apply. Although the use of English might have had a slight image-conveying and identity-building effect, the language's connotations at the time were more likely to have been less strong: people would have had fewer ideas about it, and if present, the connotations would not necessarily have resembled today's 'modernity, chic and sophistication'. As far as connecting with multiple audiences is concerned, Nielsen and Jørstad were most likely not – could not have been – identifying themselves with a community of CS by choosing to insert English into their lyrics. Norway was not yet bilingual, and hence there simply was no such community. Ideas of producing and selling Norwegian music to international (non-Scandinavian) audiences were not yet prominent, and as such it is unlikely that a desire or need to internationalize would have constituted any reason behind the choice to use English. So why use English? Well, in both cases the main function of the English insertions seems to be to create an intertextuality that contributes to the overall meaning content of the lyrics. To borrow one of Gérard Genette's terms, the English insertions in these lyrics, to a greater degree than more modern examples of CS with English, seem to work on the level of the *diegesis* – the narrative, or more generally, the 'story', of the song.[25] The title '**He is dead but he won't lie down**' obviously and inevitably takes on the function of forming an intertextual link back to Mercer's original lyrics and the film, but in that very same process, the English title is transmuted into an ironic commentary on the Norwegian lyrics' main theme. In a similar vein, '**Where have all the flowers gone**', while unambiguously pointing back to the familiar folk song, is transformed into a different kind of lament: 'what has happened to the poetry in songs'.

---

24 *Rockipedia* <https://www.rockipedia.no/utgivelser/det_vart_poesi_ta_slekt-6359/> [accessed 23 September 2013]. Lyrics printed with permission by Norsk Noteservice AS.
25 Gérard Genette, *Narrative Discourse* (Oxford: Blackwell, 1980) (Original title: *Discours du récit: essai de method*, in Figures III [Paris: Seuil, 1972]).

The earlier examples of CS do seem to be largely characterized by such *diegetic functions*. In addition to the above, we have a group of songs that are interesting for the way in which the English language itself is somehow thematized in the lyrics. The first that I want to have a look at is 'Ola var fra Sandefjord' ['Ola was from Sandefjord']. The song was written by Albert Edvin Pedersen and Per Kvist for a jazz music competition in 1929 where it came third, and was recorded by bestselling recording artist Einar Rose in the same year, as a foxtrot. It did not become a national hit, however, until it was recorded by Johnny Band in 1965, in beat style. The lyrics tell the tale of a Norwegian sailor whose ship sailed to England, where he fell in love with an English-speaking girl, the problem being that Ola could not speak English. That is – he knew just enough English to get by:

> For en ting kunne han si: **My little sweetheart**
> Og hun sa: **Yes, very well** og **I love you**
> Han sa: Jeg vil du skal bli **my little sweetheart**
> Og snart så kunne hun si: Jeg elsker du
> Det gikk på engelsk og norsk, engelsk og norsk
> Og den lille **Miss** fikk på norsk et ærlig **kiss**
> For en ting kunne han si: **My little sweetheart**
> Og hun sa: **Yes, very well** og **I love you**[26]

Interestingly, Ola is a sailor, one of the earliest groups of people in Norway to experience the need to know English and who acquired it to some degree.[27] The story of the song is of a code-switching relationship between a man (Ola) and an unnamed woman, presumably someone he met while ashore in England. Ola is a happy-go-lucky kind of fellow who deploys his limited linguistic resources, invariably with a great degree of precisely, luck. Even later on in the song, when the English girl professes to being 'sick and tired of Norwegian'

---

26 'Because he could say one thing: **My little sweetheart**/And she said: **yes, very well** and **I love you**/He said: I want you to be **my little sweetheart**/And soon she was able to say: I loves [sic] you/They would use English and Norwegian, English and Norwegian/And the little **Miss** got an honest **kiss** in Norwegian/Because he could say one thing: **My little sweetheart**/And she said: **yes, very well** and **I love you**'. Lyrics printed with permission by Norsk Musikforlag AS.

27 Simensen, p. 158.

and proceeds to be unfaithful to him with an English naval officer, he salvages his relationship in the end, by means of the very same phrases. This thematization of the issue of English proficiency, and the deep embedment of the actual phrases used in the narrative, makes this a clear case of CS in its diegetic function.

Other examples of lyrics that thematize English in some way or other as well as containing CS, are rock artist Åge Aleksandersen's 'Æ sa kjøttkak' ['I said Meatballs'] (1977); children's TV presenter and comedian Trond Viggo Torgesen's 'Hjalmar' (1978); and country and western artist Bjøro Håland's '**I love Norwegian country**' (written by Benny Borg) (1982). The story in Aleksandersen's song is that of a young country lad visiting a city and in search of a meal, who wants the regional staple dish of meatballs and potatoes. Everywhere he goes, however, he is looked down on by haughty chefs who insist on introducing him to more fancy dishes, doing so using difficult, foreign terms. This is Norway in the 1970s, so even pizza will for some segments of the population be considered exotic:

> Vi har pizza te aill
> Du får'n varm eller kaill
> **The American way**
> Eller **plain as we say**?
> Æ sa potet
> Og kokken svart: **Quarter past five**[28]

In the same way as in 'Ola var fra Sandefjord', these lyrics are in some sense about CS, but here, rather than being seen as a valuable resource to achieve one's communicative goals, the English insertions are perceived (by the country-boy narrator) as a despicable display of arrogance – trying to make yourself seem better than you are and refusing to communicate clearly.

Torgersen's 'Hjalmar' contains the story of a young boy of about nine or ten who, rather than doing his homework, spends his time singing, in what purports to be English:

---

28 'We have pizzas for everyone/You can have it hot or cold/**The American way**/Or **plain as we say**?/I said potatoes/And the chef answered: **Quarter past five**'. Lyrics printed with permission by Norsk Noteservice AS.

Hjalmar han lot leksene være
Synes selv han låt som en engelskmann
Når han sang, ropte han:²⁹

Ååååå, yug gatta rapsuly take aly
Ååååå, when yu brekandan se gobay (se gobay)
Heey, coman sipy an bickering
Takin me boy, rapsoly toy
Looseri love, you've fickeni moo³⁰

Here, a lack of proficiency is again at stake: though the young Hjalmar is struggling to learn the language, he actually thinks that he knows it rather well, something that he realizes later on in the song, when he visits England, is utterly wrong. Unlike all of the previous examples, where the CS consists of inserted words, phrases and clauses, the whole chorus is in a mix of English (e.g. '**love**', '**you've**') and nonsense words that are phonetically close to English (e.g. '**rapsoly**', '**fickeni**'). In this way, Hjalmar's limited English proficiency is put on display in a prolonged manner in a prominent place in the song, arguably making this a case of organizational style code switching. Bjøro Håland's '**I love Norwegian Country**' similarly has verses in Norwegian and a chorus entirely in English, except this time, the chorus is in plain English, and there is no comic intent. The song tells the story of the narrator and his friend travelling from Norway to the USA to play concerts, and the chorus sums up the feedback they received by audiences and record company representatives: '**I love Norwegian country/And I like the way you sing/'cause all country music 'round the world/Will always be the greatest thing**'.³¹

In all of these examples of CS used diegetically, the English insertions are tightly woven into the narrative fabric of the lyrics, and, as was pointed out initially, this seems to characterize the earlier examples in particular. This does not mean that later examples do not exist at all. In 1991, for example,

---

29 'Hjalmar didn't bother with homework/He thought he sounded like an Englishman/When he sang, he would shout'.
30 Lyrics printed with permission by Trond Viggo Torgersen.
31 Lyrics printed with permission by Norsk Noteservice AS.

singer/songwriter Kari Bremnes released the song 'Montreal', where, much like in the Håland example, we get a Norwegian narrator who tells the story of a journey in an English-speaking country. In Bremnes' song, the lyrics' narrator encounters an English-speaking female character, a seller of clothes, whose utterances are rendered untranslated in the chorus: '**I'm selling all my mother's clothes/Her lingerie, her skirts and coats/Her beauty was as pure as this affair is sordid/I'm selling all my mother's clothes/And, yes, I find it morbid**'.[32]

Interestingly, the lyrics by Håland and Bremnes do not, like the earlier examples, depict or imply a lack of proficiency, but rather the opposite: the former tells of the triumph of eliciting praise for non-native singing from native-English speakers, and the latter of the modern globe-trotter's effortless understanding of the language. This is perhaps unsurprising, as it coincides with a period where Norwegians' proficiency in English was on the rise, and it shows how songs can in fact constitute comments on the sociolinguistic situation within a linguistic community.

After the 1991 Bremnes example, the use of CS may seem to more or less disappear for a period, only to reappear in the mid-2000s, but in a different form. Alternative rock band Kaizers Orchestra are early representatives of the new trend. Their career started in 2001, and since then they have enjoyed great success, both nationally and abroad, with several albums. Before 2005, their lyrics contained very little CS. This changed, however, with their 2005 album entitled *Maestro*. The following chorus from their song '**Action**' (2005) (written by Joachim Nielsen and released on the bonus CD *Maestro Limited Edition*) is an example of a song that presents a particularly dense patchwork of CS:

> Eg ser etter **action**
> Men alt eg finner er glasskår og spy
> **Action action**
> Eg ser etter **action**
> Gi meg et eller annet
> Før dagen deres gryr[33]

---

32 Lyrics printed with permission by Kari Bremnes.
33 'I'm looking for **action**/But all I find is broken glass and vomit/**Action action**/I'm looking for **action**/Give me something, anything/Before your day dawns'. Lyrics printed with permission by Christopher Nielsen.

The lyric's protagonist is a man who wanders the streets after closing time, a predator without a sense of belonging. He is looking for action; something – we never get to know exactly what – to satisfy his dark need for excitement. And although the word '**action**' obviously has a denotation that somehow contributes to the semantic content of the lyrics, there are definite differences between the previous examples and this one. In at least some of those lyrics, i.e. 'Ola var fra Sandefjord', 'Æ sa kjøttkak', and 'Hjalmar', the stories could simply not have been told without the English insertions (at least not effectively enough to fit within the span of the song). In others, such as '**I love Norwegian Country**' and 'Montreal', the use of English functions as a characterizing device. By contrast, the word '**action**' could easily have been replaced by a Norwegian element (e.g. the word's literal translation 'handling') without the song losing its narrative backbone (or rhythm), and although the use of '**action**' may serve a weak characterizing (intra-diegetic) function, this still does not seem to capture exactly what is going on here.[34] So what does? Starting by looking at the level of discourse, we may note that '**action**' is repeated 21 times throughout the verses and the chorus. It appears in the same place at the end of each verse; it is sung on a long (and hence prominent) note in the first line in the chorus and repeated twice in the third line of the chorus, and then again once in the fourth line, making it clear that this is a case of organizational style CS. The repetitions give the song a clear identity; they signal transitions between verses and choruses, they contribute to the creation of a hook line (the first line in the chorus), hence helping to make this part of the song easy to remember. These are all very important functions on the discursive *and*

---

34 Some would argue that '**action**' constitutes a loan rather than CS. Many, however, believe there are good reasons to see borrowing and CS as phenomena on opposite ends of a scale rather than as essentially separate (see Gardner-Chloros, p. 12). The latter is the view I am adopting here. Something that starts off life as CS could eventually turn into a permanent loan, and it can sometimes be difficult to pinpoint exactly when the former has turned into the latter (for a given group of individuals). As far as '**action**' is concerned, I would argue that it is used, in these lyrics, as an instance of CS rather than as a loan. The reasons for this are the following: 1) non-naturalized spelling is used (the word can be spelt in a naturalized way, as æksjn); 2) '**Action**' is the title of the song, and the subsequent numerous repetitions of the word accentuate the word's foreignness. Kaizers Orchestra in fact often use such semi-naturalized words (like '**darling**', and '**baby**'), in foreignizing ways in their songs. Such words have the advantage of being familiar and unobtrusive to a local audience as well as recognizable by international audiences, and their foreignizing use adds interest to the lyrics.

musical levels. They could, however, just as well have been fulfilled by means of the repetition of any *Norwegian* word; so the question still remains, why did the songwriter choose an essentially *English* word? At this point, the only answer left to this question seems to be: 'because of the English-ness of that word'. And here, we are obviously back to some of the functions identified in the research presented in the previous section. What characterizes the identity-building and connection-building functions that we saw there, is that they are *extra-diegetic*: the crucial thing is not the denotations of the words used and how they contribute to the narrative, but rather how the choice to code-switch and the language choice in and of itself carry various connotations, which help songwriters and artists express something over and beyond the actual content of the lyrics, and connect with those who are able to recognize those meanings.

Kaizers Orchestra exploit the connotations of English on several levels. For a start, in their oeuvre as a whole, they exploit the regional and historical connotations of German and English, as well as English sung in a distinctly German accent, to create the gloomy, European, between-the-wars atmosphere that became so typical of their records.[35] Furthermore, they obviously, like so many other modern pop and rock artists, exploit the sociocultural connotations of English. Using English, either exclusively or as a lyrical spice, signals modernity, progress, and globalization.[36] The English-language insertions are linguistic tattoos that anchor the band's and their music's identities to a generation and a given historical period, both locally, and globally. Words, phrases and clauses that are known and understood (or at the very least recognized as being English) trigger shared associations and a sense of familiarity that create an important foundation for developing loyalties and allegiances. We see this with J-Pop and K-Pop, which, unlike much non-English-language pop music, have managed to build considerable fan-bases world-wide, including in Anglophone countries. In light of this, it is interesting to note that Kaizers Orchestra's

---

35   It could, of course, be discussed whether this is in fact part of the diegesis; here, I choose to see this function as one that forms a bridge over to the more clearly extra-diegetic functions of the use of English in Kaizers Orchestra's work.
36   Ingrid Piller, 'Advertising as a site of language contact', *Annual Review of Applied Linguistics*, 23 (2003), 170–83 (p. 175).

transition to a greater amount of code-switching in 2005 also coincided with their major breakthrough in continental Europe.[37]

Another Norwegian artist who has recently used CS with English extensively in her work is Norwegian-Grenadian R&B artist Sichelle. Unusually for this genre, Sichelle chooses to sing in the local language; being quite a marked linguistic act, this may have contributed to her relatively high degree of visibility as an artist and thus the great success of her eponymous album *Sichelle* in 2008. Many of the lyrics represented on the album contain CS. Some are musical fillers, as in the song 'Hvis du går' ['If you Leave (me)'] ('**yeah**', '**oh**'); others are single-word switches, such as in the songs '**Fuck** deg' ['**Fuck** you'] (which is a translation of a Danish original where the same code-switched element occurs in the same places in the song), '**Keen**', and '**Freaky**'. These lyrics use CS in a quite similar way to Kaizers Orchestra's '**Action**': the English language insertion appears in the title and otherwise in structurally prominent places in the songs. In Sichelle's case it is also tempting to suggest that the English insertions do the job of ensuring that the songs stay sufficiently within the genre: musical fillers, for example, are very typical within R&B and they do tend not to sound right if translated into Norwegian. Finally, the connotations spoken of earlier are of course inevitably there, simply because all current use of English by non-English speakers in non-English-speaking countries invites them. In Sichelle's case, however, their presence has not (yet) led to any significant degree of international success, indicating the obvious fact that CS alone will never be a guarantor that this will happen.

Rap – a genre that is very much defined by profuse CS and culture-mixing – also has its Norwegian representatives, and provides many current examples of CS in its extra-diegetic functions. Erik og Kriss is a Norwegian rap duo who struck gold via the Internet in 2004 with their song 'Bærumsgrammatikk' ['Bærum Grammar'], a song in which they indirectly identify borrowing/CS with English as a phenomenon particular to Bærum, the wealthy area in Oslo where the artists themselves grew up. Interestingly, 'Bærumsgrammatikk', in thematizing the English language like we have seen in earlier examples, is in fact a case of diegetic, not extra-diegetic, use of CS:

---

37 'Kaizer's Orchestra', *Wikipedia* <http://no.wikipedia.org/wiki/Kaizers_Orchestra> [accessed 5 August 2013].

En dvask kar er **chubby**
Kødding er betegnelsen på tull
Og venn er **buddy**[38]

Like in the earlier examples, the narrative constitutes an interesting comment on where Norwegians see themselves within the current linguistic landscape, with regard to English. In this 2004 song, CS is used to draw attention to the CS phenomenon itself, to its group of users, and to how the phenomenon contributes to defining them socially. In this song, like in Aleksandersen's 'Æ sa kjøttkak', people who use CS are portrayed as people who see themselves as being better than others (a great, social *faux pas* in Norway until very recently): however, while Aleksandersen criticises this attitude, Erik og Kriss, who belong to the group they are singing about, defend their right to think of themselves as better (using extra-diegetic CS):

Klysete eller ikke **bitch**
Det her er sånn vi **putter** det
Om du ikke riktig **digger** det eller blir kvalm av det
Kan du bare drite i det
Det her er sånn vi skal ha det[39]

Extra-diegetic CS also characterizes the remainder of Erik and Kriss' work. In 2011 the duo released the single '**My City**' together with Danish rappers Nik & Jay. The former rap in Norwegian, while the latter do so in Danish, both with single-word and phrasal switches into English (such as '**cityfella**', '**baby**', '**chicksa**', '**icebreaker**', '**my city**'). In addition, the whole chorus is in English, sung (apparently) by all four rappers: '**You know, you know/We don't hit the club until after 2 o'clock/Put whatever in ya cup, that's whats up/We got the most beautiful girls/Might be the best place in the world/My city baby**'. The fact that all four of them join in the chorus, and that this chorus is sung entirely

---

38 'A slightly fat guy is **chubby**/Kødding is the term for silliness/And friend is **buddy**'. Lyrics printed with permission by Erik og Kriss.
39 'Snotty or not **bitch**/This here is how we put it/If you can't dig it or it makes you feel sick/Then stop giving a shit/This is how it is going to be'. Lyrics printed with permission by Erik og Kriss.

in English, is interesting in this particular context because of the role that English increasingly plays in Norwegian-Danish communication. In Norway, there is currently a common perception that Norwegian and Danish, despite being very closely related, are becoming less and less mutually intelligible in their spoken form. This often triggers the use of English as a *lingua franca* between Norwegians and Danes. Thus, although verses in local languages and (full) choruses in English are not unusual in a rap context – this way of doing it is both an excellent structuring device, and allows the artist to connect with international rap audiences – there may, here, also exist an additional, more local explanation why English is chosen: the language quite simply constitutes common ground for artists who would otherwise have struggled to accommodate each other linguistically.

My final example in this chapter is taken from a Norwegian rock group, The BlackSheeps, demonstrating that CS is a phenomenon that spans a large number of sub-genres of popular music. The deliberately incorrect use of the plural –s in the group's name signals a playful attitude to language, which is definitely borne out by their lyrics. In 2008, the group caused everybody's ears to prick up with their song 'Oro jaska beana',[40] which secured them victory in the Norwegian Junior Eurovision Song Contest. The song quite unusually contained CS between Saami and Norwegian, and its initial success is perhaps testimony to the attention-getting function of CS in certain of its manifestations.[41] As part of a PR campaign for the dairy company TINE, the group also recorded a version of Herman's Hermit's 'No milk today', translating parts of the lyrics into Saami.[42] In 2011, they came second in the Norwegian Eurovision Song Contest final with the song '**Dance Tonight**'. In these lyrics the verses are in Norwegian, with one inserted Saami phrase, while the entire chorus is in English:

---

40   Saami for 'Shut up, Dog'.
41   Jamie Shinee Lee, 'Linguistic hybridization in K-Pop', p. 435.
42   'The Blacksheeps', *Wikipedia* <http://no.wikipedia.org/wiki/The_BlackSheeps> [accessed 5 July 2013].

Inatt, du og jeg på gulvet
Og du vil få meg til å le og le og le
Inatt, du **ja mu ciegusvuohta**
Og du og du og du og du vil få meg til å le[43]

Let's do the dance tonight (x3)
Tonight, you and I
Let's do the dance tonight (x3)
Tonight, you and I[44]

The Saami insertion first and foremost serves the function of reminding audiences of what made the group famous in the first place, as well as re-asserting their Saami identities. The English insertions perform more of a structuring role, at the same time as contributing to forging a new, more globally oriented identity for the band. Moreover, we have in the case of this particular song an interesting twist on the censorship-avoidance function.[45] Unlike in the Asian communities dealt with by Lee, censorship with regard to sexually explicit material is not really very strong at all in Scandinavia. The degree of sexual explicitness of this song is moreover not particularly high. This being the case, the strategy used to titillate audiences rather seems to be that of using a foreign language to mask content *as if* it were necessary to mask this content. This is arguably one of the functions of the Saami insert (which, upon closer inspection turns out to contain merely another bland metaphor for sex).[46] As far as the English inserts are concerned, it is, in a Norwegian context, not possible to literally hide away explicit material here, although such materials can certainly be somewhat ameliorated by being sung in English rather than in the audience's mother tongue. As it happens, the contents of this particular chorus are, as already pointed out, *not* explicit but again, since the use of English may produce an impression of a hiding-away/ameliorating act, the weak sexual implications of 'doing the dance' may become stronger than they originally were.

---

43   'Tonight, you and me on the floor/And you will make me laugh and laugh and laugh/Tonight, you **and my secret**/And you and you and you and you will make me laugh'.
44   Lyrics printed with permission by Emilie Nilsen and Agnete Kristin Johnsen.
45   Jamie Shinee Lee, 'Linguistic hybridization in K-Pop', p. 437ff.
46   Morten Hegseth, 'The Blacksheeps til finalen med sextekst' ['The Blacksheeps to the final with sex lyrics'], *VG* <http://www.vg.no/musikk/grand-prix/artikkel.php?artid=10013651> [accessed 5 July 2013].

Discussion and conclusions

To sum up, the clearest tendency in the material is the transition from a predominantly diegetic to a predominantly extra-diegetic use of Norwegian-English CS in song lyrics in the period from the 1960s to the 2000s. This transition can furthermore be seen in connection with the increase in English proficiency across the Norwegian population within the same period and the growing importance of the role of the English language, which for artists functions both as a tool for acquiring international appeal, and for asserting oneself intranationally.

The diegetic examples span the 1960s and early 1980s, with a couple of examples stranded in later decades. This period (1960s to 1980s) corresponds to what could be called an early appropriation period in regard to English in Norway, with English becoming a compulsory subject in the school curricula, enabling more efficient acquisition of the language on the basis of the ever growing amount of English input through the media. As far as Norwegian music artists' engagement with English is concerned, this is a period where they either chose to stay safely with Norwegian, or began to explore the creative opportunities in using English, by using CS, as we have seen, or by writing all-English lyrics. On the content side, the lyrics that contain CS, such as 'Ola var fra Sandefjord', 'Æ sa kjøttkak', and 'Hjalmar', tell stories of the linguistic promise, insecurities and prejudice involved in the move towards societial and invividual bilingualism. It is also interesting to consider the humorous, but also at the same time serious, didactic message of the last of these songs, 'Hjalmar'. After practising singing in English in front of the mirror at home, the boy Hjalmar leaves school to go to England, only to discover that his English is not quite up to scratch:

> Dette er ikke engelsk min venn
> Du må starte fra bånn igjen
> Du tror du låter som Elton John
> Men det er ingen som snakker sånn[47]

---

47 'This isn't English my friend/You'll have to start from scratch/You think you sound like Elton John/But nobody speaks like that'. Lyrics printed with permission by Trond Viggo Torgersen.

In this bridge, the song warns of the dangers of being over-confident about one's foreign language abilities. The potential punishment is humiliation and the source of this humiliation is seen to be the native speaker (portrayed here by the singer, singing in Norwegian with a mock-English accent), the ultimate judge of what constitutes passable English. And the message to the fourth-grader is clear: you'll need to work on your proficiency.

During the period from approximately 1980 to the mid-2000s there is a discernible temporal gap where hardly any CS seems to be taking place. Looking at *VG-lista topp 20* we find that what is going on in this gap is Norwegian singers trying to find their musical and artistic identities by singing (exclusively) in English (see introduction). Although some artists continued to sing in Norwegian, this very prominent 'English turn' in pop music is nevertheless indicative of an intensive appropriation period, of an intense striving to imitate and emulate Anglo-American sources, both musically and linguistically. In portraying the confident non-native English speaker abroad, the examples of diegetic CS found in this period ('**I love Norwegian Country**' and 'Montreal') neatly illustrate how these efforts were, in many cases, crowned with success: Norwegians were getting better at English. At the peak of this period, the head of Norwegian radio's music channel P3, Nils Heldal proclaimed in one of Norway's largest tabloids, *Dagbladet*:

> Norske artister kan like godt slutte å synge på norsk. I den globaliserte verden vi lever i er det meningsløst å gni og gnukke på norsken. Det er langt viktigere å kommunisere med hele verden enn å bevare noe som bare er vårt.[48]

Heldal's statement in fact marked the beginning of the decline of the intensive appropriation period. Another linguistic turn was about to happen, when a number of Norwegian bands, among them Kaizers Orchestra, instigated a reappraisal of Norwegian as a viable language of pop music.[49] This turn is cur-

---

48 'Norwegian artists may as well stop singing in Norwegian. In our globalised world it is meaningless to keep on grinding and grating the Norwegian language. It is far more important to communicate with the whole world than to preserve something that is merely ours'. In Per Kristian Olsen, Asbjørn Bakke and Sigrid Hvidsten, *Norsk rocks historie. Fra Rocke-Pelle til Hank von Helvete* [*The History of Norwegian rock. From Rocke-Pelle to Hank von Helvete*] (Oslo: Cappelen Damm, 2009), p. 357.
49   Ibid.

rently manifesting itself as a modest Norwegian wave, with artists who used to write and sing in English now releasing albums entirely in Norwegian (e.g. World Idol winner Kurt Nilsen).[50] The mid-2000s constitute the beginning of what one could call a late appropriation period, where Norwegians, including Norwegian artists, have become relatively adept at using English, and very used to wearing it as a second cultural coat, to the extent, perhaps, that it has started to lose some of its allure, allowing a re-orientation towards the Norwegian language. With English lyrics being the going rate, using Norwegian has in fact recently been a good strategy for some artists to get noticed.

More writing in Norwegian has also created a space for the renewed use of CS. Most of the CS from within this period is, however, not of the diegetic kind. The artists in question do not sing songs 'about language': instead, they use English for effect.[51] Choosing not to sing lyrics in English, they nevertheless try to have their cake and eat it. The Norwegian matrix allows them to build a strongly authentic image as someone who is firmly rooted in who they are and what they know – they are not someone who needs to hide away poor songwriting skills behind semi-transparent English clichés. At the same time, the English inserts allow them to establish a complex, glocal, identity, which enables them to connect with audiences virtually everywhere (albeit probably least easily in countries where English is spoken as a mother tongue). The one, diegetic example of CS identified within this period, 'Bærumsgrammatikk', portrays a group of confidently bilingual code-switchers (which includes the rappers themselves, who are, precisely, artists). As such, this song concludes – for now – the story about the changing role of the English language in Norway. Future instalments are no doubt forthcoming.

---

50   Stein Østbø, 'Kos med Kurt' ['A nice time with Kurt'], *VG* <http://www.vg.no/musikk/artikkel.php?artid=10072162> [accessed 5 August 2013].
51   Simon Frith, 'Why do songs have words?', p. 91.

Bibliography

Awedyk, Witoslaw, 'Attitudes of Norwegians towards the growing influence of English', *Folia Scandinavica*, 10 (2009), 143–53.

Bentahila, Abdelali and Eirlys A. Davies, 'Language mixing in rai music: Localisation or globalisation?', *Language and Communication*, 22 (2002), 187–207.

Blom, Jan-Peter and John J. Gumperz, 'Social meaning in linguistic structures: Code-switching in Norway', in *Directions in Sociolinguistics: The Ethnography of Communication*, ed. by John J. Gumperz and Dell Hymes (New York: Holt, Rinehart and Winston, 1972), pp. 407–34.

Frith, Simon, 'Why do songs have words?', *Contemporary Music Review*, 5.1 (1989), 77–96.

Gardner-Chloros, Penelope, *Code-switching* (Cambridge: Cambridge University Press, 2009).

Genette, Gérard, *Narrative Discourse* (Oxford: Blackwell, 1980).

Hegseth, Morten, 'The Blacksheeps til finalen med sextekst', *VG* <http://www.vg.no/musikk/grand-prix/artikkel.php?artid=10013651> [accessed 5 July 2013].

Larkey, Edward, 'Just for fun? Language choice in German popular music', *Popular Music and Society*, 24.3 (2008), 1–20.

Leppänen, Sirpa, 'Youth language in media contexts: Insights into the functions of English in Finland', *World Englishes*, 26.2 (2007), 149–69.

Moody, Andrew J., 'English in Japanese popular culture and J-Pop music', *World Englishes*, 25.2 (2006), 209–22.

Olsen, Per Kristian, Asbjørn Bakke and Sigrid Hvidsten, *Norsk rocks historie. Fra Rocke-Pelle til Hank von Helvete* (Oslo: Cappelen Damm, 2009).

Pennycook, Alastair, *The Cultural Politics of English as an International Language* (New York: Longman, 1994).

Pennycook, Alastair, 'Global Englishes, Rip Slyme, and performativity', *Journal of Sociolinguistics*, 7.4 (2003), 513–33.

Piller, Ingrid, 'Advertising as a site of language contact', *Annual Review of Applied Linguistics*, 23 (2003), 170–83.

Preisler, Bent, 'Functions and forms of English in a European EFL country', in *Standard English: The Widening Debate*, ed. by Tony Bex and Richard J. Watts (London: Routledge, 1999), pp. 239–67.

Regjeringen.no <https://www.regjeringen.no/nb/dokumenter/rundskriv-f-003-06/id109627/> [accessed 22 January 2015].

Rockipedia <https://www.rockipedia.no/utgivelser/det_vart_poesi_ta_slekt-6359/> [accessed 23 September 2013].

Sarkar, Mela and Lise Winer, 'Multilingual codeswitching in Quebec rap: Poetry, pragmatics and performativity', *International Journal of Multilingualism*, 3.3 (2006), 173–92.

Shinee Lee, Jamie, 'Linguistic hybridization in K-Pop: Discourse of self-assertion and resistance', *World Englishes*, 23.3 (2004), 429–50.

Simensen, Aud Marit, 'Europeiske institusjoners rolle i utviklingen av engelskfaget i norsk skole', *Didaktisk Tidsskrift*, 20.3 (2011), 157–81.

VG-lista – Topp 20 <http://lista.vg.no/> [accessed 1 July 2013].

Wikipedia http://no.wikipedia.org/wiki/He_Is_Dead,_But_He_Won%27t_Lie_Down [accessed 2 August 2013].

Wikipedia <http://no.wikipedia.org/wiki/Kaizers_Orchestra> [accessed 5 August 2013].

Wikipedia <http://no.wikipedia.org/wiki/The_BlackSheeps> [accessed 5 July 2013].

Østbø, Stein, 'Kos med Kurt', *VG* <http://www.vg.no/musikk/artikkel.php?artid=10072162> [accessed 5 July 2013].

11 'Your multilingual business friend might make you a better reader': Multilingualism and song lyrics in Kjartan Fløgstad's prose

Anne Karine Kleveland

> The mirror on reflection has climbed back upon the wall, for the floor she found descended and the ceiling was too tall. Resepsjonen var imponerande med sine glasdører, teaklister og marmorplater. Eg sette meg i ein mjuk, skinnkledd stol medan eg venta.[1]

This bilingual excerpt is taken from Kjartan Fløgstad's first prose collection, *Den hemmelege jubel* [*The Secret Cheer*], published in 1970. Preceded only by two collections of poems, it is here that we find the first fragments of song lyrics in his works. Since then, song lyrics have been part of the author's literary voice. Given the fact that these lyrics often bring other languages into play, they make a good starting point for a study of multilingualism in Fløgstad's works.

Kjartan Fløgstad frequently inserts song lyrics written by others into his novels and short prose. These often interrupt the fluency of the reading, as one or more verses are inserted. On other occasions they are hidden within his writing as intertextual references. We find both lyrics in their original language and lyrics that have been translated into Norwegian. We even find different translations into Norwegian of the same song fragment. The author also

---

[1] Kjartan Fløgstad, *Den hemmelege jubel* (Oslo: Samlaget, 1970), p. 84. Translation of book title and all other translations are mine.

composes his own lyrics that are inserted into his novels. These are commonly attributed to a fictional band or musicians who are characters in the novel where they appear. They usually emerge without any introduction, sometimes interrupting the plot. The self-composed lyrics are mostly in Norwegian, but some are bilingual, for instance 'Høysang' ['Hymn'] from *Dalen Portland* (1977) that mixes Norwegian with Spanish.[2] Sometimes the author writes verses completely in another language, as in his last novel *Nordaustpassasjen* [*Northeast Passage*] (2012) where we find 'Points of You', a song lyric in 'broken English'.[3]

In the 1990s the author's poems and song lyrics were collected in a volume named *Dikt og spelmannsmusikk*.[4] The fact that Fløgstad's editor has published these fragments in a collection which appeared in two editions within three years (the first in 1993 and the second in 1996) suggests that these texts are quite numerous.[5] More importantly, a separate publication implies that the publisher holds these lyrics in high esteem and wishes to share them with a broader readership. Although the publication was also most likely of commercial interest, given that Fløgstad at this point had become one of the best-known Norwegian authors, it is ultimately an argument for the quality of the author's poems and songs.

From a reader's point of view, these inserted songs and song fragments can be considered foreign or strange. Many of them disrupt the flow of the narrative and unsettle the act of reading. Their mere presence may therefore be said to cause what Berthold Brecht called *Verfremdung* or perhaps what Victor Schlovsky called *ostranenie* – both terms which are commonly translated into English as 'estrangement', 'defamiliarization' or 'alienation'. The fact

---

2 Kjartan Fløgstad, *Dalen Portland* (Oslo: Samlaget, 1977), pp. 216–20. I will come back to this particular song.
3 Kjartan Fløgstad, *Nordaustpassasjen* (Oslo: Gyldendal, 2012), p. 333. 'Points of you' is composed by the fictional character Kjell Kistefjell as he sits in a bar listening to a mariachi band. This song includes several puns, also a recurrent stylistic device in the Fløgstad's writing. All future references are given by page number and in parenthesis in the text, and are taken from this edition.
4 Poems and folk music. Vid. Kjartan Fløgstad, *Dikt og spelmannsmusikk: 1968–1993* (Oslo: Gyldendal, 1993); and Kjartan Fløgstad, *Dikt og spelmannsmusikk: 1968–1996* (Oslo: Gyldendal, 1996).
5 A few pieces in the collection are translations of poems and songs by others, but the majority of the writings are Fløgstad's own.

that these lyrics also introduce languages other than Norwegian, most commonly English, Spanish or German, enhances the alienating effect. Brecht and Schlovsky shared the idea that an author or playwright can use certain elements in the literary text or the theatrical play in order to force readers or spectators to distance themselves from what they read or watch. They differed, however, in their view of art in a socio-historical perspective. Schlovsky suggested that the use of estrangement in literary texts de-automatized readers' perception of things, words, and the world, thus allowing them to appreciate art. In 'Art as Technique' (1917) he argues that:

> art exists [so] that one may recover the sensation of life; it exists to make one feel things, to make the stone *stony*. The purpose of art is to impart the sensation of things as they are perceived and not as they are known. The technique of art is to make objects 'unfamiliar', to make forms difficult, to increase the difficulty and length of perception because the process of perception is an aesthetic end in itself and must be prolonged.[6]

Brecht, apart from theorizing about the alienating techniques, used these actively in his plays, forcing the spectators out of their role as passive consumers so that they could become critical interpreters of the words and gestures that took place on stage. After a brief look at song lyrics and multilingualism in literature in general, I will present an analysis of a number of examples in Fløgstad's prose where perception, I argue, is made difficult and – as Schlovsky suggested – prolonged. I will also propose that the author's use of multilingual song lyrics is a defamiliarizing technique that forces the reader to participate actively in the construction of meaning, to question her own reading process, ultimately making the reading process richer.

---

6   Viktor Schlovsky, 'Art as technique', in *Modern Criticism and Theory. A Reader*, ed. by David Lodge (London and New York: Longman, 1988), p. 20.

Song lyrics and multilingualism in literature

If we go back in time, we find that the inclusion of song lyrics is not at all new to prose. The medieval *cantefable*, for example, was a tale of adventure told in alternating sections of sung verse and recited prose, the most famous example being the anonymous French work *Aucassin et Nicolette*, from the 13th Century.[7] In Miguel de Cervantes' *Don Quixote de la Mancha* (1605), often considered the first modern novel, occasional song lyrics are part of the narration in several chapters.[8] More recent examples from fantastic literature are, of course, J.R.R. Tolkien who uses songs in *The Lord of the Rings* (1954/55), and George R.R. Martin who does the same in his series *A Song of Ice and Fire* (August 1996 until present), better known as the *Game of Thrones*. These contemporary authors have even invented imaginary languages as part of their fiction.[9] But despite the recent example of R.R. Martin, song lyrics are not that common in today's best-selling novels, and can still be considered extravagant or surprising.

Like song lyrics, multilingualism is not new to literature either. In a European context we can trace it back to the Roman Empire. As Alex Mullen points out in 'Latin and Other Languages: Societal and Individual Bilingualism', the Roman Republic and Empire were Greco-Roman, that is, bicultural from the outset. According to Mullen, code-switching from Latin into Greek seems to have been an in-group, high-status game among elite Romans. Examples of this practice are found for instance in Cicero's letters.[10] Leonard Forster's *The Poet's Tongues: Multilingualism in Literature* (1970), a modern classic in this

---

7 'Chantefable' in *Encyclopædia Britannica* <http://www.britannica.com/EBchecked/topic/105867/chantefable> [accessed 24 July 2013].
8 For instance in chapter XI and XIIII (Miguel de Cervantes, *Don Quixote de la Mancha*, in *Centro Virtual Cervantes* <http://cvc.cervantes.es/literatura/clasicos/quijote/> [accessed 24 July 2013]).
9 There are many examples of songs in *The Lord of The Rings*, for instance in The Two Towers, in chapter four entitled 'Treebeard' where Treebeard sings Ent songs, and in chapter eleven called 'The Palantir', where Gandalf sings (J.R.R. Tolkien, *El señor de los anillos. Las dos torres* [New York: Rayo, 2009], pp. 77–8, 83–4, 94–6 and 260). In George R.R. Martin's *A Storm of Swords*, the third volume of the series includes songs in the chapters 'Jon' and 'Tyrion' (George R.R. Martin, *Tormenta de espadas* [Buenos Aires: Random House Mondadori, 2012], pp. 223 and 433). In Cervantes' works, as in those of Tolkien and Martin, these songs help build the imagined worlds, as the reader is offered fragments of its popular culture. In the latter two, both fantasy novels, the songs are perhaps even more important since they contribute to building a whole mythology.
10 Alex Mullen, 'Latin and other languages: societal and individual bilingualism', in *A Companion to the Latin Language*, ed. by James Clackson (Oxford: Blackwell Publishing, 2011), pp. 527–48.

research field, provides an overview of multilingual texts from Mediaeval times and up until the twentieth Century.[11] In most of his examples, Forster suggests that multilingualism is an aesthetically or intellectually motivated stylistic device. In this way they are comparable to Kjartan Fløgstad's use of multilingualism.

In the last decades there has been a tendency towards multilingual writing in many parts of the world. It is often apparent in literature from former colonies, in works signed by authors with migration background, or in texts by authors that belong to minority groups. We find examples in African Francophone writers like Abdelkhebir Khatibi and his *Amour Bilingue* (1983) where he shifts between several languages; mainly classical Arabic, the spoken Moroccan dialect and French. A more recent example is Mongo Beti's *Trop de soleil tue l'amour* (1999), where he code-switches between different European languages, mostly French and English, apart from his mother tongue Éwondo.[12] There is an equal tendency towards code-switching between English and different varieties of Spanish in US-literature. Well-known examples of this are Gloria Anzaldúa's *Borderlands/La Frontera: The New Mestiza* (1987), and the recent Pullitzer prize-winning novel by Junot Díaz *The Brief Wondrous Life of Oscar Wao* (2008).[13] These are just a very few among the many authors that use multilingualism worldwide. Despite these recent examples, and despite the fact that we live in a globalized world where people both read and use several languages in their day to day life, the use of only one national language still seems to prevail in the bestselling prose.[14] Thus the world of prose fiction for the

---

11   Leonard Forster, *The Poet's Tongues: Multilingualism in Literature* (New York: Cambridge University Press, 1970).
12   Abdelkhebir Khatibi, *Amour Bilingue* (Montpellier: Fata Morgana, 1983), and Mongo Beti, *Trop de soleil tue l'amour* (Paris: Éditions Juillard, 1999). See also Inger Hesjevoll Schmidt-Melbye, this volume.
13   Gloria Anzaldúa, *Borderlands/La Frontera: The New Mestiza* (San Francisco: Aunt Lute Books, 1987), and Junot Díaz, *The Brief Wondrous Life of Oscar Wao* (New York: Riverhead Trade, 2008). For an overview of code-switching in contemporary US-Latino writers, see Cecilia Montes-Alcalá, 'Code-switching in US-Latino novels', in *Language Mixing and Code-Switching in Writing. Approaches to Mixed-Language Written Discourse*, ed. by Mark Sebba, Shahrzad Mahootian and Carla Jonsson (New York: Routledge, 2012), pp. 74–84.
14   We can of course ask ourselves whether this is likely to continue to be the case very much longer, since fragmented text composition is the leading tendency in the highly influential and currently ubiquitous blogosphere. It is possible that readers are getting so used to fragmented texts composed in a multilingual environment that they are already on the way towards considering this way of writing the norm rather than the exception.

most part allows readers to consume literature without too many 'uncomfortable' interruptions, which means that it is not inconceivable that readers should experience a sense of estrangement in the presence of inserted song lyrics or code-switching. Consequently, it may well be fruitful to approach multilingual texts taking the concept of defamiliarization as a point of departure.

Song lyrics and multilingualism in Kjartan Fløgstad's prose

In the following I present examples of how song lyrics introduce other languages in Kjartan Fløgstad's prose. I consider what these lyrics may tell us about the author's literary language and show how they demand a specific reading process. By way of demonstrating that these songs prevail throughout Fløgstad's *oeuvre*, two of the examples are taken from his early work in the 1970s and two from his recent novel, *Nordaustpassasjen*. I have selected examples that allow us to appreciate the diversity of how song lyrics are used in the author's prose. I first show how Fløgstad uses lyrics by other writers and then comment on a bilingual text composed by himself. In the analysis I refer to a hypothetical reader, on the grounds that this gives me an analytical distance to the text excerpts and provides a possibility of considering other reactions than my own. On one occasion I mention a specific reader I once helped with a translation. Writers operate with imagined readers, just as literary scholars do. The Argentinian writer Julio Cortázar, who has been a great inspiration to Fløgstad, above all hoped to reach a 'lector cómplice', a 'co-conspirator'. This is a reader who is not a passive consumer of the text, but one that actively helps to construct it. In his essay *Tyrannosaurus text* Fløgstad describes a similar reader, which he calls an 'utopisk leser', a 'utopian reader'. Like Cortázar's, Fløgstad's ideal reader is someone who interacts with the text to create meaning.[15] In the examples to be discussed we will see how Fløgstad's prose favors an active, participating reader.

---

15   Kjartan Fløgstad, *Tyrannosaurus text* (Oslo: Samlaget, 1988), p. 51.

I start the analysis with the excerpt from *Den hemmelege jubel* cited initially:

> The mirror on reflection has climbed back upon the wall, for the floor she found descended and the ceiling was too tall. Resepsjonen var imponerande med sine glasdører, teaklister og marmorplater. Eg sette meg i ein mjuk, skinnkledd stol medan eg venta.[16]

These lines belong to 'Den svarte tulipanen' ['The Black Tulip'], a very experimental *collage* of only five book pages, whose title alludes to Alexandre Dumas Senior's novel *La tulipe noir* (1850). The English phrase in Fløgstad's text is taken from the first stanza of the progressive rock band Procol Harum's song 'Homburg'. It constitutes the last four lines of the stanza, which actually opens with a reference to multilingualism: 'Your multilingual business friend has packed her bags and fled, leaving only ash-filled ashtrays and the lipsticked unmade bed'.[17] Those of us who know the whole stanza thus understand that the English phrase both originally belongs to a context where multilingualism is a topic, *and* adds bilingualism to Fløgstad's text. The stylistic device applied by the author directly reflects one of the topics treated in the fragment he has borrowed. We can say that Fløgstad's text is intertextually related to Procol Harum's lyrics both thematically and stylistically. But the phrase that reveals this is not quoted. And the phrase that the reader of 'Den svarte tulipanen' suddenly bumps into, in English and without quotation marks or other typographical markers, does not fit the context semantically.

The English insertion constitutes a foreign element, and moreover one that is foreign in several ways: it points towards another text, another author and another context, it belongs to another genre and it introduces another language. In this way the element illustrates what Michail Bakhtin calls *tjusjuoje slovo*, that is, another's word, another's discourse, even another's language or text.[18] Following Bakhtin we can say that Fløgstad's text enters into a dialogue with Procol Harum's words, discourse, language and verses. From a reader-

---

16 'The mirror on reflection has climbed back upon the wall, for the floor she found descended and the ceiling was too tall. The lobby was impressive with its glass doors, teak moldings and marble slabs. I sat in a smooth, leather-clad chair while I waited'. Kjartan Fløgstad, *Den hemmelege jubel*, p. 84.
17 Gary Brooker and Keith Reid, 'Homburg' (United Kingdom: Regal Zonophone – RZ 3003, 1967).
18 Michail M. Bakhtin in Nina Møller Andersen, *I en verden af fremmede ord. Bachtin som sprogbrugsteoretiker* [*In a World of Foreign Words. Bachtin as Theorist of Pragmatics*] (Viborg: Akademisk Forlag, 2002), p. 94. Original source: Michail M. Bakhtin, *Estetika slovesnogo Tvortjestva* (Moskva: Iskusstvo, 1979), p. 269.

oriented perspective, the song fragment can certainly have an estranging effect. Both the semantic incongruity and the foreign language hinder a relaxed and automatized reading and force the reader to question the foreign element, to enter into dialogue with it. Only the dedicated reader will figure out the connection and enjoy this multilingual 'divertimento'.

Since 'Den svarte tulipanen' is a literary *collage*, the reading is necessarily a process of dialogue between the reader and the text, a process where the reader's role is essential in the creation of the work of art. Does it matter then, whether the reader recognizes the source of the song fragment or not? Being a *collage*, we could argue that it does not make any difference, since the other's words now enter into a new context, a new piece of art. But if the reader does recognize the lines from 'Homburg' she will observe that multilingualism is a topic both in the song and in Fløgstad's *collage* as a whole. She might also realize that someone is abandoned in Procol Harum's song, and that loneliness and the feeling of being foreign are the main topics of 'Den svarte tulipanen'. This will teach her something important about how Fløgstad creates his literary language: she will understand that a small fragment can offer a clue to interpreting the text as a whole. She will also understand that the author's literary language is meticulously composed and offers layers of meaning beyond the direct semantic meaning of a phrase in its immediate context. Interpretation must then proceed by association, as in poetry. And the reader must be willing to fill in the gaps, what Wolfgang Iser called *Leerstellen*, in this case the semantic ellipsis that consists of the first lines of the relevant stanza in Procol Harum's song.[19] This is ultimately a way of exploring language and the way in which it is used to compose literature. Bilingualism is part of this exploration.

In 'Den svarte tulipanen' there are actually two other song excerpts – a line from 'A Whiter Shade of Pale' (1967) by Gary Brooker, Keith Reid, Matthew Fisher, also performed by Procol Harum, and 'Butterfly of Love' (1966) written and sung by Bob Lind. Both are inserted into the text in the same way as in the example we have just seen. There are also two passages from William Faulkner's *The Sound and the Fury* (1929), also included in their original versions, although in italics.[20] Additionally, there are fragments of conversation

---

19   Wolfgang Iser, *Der Akt des Lesens: Theorie ästhetischer Wirkung* (München: Fink, 1976).
20   Faulkner's *The Sound and the Fury* has different narrative styles and voices, and Fløgstad's 'Den svarte tulipanen' can be interpreted as a metaliterary comment on, or *hommage* to, Faulkner.

in Spanish, inserted without any typographical markers. The text also bears a dedication in French – 'A la petite Chelo'. Thus, we see that multilingualism, intertextuality and fragmentation are key words to describe the composition of this text. It provides an early example of how code-switching is used in Fløgstad's literature, and it suggests that song lyrics are just one option among many for introducing other languages – and another's word in the Bakhtinian sense – as part of the prose.

The questioning of the possibilities of language through code-switching as well as the importance of association in the process of creating meaning are found in most of Fløgstad's prose. They are definitely present in *Nordaustpassasjen* from 2012. In this work we find a great quantity of references to song lyrics and also fragments of many of them, in Norwegian, in English and in Spanish. Part of the novel is set in Norway, and part in the Spanish-speaking countries of Mexico and Spain.[21] We find examples of code-switching between Spanish and Norwegian in chapter 15, which starts with the arrival of the protagonist and first person narrator Kjell Kistefjell at the city of Veracruz, where he is going to start his new job as the host of a radio show. The show is actually broadcast from a ship that is permanently anchored in the harbor, and Kistefjell's job will be to play popular music, mixed with a minimum of small talk. The chapter's title is 'La Bamba'; in itself a reference to a well-known Mexican song, made popular in the 1980s by Los Lobos, and before them by Richie Valens in the late 1950s. In fact this song is a folk song from the region of Veracruz, which makes sense given that the chapter mainly takes place in this city.

A small fragment of 'La Bamba' is also inserted into the running text of the chapter:

---

21   Nonetheless, a reader of Fløgstad will know that the author does not need a Spanish-speaking context as an excuse to use this language in his texts. In his novel *Grense Jakobselv*, for instance, the story mainly takes place in Norway and Germany, with only occasional mention of Spanish-speaking countries. Here, the author inserts a Mexican song on several occasions, always in a German or Norwegian setting.

> Kan songen gje meg venger? Det kunne den. Det kunne eg, det fór det gjennom hovudet mitt medan jarocho-versjonen av folkesongen 'La Bamba' tona ut, etter at vokalisten igjen og igjen har forklart at han ikkje er sjømann, men kaptein, han er kaptein! *Yo no soy marinero, yo no soy marinero, ¡soy capitán, soy capitán, soy capitán!*²² (p. 327)

The detailed information about the specific recording of 'La Bamba' that is fading out, 'jarocho-versjonen' ['the Jarocho version'], shows that Fløgstad is very much aware that this song comes from Veracruz: Jarocho is a particular style of folk music played in this area. This example helps us understand a bit more about how the author uses song lyrics during the process of composition: the many song fragments in this novel are used with care. In this case, the chapter's title 'La Bamba' holds a tiny bit of cultural information relevant to a chapter that takes place in Veracruz, where the protagonist is hosting a radio-show broadcast from a ship. Interestingly, the protagonist of Fløgstad's story will eventually become a captain himself, or as the song puts it, *capitán*. He will be a part of 'La Bamba', that is, the chapter of the book, and also somehow play a role similar to the alleged captain within the song: Kjell Kistefjell's position in the mediocre radio-show is just as unglamorous as the undeserved captain's title claimed by the sailor in the popular song.

At first sight it is not obvious why the chapter is titled 'La Bamba', but, as we have seen, the reference to and use of this popular song provide intricate intertextual links. Just as in the excerpt from 'Den svarte tulipanen', we understand that specific details from a song point towards information that is not explicit but makes the text richer for an observant reader – that is, a reader who is willing to cooperate actively with the text, to put together bits of information from different parts of the text. Once again, the interpretation must rely on a process of association. Julie Hansen addresses a similar procedure in her recent article about translingual puns in Olga Grushin's works, calling it a 'delay in the completion of the pun'. ²³ Fløgstad's use of the Mexican song lies

---

22 'Can the song give me wings? It could. I could, that is what went through my head while the Jarocho version of the folk song 'La Bamba' faded out, after the vocalist again and again has explained that he is not a sailor, but captain, he is captain! *Yo no soy marinero, yo no soy marinero, ¡soy capitán, soy capitán, soy capitán!*'.
23 Julie Hansen, 'Making sense of the translingual text: Russian wordplay, names and cultural allusions in Olga Grushin's *The Dream Life of Sukhanov*', *Modern Language Review*, 107.2 (2012), 540–58 (p. 546).

closer to a riddle than a pun: the chapter's title 'La Bamba' will initially seem enigmatic to the reader, and the posterior use of a fragment from this song then provides information that leads the reader towards a possible answer to the enigma. If we apply the concept of estrangement to this example, we find that the puzzling title might cause the reader to slow down the reading process, put questions to the text and ultimately discover that the chapter's name adds a small piece of information that helps construct the diegesis. Through this example, the reader might also acquire new insight into how literature is composed and how a literary writer sometimes chooses to communicate with the reader.

We notice that in this last example the author has paraphrased the content of the song in Norwegian immediately before the lines in Spanish: '[…] etter at vokalisten igjen og igjen har forklart at han ikkje er sjømann, men kaptein, han er kaptein!' This is an example of how the act of translating is an integral part of the author's literary voice.[24] It also suggests that the author does not consciously use bilingualism as an estranging element in this case. This is a change from his early work, illustrated previously by the extract from 'Den svarte tulipanen', where foreign languages are usually left untranslated and thus become more defamiliarizing. In the case of 'La Bamba' it is the composition of the text that causes estrangement and that allows for the possibility of new insights.

In *Nordaustpassasjen* we also find song lyrics where the original words are altered. This is never pointed out to the reader, but sometimes the use of capital letters suggests that something is going on. The chapter 'La Bamba' provides a curious example:

> Inne bak glasveggen til sendestudio sat programverten […]. Så la han på ein reklamesnutt for tequilamerket Sauza, før det braka laus med ein øyredøyvande narcocorrido. Ikkje heilt apropos, men i alle fall med stor entusiasme ropte han det gamle slagordet ¡ESTADOS UNIDOS JAMÁS SERÁN VENCIDOS! straks musikken var tona ned.[25] (p. 320)

---

24 Translation is in fact a *leit-motif* in Kjartan Fløgstad's novels. I will not look into this in any detail here, only mention that in the chapter 'La Bamba', the author actually offers two different translations of a verse from another Mexican song, 'Veracruz' by Agustín Lara. This kind of search for the best possible translation is a direct way of questioning language, showing that it is not given which words we choose, thus opening up a meta-discussion about language.
25 'The radio host sat behind the glass wall of the studio […]. Then he put on an advert for the

This passage describes the protagonist Kjell Kistefjell's first impression as he enters the waterborn radio studio where he will be working. The radio host shouts out an old political slogan, reproduced in capital letters in the text. Thus the switch from Norwegian to Spanish is foregrounded by the use of capital letters as well as the Spanish upside-down exclamation marks: '¡ESTADOS UNIDOS JAMÁS SERÁN VENCIDOS!' An English translation of the foregrounded phrase would be 'the United States will never be defeated!' This is a modification of the well-known slogan '¡el pueblo unido jamás será vencido!' ['the people united will never be defeated!'], initially used during Salvador Allende's presidential campaign of 1970 in Chile. Allende represented the *Unidad Popular* [*Popular Unity* or *People's Unity*] party, and although elected he was overthrown by Augusto Pinochet's military coup in 1973. The slogan, however, was also the title of a song, with lyrics by the Chilean group Quilapayún, which featured during the presidential campaign. After the coup, this song became a symbol of Chilean resistance abroad.[26]

In Fløgstad's novel *Nordaustpassasjen*, the reader enters a world that looks different from today. Among others, The United States is no longer united, but split up into smaller administrative units, some controlled by drug lords. This context is not clearly stated in the passage under discussion, but, as we see, the narrator suggests that the slogan is out of context: 'Ikkje heilt apropos' ['Not quite à propos']. It definitely is – and not just because the United States *is* in fact defeated in the novel, or because the slogan does not match the *narcocorrido* in the background that fades out just as the slogan is shouted out. It is out of context because the slogan is altered. It is also out of context because the CIA, an organization from the United States, supported the Pinochet coup. It is more than ironic then, that the North Americans should use a slogan from the Chilean resistance in the seventies.

We understand that this use of a slogan and song title, which at first glance may seem unnecessary or illogical, gives the paragraph an extra layer of

---

tequila brand Sauza, before all hell broke loose with an ear-splitting narcocorrido. Not quite à propos, but in any event with great enthusiasm, he shouted out the old slogan ¡ESTADOS UNIDOS JAMÁS SERÁN VENCIDOS! as soon as the music faded out'.

26 Fløgstad is aware of this, without a doubt. In a conversation I had with him in January 2013, he told me that he had been in contact with a great number of Chileans exiled in Scandinavia after the coup.

meaning. It is an ironic statement, constructed by creating a new slogan out of an old one. Only those familiar with the old slogan will be able to notice the twist. As in previous examples, the reader' ability to make associations is fundamental to the process of creating meaning: it is necessary to know the original context of the foreign element to understand its meaning, and under such conditions the reader can easily feel estranged – not only because of the code-switch between Norwegian and Spanish, but because she lacks important cultural knowledge. Again, a tiny detail reveals how thorough the author is when he composes his prose. One sole phrase introduces various elements at the same time: another language, and a fictional slogan that is in fact an alteration of a well-known political slogan and a song title. The use of this phrase can be read as a tongue-in-cheek comment about US politics. All in all, the example shows the great semantic density displayed in Fløgstad's literary language.

Let us consider one last example in order to appreciate yet another way of using song lyrics in Fløgstad's prose. This example is taken from an earlier novel, *Dalen Portland* from 1977 (*Dollar Road* in its official translation into English), for which Fløgstad won the prestigious Nordic Council Literature Prize in 1978.[27] In this novel we find a bilingual song composed by Fløgstad that seems to interrupt the narrative flow. The song title 'Høysang' ['Hymn'] uses the figure of *paronomasia* to pun on the last name of the protagonist Rasmus Høysand – the song title and surname differ only by a single consonant.[28] This ludic technique links the protagonist to the song and might function as a hint to the reader, facilitating the interpretation of the text. The song is an epic narrative with a first person narrator, presumably Rasmus Høysand, although this is not clearly stated.[29] As in the previous examples, the reader must use her associating skills to complete her interpretation of the narrative.

---

27 The novel was translated into English and published in the United States, where it won the Pegasus Prize for Literature in 1989. See Kjartan Fløgstad, *Dollar Road*, trans. by Nadia Christensen (Baton Rouge: Louisiana State University Press, 1989).
28 Kjartan Fløgstad, *Dalen Portland*, pp. 216–20.
29 The title can also be associated with the Biblical *Song of Songs* or *The Song of Solomon*, which in Norwegian is called 'Høysang' or 'Salomos Høysang'. Fløgstad's song is also a love song, but the Biblical parallel stops there.

'Høysang' starts with images that resemble the verses of Pablo Neruda's 1950 *Canto General* [*General Song*].[30] This makes sense since Fløgstad translated Neruda into Norwegian during the same period that he wrote the novel. In *Canto General* Neruda talks about the different regions and myths of Latin America. Fløgstad's song brings us to Colombia, where part of the novel takes place. It tells the story of a wounded man found on a beach by a woman called Angelina. She brings him back to life, but is later killed. He avenges her death and then leaves the country.

From a critical point of view it is fascinating to notice that this song works like a *cantefable*. If we agree that the first person narrator in the song is in fact Rasmus Høysand, the verses continue the plot from the previous book chapter, and when the last chorus fades away the plot continues in the next chapter.[31] Although it fits the context semantically, this structural technique is so uncommon in Norwegian novels than it might cause the feeling of estrangement in a reader. Unlike the verses of a *cantefable* 'Høysang' is not sung, and there was no tradition for performing a novel in Norway at the time *Dalen Portland* was published. But the Norwegian musician Guttorm Guttormsen recorded the song one year after the book was published, on an album entitled precisely 'Høysang'.[32] In a sense we can say that Guttormsen's recording makes tangible something latent within Fløgstad's writing at this point in the text; allowing those aspects that resemble and invoke the *cantefable* to become even clearer. Listening to the musical adaptation thus enables us to hear the generic complexities of the original better, and allows us to perceive the words and Fløgstad's word-art in a new way.

Let us consider code-switching in 'Høysang'. The song has eighteen verses and a chorus that is repeated five times, but I will focus on the last verse and chorus:

---

30   Pablo Neruda, *Canto General* (Mexico City: Imprenta Juárez, 1950).
31   The novel contains three more songs that are part of the plot in the same way as the example under discussion here – for instance in *Dalen Portland*, pp. 33, 54 and 63.
32   Lars Klevstrand and Guttorm Guttormsen Kvintett, *Høysang* (Nordisc, NORLP 311, 1978).

Gatene er tomme, men eg har halde ord
Santísima María, kviskrar portane, Madre de Dios
Eit skip ligg på reia med kurs mot nord
Hundane gøyr da vi kastar loss

Vi startar motoren og drar
No quedan grandes esperos
Es tan difícil olvidar
Aquellos tiempos pasajeros[33]

We see how the author switches between Norwegian and Spanish. In this song Spanish is used consistently in the last three lines of the chorus, and in nouns that refer to Latin American culture, that is, culture specific nouns or *culturemas*. In the extract we find two exclamations: 'Santísima María' ['Most Holy Mary'] and 'Madre de Dios' ['Mother of God']. A closer look at the excerpt tells us how intricately Spanish and Norwegian are woven together: 'Madre de Dios' rhymes with 'vi kastar loss', and the rhythm in the two phrases is very similar. Rhyme is also found in the pair of line endings, 'og drar' vs. 'olvidar'. Taken in isolation, the rhythm here might appear not to have been sustained, but the lines themselves ('Vi startar motoren og drar' and 'Es tan difícil olvidar') are part of a verse structure (rhyming *abab*) that links them, and where the metre is identical (iambic tetrameter). We can call this translingual rhyming, a technique that is repeated throughout 'Høysang', albeit not consistently. Interestingly, this translingual rhyming technique is also found in European Mediaeval literature. A well-known example is the anonymous Christmas song 'In dulci jubilo' from the fifteenth century, where each stanza contains lines in Latin and German which rhyme.[34] In this way, 'Høysang' harks back to mediaeval literature in two ways: it resembles the *cantefable*, and the use of translingual rhyme is similar to that of a renowned mediaeval song.

---

33 'The streets are empty, but I've kept my word/Santísima María, whisper the gates, Madre de Dios/A ship is on the roadstead heading north/The dogs are barking as we set off/We start the motor and depart/No quedan grandes esperos/Es tan difícil olvidar/Aquellos tiempos pasajeros'. Fløgstad, *Dalen Portland*, p. 220.
34 In most of the verses lines 1, 4, 6 and 7 are in Latin, and lines 2, 3 and 5 in German. See Leonard Forster, *The Poet's Tongues*, pp. 10–11. Code-switching between Latin and a vernacular language is generally referred to as vertical code-switching, while code-switching between two vernacular languages, like in Fløgstad, is called horizontal.

In the excerpt under consideration we also find a somewhat puzzling rhyme, where both elements are apparently in Spanish: 'esperos' and 'pasajeros'. But the word 'esperos' is not Spanish, nor is it Norwegian. Judging from the context the poetic voice is actually aiming to express 'hope' – 'esperanzas'. The problem is that 'esperanzas' does not rhyme with 'pasajeros'. If we look at this rhyme from the perspective of authorial intent, we might suspect that the author has had limited knowledge of Spanish and chose to use a word he thought was correct. My knowledge of the author suggests this is not the case. Fløgstad knows the language too well for this to be an actual error. And his use of language is in general always well thought through, which suggests that the use of 'esperos' is a purposeful choice. The author has simply created a quasi-Spanish word in order to create a better rhyme, using an adapted form of the verb 'esperar' [to hope] in the first-person singular ('espero'). This is evidence of a translingual rhyme between a Spanish and a mock-Spanish word. Ultimately it is an example of how the author plays with languages. If we look to his other novels, it can be considered one of many examples of sound-games in his works. In addition, it can be given a further interpretation: Rasmus Høysand, the protagonist of the song, is a stranger in a Spanish speaking country. He surely makes linguistic mistakes; perhaps he even mixes 'esperos' and 'esperanzas'. From this perspective the erroneous word corresponds to an example of intradiegetic logic.

Contrary to the example from 'Den svarte tulipanen' and '¡ESTADOS UNIDOS …' from *Nordaustpassasjen*, the foreign words in 'Høysang' are not decontextualized but fit well in with the plot of the song. Semantically, then, they are not alienating elements. Considering the song as a whole, the function of the code-switching is to foreground topics specific to the region where the plot takes place (for readers with some understanding of the Spanish language), to evoke an exotic feeling or to add local color. When it comes to the Spanish phrases of the chorus, I have personally translated them for a Norwegian literary scholar, so I know they can impede comprehension for a Norwegian reader. For this kind of reader, they can be considered estranging. For a bilingual reader of Norwegian and Spanish the text will of course be experienced as less so. She will, however, find the word 'esperos' estranging, since it does not exist. It is thus possible that the translingual rhyme will seem exotic to both groups of readers, just as it is plausible that both groups will find that the change of style from narrative to epic song disturbs the reading process. The inserted song definitely requires an effort from the reader. It will presumably slow down the reading process and make the reader question the text. Hence Fløgstad's strategy helps create a more alert and active reader.

Concluding remarks

The examples discussed in this article show different uses of multilingual song lyrics and one song title in Fløgstad's early and recent prose. Giving off a playful and sometimes mischievous impression, they can be considered poetical fragments in a prose text. That is, they bring a different literary language as well as a different national language into the prose, while also allowing room for tongue-in-cheek comments, puns and wordplay. As I have suggested, the interpretive act must then be an associative and participatory one, as in the reading of poetry. Fløgstad's use of multilingual lyrics invites the reader to perceive the written word in new ways. His texts suggest that she needs to look beyond the explicit meaning of the words on the page, as well as beyond the cultural and lexical contexts within which words normally derive their meanings. Mélange can thus be seen as a central device in Fløgstad's fiction, a tool with which to unsettle readers into appreciating the full communicative potential of language and literature – while enjoying its aesthetic and ludic spaces.

Bibliography

Anzaldúa, Gloria, *Borderlands/La Frontera: The New Mestiza* (San Francisco: Aunt Lute Books, 1987).
Bakhtin, Michail M., in Nina Møller Andersen, *I en verden af fremmede ord. Bachtin som sprogbrugsteoretiker* (Viborg: Akademisk Forlag, 2002).
Beti, Mongo, *Trop de soleil tue l'amour* (Paris: Éditions Juillard, 1999).
Brooker, Gary, and Keith Reid, 'Homburg' (Regal Zonophone, RZ 3003, 1967).
Cervantes, Miguel de, *Don Quixote de la Mancha*, in *Centro Virtual Cervantes* <http://cvc.cervantes.es/literatura/clasicos/quijote/> [accessed 24 July 2013].
Díaz, Junot, *The Brief Wondrous Life of Oscar Wao* (New York: Riverhead Trade, 2008).
Encyclopædia Britannica <http://www.britannica.com/EBchecked/topic/105867/chantefable> [accessed 24 July 2013].

Fløgstad, Kjartan, *Den hemmelege jubel* (Oslo: Samlaget, 1970).
Fløgstad, Kjartan, *Dalen Portland* (Oslo: Samlaget, 1977).
Fløgstad, Kjartan, *Tyrannosaurus text* (Oslo, Samlaget, 1988).
Fløgstad, Kjartan, *Dollar Road*, trans. by Nadia Christensen (Baton Rouge: Louisiana State University Press, 1989).
Fløgstad, Kjartan, *Dikt og spelmannsmusikk: 1968–1993* (Oslo: Gyldendal, 1993).
Fløgstad, Kjartan, *Dikt og spelmannsmusikk: 1968–1996* (Oslo: Gyldendal, 1996).
Fløgstad, Kjartan, *Nordaustpassasjen* (Oslo: Gyldendal, 2012).
Forster, Leonard, *The Poet's Tongues: Multilingualism in Literature* (New York: Cambridge University Press, 1970).
Hansen, Julie, 'Making sense of the translingual text: Russian wordplay, names and cultural allusions in Olga Grushin's *The Dream Life of Sukhanov*', *Modern Language Review*, 107.2 (2012), 540–58.
Iser, Wolfgang, *Der Akt des Lesens: Theorie ästhetischer Wirkung* (München: Fink, 1976).
Khatibi, Abdelkhebir, *Amour Bilingue* (Montpellier: Fata Morgana, 1983).
Klevstrand, Lars and Guttorm Guttormsen Kvintett, *Høysang* (Nordisc, NORLP 311, 1978).
Martin, George R.R., *Tormenta de espadas* (Buenos Aires: Random House Mondadori, 2012).
Montes-Alcalá, Cecilia, 'Code-Switching in US-Latino Novels', in *Language Mixing and Code-Switching in Writing: Approaches to Mixed-Language Written Discourse*, ed. by Mark Sebba, Shahrzad Mahootian and Carla Jonsson (New York: Routledge, 2012).
Mullen, Alex, 'Latin and other languages: societal and individual bilingualism', in *A Companion to the Latin Language*, ed. by James Clackson (Oxford: Blackwell Publishing, 2011), pp. 527–48.
Neruda, Pablo, *Canto General* (Mexico City: Imprenta Juárez, 1950).
Schlovsky, Viktor, 'Art as technique', in *Modern Criticism and Theory. A Reader*, ed. by David Lodge (London and New York: Longman, 1988).
Tolkien, John Ronald Reuel, *El señor de los anillos. Las dos torres* (New York: Rayo, 2009).

12 'Famous Blue Raincoat' in translation

Anja Angelsen and Domhnall Mitchell

Translations and performances by others of Leonard Cohen's iconic 'Famous Blue Raincoat' can give the impression that they are built on a solid and unchanging foundation which is textually and semantically stable, fixed forever at the time of its first release in 1971.[1] But those same versions, not least that of Jennifer Warnes in 1987 – where not only the gender but also the perspective of the singer were adapted by Cohen himself – involve subtle but important alterations, alerting us to latent indeterminacies in the source, and suggesting that it is more permeable than it might appear. In this essay, we investigate the cultural situatedness of various references in both 'Famous Blue Raincoat' itself, and in three of its translations into Scandinavian languages. We show how an allusion to Lili Marlene is more complex than might first appear, and trace how Cohen's imagery is informed by an English language translation of the German original. We also argue that 'Famous Blue Raincoat' in translation opens up for other transformations which are as cultural as they are linguistic and creative. Thus, Cohen's text can be seen as a brief but important station in the creative migration of several artistic works through and across different cultures and languages. The versions of 'Lili Marlene' and 'Famous Blue Raincoat' that we look at, show how this migration is continuous but also changing: art in translation not only instigates a process of cultural mélange, but is itself a product of it.

---

1   Although we do make references to and comment on performances of the song 'Famous Blue Raincoat', we are primarily interested in the lyrics as text and relate to text both as source and target.

Famous Blue Raincoat

'Famous Blue Raincoat' is a well-crafted lyric, with an epistolary structure, rhyming couplets and a clear metrical pattern, its first lines combining predominantly iambic and anapestic feet in a catalectic (or incomplete) line. First released on the 1971 album *Songs of Love and Hate*, it takes the form of a letter from an 'L. Cohen' to an anonymous 'you' who is seen as a competitor for the affections of a woman called Jane.[2] The lyrics are usually interpreted as referring to a complex love triangle, mainly focusing on the relationship between two male love rivals. Their rivalry is reflected in the descriptions of 'you' as a 'thin gypsy thief' and 'my brother, my killer', and in the reference to Lili Marlene, a song set in wartime, and therefore suggestive of conflict but also of thwarted or unfulfilled love.[3] The complexity of the lyrics allows for other scenarios that complicate this idea of a classic love triangle – the rivalry could be seen as an internal conflict in the narrator, rather than a relation between two (male) protagonists. This textual openendedness offers a challenge, but also opportunity, for interpreters of the song, and it has been widely translated, with several versions in four of the five Scandinavian languages. In our study, we focus on the most widely distributed Norwegian, Danish and Swedish translations. Aspects of the text that have a clear cultural prominence or situatedness in the source language will be given special attention, but other intertextual elements of the original song are also explored.

---

2   Leonard Cohen, *Songs of Love and Hate* (Columbia, C 30103, 1971). That the correspondent and the composer share the same first initial and surname should not be taken as evidence that they are the same person. If anything, it is the rival who seems to have more in common with Cohen himself: like Cohen did later, he goes off on a retreat from the world; like Cohen, he once had an interest in Scientology; like Cohen, he wore a blue raincoat; he is even described as 'my brother, my killer', and the original fratricide was Cain, a name that does not sound entirely unlike Cohen.

3   Cohen almost certainly had the 1944 American version of the song, popularly attributed to Mack David, in mind when he wrote his own song, since David's version of the lyric includes references to evening, a lock of hair, and a rose – all of which feature in 'Famous Blue Raincoat'. It has to be said that there is no evidence that the relationship between the rival and Jane was ever sexual: we are told only that the rival gave her a lock of his hair, and that when she returned Jane 'was nobody's wife' – a beautifully ambiguous phrase suggesting independence from the writer (she was no longer to be defined as belonging to a man – as married women in the sixties and seventies took the surnames of their husbands) and his humiliation (having been with a more charismatic man, she returns to a lesser one – a nobody). In the verse 'Well, I see you there with the rose in your teeth/One more gypsy thief', it seems likely that the images are the speaker's jealous projections rather than actual memories: the rival is the generic gypsy thief from folk songs and stories such as 'The Raggle Taggle Gypsy' who 'steals' married women away from economically more powerful husbands. The rose in the teeth is similarly melodramatic, and reminiscent of Bizet's *Carmen* (1875).

One of those elements is the title itself, which refers to a garment that has come in many ways to be emblematic of the artist himself, and the traces of which are interesting to follow in the Nordic versions. The iconic status of this artifact has been further reinforced by a number of paratextual elements: Cohen discusses it in the liner notes of his 1975 *Best of Leonard Cohen* album; it provides the title and cover illustration for Jennifer Warnes' 1986 *Famous Blue Raincoat*; and it has attained a cult status among Cohen's fans across the globe.[4] That the song has been covered by and amended for a number of women artists – including Warnes and Joan Baez – in ways which actualize a latent but intermittent female perspective in the original, is an aspect of its meaning which we will pay particular attention to in its translated forms.

The opening verse creates a geographical and cultural setting for the song, and this is where we find some of the most interesting elements for discussion – particularly in the place names and in the references to location:

> It's four in the morning, the end of December
> I'm writing you now just to see if you're better
> New York is cold, but I like where I'm living
> There's music on Clinton Street all through the evening.
>
> I hear that you're building your little house deep in the desert
> You're living for nothing now, I hope you're keeping some kind of record.
>
> Yes, and Jane came by with a lock of your hair
> She said that you gave it to her
> That night that you planned to go clear
> Did you ever go clear?

---

4   In the liner notes to the 1975 collection *The Best of Leonard Cohen*, Cohen writes 'I had a good raincoat then, a Burberry I got in London in 1959. Elizabeth [Kenrick, a friend from London in 1960] thought I looked like a spider in it. That was probably why she wouldn't go to Greece with me. It hung more heroically when I took out the lining, and achieved glory when the frayed sleeves were repaired with a little leather. Things were clear. I knew how to dress in those days. It was stolen from Marianne's loft in New York sometime during the early seventies. I wasn't wearing it very much toward the end'. It is interesting that Cohen uses a similar phrase to 'things were clear' in the song. Cohen himself went on a Buddhist retreat to the Mount Baldy Zen Buddhist monastery in 1994 – which postdates the composition of the song, of course, but suggests a religious – or more properly a spiritual – sensibility which is not entirely at odds with the rival's interests. Leonard Cohen, *The Best of Leonard Cohen* (CBS, 69161, 1975).

Ah, the last time we saw you you looked so much older
Your famous blue raincoat was torn at the shoulder
You'd been to the station to meet every train
And you came home without Lili Marlene
And you treated my woman to a flake of your life
And when she came back she was nobody's wife.

Well I see you there with the rose in your teeth
One more thin gypsy thief
Well I see Jane's awake –
She sends her regards.

And what can I tell you my brother, my killer
What can I possibly say?
I guess that I miss you, I guess I forgive you
I'm glad you stood in my way.

If you ever come by here, for Jane or for me
Your enemy is sleeping, and his woman is free.

Yes, and thanks, for the trouble you took from her eyes
I thought it was there for good so I never tried.

And Jane came by with a lock of your hair
She said that you gave it to her
That night that you planned to go clear.

– Sincerely, L. Cohen

The phrase 'my brother, my killer' in the seventh stanza clearly invokes the story of Cain and Abel: a number of allusions taken from different religious traditions underpin the narrative. Similarly, the 'little house deep in the desert' is both a contemporaneous and an older reference: the sixties and seventies were full of individuals and groups who sought out alternative lifestyles and communities in places like the Mohave desert of California, but there are echoes here too of early hermits and ascetics such as St Anthony (251–356) and St Jerome (347–420), both of whom retreated from worldly and fleshly temptations into the desert.[5] This is not to imply that the rival's motives for seeking seclusion are solely or even partly Judeo-Christian: 'living for nothing' suggests that he might have embraced nihilism or Buddhism, while the phrase 'go clear' can be understood as deriving from Scientology.[6] The song's referential landscape is inherently hybrid then – it contains elements of Eastern and Western religions, European popular culture in a mediated form, contrasting topographies and social history (in the shape of open relationships and sexual liberation, social and spiritual experimentation and the rise of feminism during the sixties).

This cultural hybridity or blend that we speak of has been identified as a defining characteristic of the North American culture that Cohen partly embodies:

> Probably part of the profound and peculiar appeal of American popular culture is precisely its mixed and 'traveling' character, its 'footloose' lightness, unhinged from the feudal past. In this culture, the grammars of multiple cultures mingle, and this intercultural density may be part of the subliminal attraction of American popular media, music, film, television: the encounter, and often enough the clash, but an intimate clash, of ethnicities, cultures, histories. The intermingling of culture grammars then makes up the deeply human appeal of American narratives and its worldly character, repackaging elements that came from other shores, in a 'Mississippi Masala'.[7]

---

5 Christ is another possible candidate – he spent 40 days in the desert. Beset by devils, St Anthony shut himself into an old Roman fort at one stage. St Jerome seems the best candidate, because he had to defend himself against charges of improper relationships with widows in Rome, and in the desert experienced visions of tempting women. '[L]iving for nothing' has other potential meanings, of course: the rival has nothing to live for, for example, or he is surviving on very little money – life in the desert is cheap, which may be one of its attractions. The Norwegian version of the song hints at this in its line 'Syns du skal føre et slags regnskap' [Think you should keep some kind of record], where 'regnskap' suggests a literal account as well as a record. But Cohen increases the ambiguity or indeterminacy of the line by writing 'living for nothing' and not 'nothing to live for': the difference is crucial.
6 Sylvie Simmons, *I'm Your Man: The Life of Leonard Cohen* (London: Jonathan Cape, 2012), p. 216.
7 Jan Nederveen Pieterse, *Globalization and Culture: Global Mélange* (Maryland: Rowman and Littlefield, 2009), p. 56.

Lili Marlene

The travelling or movement under discussion here is not confined to America or modern times, but Anglo-American popular culture – as well as cultures that have emerged from or been in close contact with it – seems to be more tolerant or susceptible to this form of lending and blending of cultural referents. A good example of this 'travelling' element in 'Famous Blue Raincoat' is the allusion to Lili Marlene, a figure who originally appeared in a poem by German author Hans Leip, 'Das Lied eines junges Soldaten auf der Wacht', written during World War One. The poem was set to music in 1937 and the song was widely broadcast to the opposing forces during World War Two, both in German and English language versions.

There are several striking parallels between 'Das Lied eines junges Soldaten auf der Wacht' and 'Famous Blue Raincoat': both have a clear poetic quality but are best known as song lyrics; both have been widely covered and translated into a number of different languages; both involve a form of direct address (the soldier to his woman, Lili Marlene, and L. Cohen to his 'brother, his killer'); and finally they both deal with longing and with lovers that are, for some reason, unattainable or out of reach.[8]

But our main interest is in the details of one of the translations of Lili Marlene. Several versions of the text exist in English, and one of these, performed by Marlene Dietrich, departs more from the lyrics of the German 'Lili Marlene' than most other English renditions. This translation includes a number of references that are not present in the source text and seems to opt for equivalence in function rather than in referential meaning. Neither the content nor the form of the five stanzas are a perfect match. The stanza that is most clearly reflected in Cohen's lyric is the third:

> Give me a rose to show how much you care
> Tied to the stem, a lock of golden hair
> Surely, tomorrow, you'll feel blue
> But then will come a love that's new
> For you, Lili Marlene.

---

8 Hans Leip composed a melody for the poem the very day he wrote it. Liel Leibovitz and Matthew Miller, *Lili Marlene: The Soldiers' Song of World War II* (New York: W.W. Norton & Company Ltd., 2008), p. 18.

The intertextuality is clearly visible in the components that are echoed in Cohen's song: the mention of the colour blue, albeit in a metaphorical sense, as well as the rose and the lock of golden hair. These elements that do not exist in the original German lyrics find their way, more or less literally, into Cohen's 'Famous Blue Raincoat'. This appropriation is an excellent example of how the travelling Lili Marlene picks up new luggage, which is inspired by the sentiment of the German Lili, as she enters into Anglo-American culture via Mack David's translation, and this is carried over into the context of 'Famous Blue Raincoat'. Lili Marlene, 'a lock of your hair', a 'rose in the teeth', and 'your famous blue raincoat' resonate against the backdrop of the history of Lili Marlene from World War One to the late 1960s. In other words, there is an intertextual dimension to 'Famous Blue Raincoat' which is not limited to individual references to a previous work of art, but which also encompasses the cultural and historical phenomena of 'Lili Marlene' and its era.

Din gamle blå frakke

'Din gamle blå frakke' (literally 'Your old blue coat'), one of several Danish versions of 'Famous Blue Raincoat', was translated by Anders Dohn for a Danish tribute album to Cohen.[9]

> Fire om natten – sidst i december
> Jeg skriver i håb om du har det lidt bedre
> Her er koldt i New York men jeg er vild med Manhattan
> Musikken i Clinton Street er høj hele natten[10]
>
> Jeg hører du bygger dit lille hus i en fjern, fjern krog
> Du lever for ingenting, Gad vidst om du fører bog?
> Men Jane kom forbi med en lok af dit hår

---

9   Leonard Cohen, *På Danske Læber: Leonard Cohen – Sange i Danske Fortolkinger*, Swan Lee, trans. Anders Dohn (Auditorium, TRBL 112, 2004). The song was the eighth track in a tribute collection featuring different Danish acts performing live. Swan Lee, a Danish band fronted by Pernille Rosendahl, was active between the years of 1996 to 2005.
10   'Four in the night – the end of December/I write in the hope that you are feeling a bit better/It is cold here in New York, but I love Manhattan/The music on Clinton Street is loud all through the night'.

Som du gav hende den nat i fjor
Da du valgte at gøre dig fri
Slap du virkelig fri?[11]

On the surface, 'Din gamle blå frakke' appears to have remained very faithful to the source text as many of the referential items are retained in their original form: Jane is mentioned, as are the blue raincoat and, unlike the Norwegian and (especially) the Swedish translations, the particular coordinates of the American cityscape. And yet, there are slight differences: Manhattan is added to the list of names in the opening verse which, mediated through the Danish language, contributes to the sense of a legendary New York seen by an outsider – different from the allusion to Clinton Street which implies someone who knows the city well, and possibly also an addressee who shares that familiarity, either because he has also been there, or because Clinton Street was known as a place for good music. So despite the translation's apparent faithfulness, the preservation of referential elements contributes to a transformation from being a melancholic song involving multiple forms of regret, to an excited travelogue: instead of someone who 'like[s] where [he's] living', this speaker is 'vild med Manhattan'; instead of the slightly more sedate 'music on Clinton Street all through the evening', it is 'høj hele natten'. In opting to reproduce as much as possible of the referential elements of the source, the Danish version seems to create a very different persona than the source text does.

This attempt to stay loyal or faithful to the cultural references of the original – the locality, Lili Marlene and Jane – can be seen as a foreignizing strategy which moves the reader towards the source (con)text. But the notion that New York constitutes a foreign element in Danish culture in 2004, in the era of globalization and travelling, is of course highly questionable, especially considering that the genre and context of the text is popular music. Perhaps a more fruitful approach is to see the referential elements – cultural entities, including place names, that have some form of global or universal value – as inherently

---

11   'I hear you are building your little house in a far, far corner/You are living for nothing, I wonder whether you are keeping records?/But Jane came by with a lock of your hair/That you gave her that night last year/When you chose to make yourself free/Did you really become free?'

hybrid in that their meaning heavily depends on the vantage point of the interpreter: Jane, New York, and Clinton Street retain their source language form and their reference in the Danish text, but the concepts have changed in that they carry with them another set of connotations in the target language. There is no perfect formal equivalence, either in terms of sense and connotation or phonetic form. The written representation is identical, but in the performance of the song, the sounds of the foreign names are slightly accommodated to the Danish phonological system. This intralinguistic transfer of phonological content is 'based on perceived dimensions of phonetic similarity'.[12] We may regard this as a form of transliteration – the source language pronunciation is mimicked, but it is not the same.

This mimicry is mirrored and magnified when it comes to the cultural significance and connotations of these same cultural entities. The placement of the referents of the 'foreign' names in a new language and cultural context involves a real shift in meaning. The transposition of Lili Marlene, New York, Manhattan and Clinton Street to the Danish language context provides us with a different vantage point – we look at the New York setting from the distance, we are not immersed in the cultural setting and a place. The American landscape and setting of the Danish text, and the process of importing the original setting into the Danish language and culture, draw attention to difference rather than sameness.

Kom du nånsin iväg

The tone of 'Famous Blue Raincoat' can be read in different ways: 'You're living for nothing now, I hope you're keeping some kind of record' can be performed as sarcasm or as concerned interest (and indeed the earlier and later versions of the song by Cohen himself might be argued to have moved from the former to the latter). Of the three versions of the song, the Swedish one, performed and translated by Ulf Lundell, seems to align itself most clearly with aspects of bleakness, hurt and aggression in the source:[13]

---

12 Chris Wen-Chao Li, 'Foreign names into native tongues', *Target* 19.1 (2007), 45–68 (p. 47).
13 Ulf Lundell, *Sweethearts* (EMI, 1361401, 1984). This is a collection of covers of songs by different artists, including Bob Dylan, Van Morrison, Elvis Costello and others. 'Kom du nånsin iväg' is the eighth song, originally the second on the B side.

> Fyra på morgon, det är svart i December
> Jag skriver till dej är du bättre eller sämre
> Stockholm är kallt men det här är mitt hem
> Vattnet som ryker och trängseln vid fem
> Det säjs att du bor i en stuga nu, långt ute i skogen
> Du fyller din dagbok full med minnen från förr[14]

Both the Swedish and Norwegian translations shift the location of the song to the capital of the country whose language it is written and performed in, and therefore represent a more radical departure from the physical, cultural and emotional landscape of the source text. The lyric/letter unfolds against a bleak backdrop – December is literally black ('svart') – and the attractions of the urban environment of the original are dropped: there are no references to how a specific district, a café, or music are 'like[d]'. The topography here is more recognizably particular to Stockholm, a coastal city made up of many different islands: here the speaker sings of 'Vattnet som ryker och trängseln vid fem'. The famous blue raincoat, demoted from its prominent titular position in the source text to a brief mention in the fourth verse ('rocken din stolthet' – the coat your pride), is in an even worse condition, being both 'smutsig' [dirty] and 'trasig' [torn].[15]

Lili Marlene is discarded, and the prospects for the speaker's love rival are grim – there is no potential new lover, no lady in waiting, and all that is left are 'tomma perronger' [empty platforms].[16] Although the lock of hair is retained, the links to the hypotextual Lili Marlene of the source text are severed, while the gypsy thief with a rose between his teeth is replaced with the more generalized 'blommande park' [flowering park] and 'skälvande mark' [quivering

---

14 'Four in the morning, it is black in December/I am writing to you are you better or worse/Stockholm is cold but this is my home/The water that smokes and the crowds at five/It is said that you live in a cottage now, far out in the woods/You fill up your diary with memories from the past'.
15 The detail of the torn shoulder of the original can be seen as another in a series of covert, but different, religious references: the rival is a fallen angel who no longer has wings, and one of the ironies of his waiting for trains is that he is not capable of any kind of transport or transcendence himself.
16 The deletion of Lili Marlene is interesting: in the source text, it is part of an undercurrent of a conflict between the 'I' and 'you', but it also hints at how pitiable the rival then was in the speaker's eyes, waiting for an idealized lover who never would or could appear. Cutting Marlene reduces that note of sympathy which the song carries, making him even more pathetic.

field]. Also modified are the religious dimensions of the source text: the little house in the desert becomes 'a cottage, far off in the woods', a more secular location (and one that is similar to the island off the coast in the Norwegian version, discussed later).[17] Whereas Cohen's text can be argued to shift between a past anger that occasionally bleeds into the present, and a more conciliatory stance at the end ('Your enemy is sleeping' is wonderfully poised between hibernation and disarmament, and there is gratitude for 'the trouble you took from her eye'), the Swedish version seems more tense: the word 'fiende' [enemy] appears twice in the final verse, and the rival is described as 'fientlig' [hostile] – a departure from the original where we know very little about his actual feelings. In addition, the distance between the past and the present is minimized in the Swedish version: in Cohen's song, Jane received a lock of hair 'that night you planned to go clear', but in Lundell's rendering it is 'i går' [yesterday], so that the sense of injury is much more recent. 'Men det jag har sett har jag sett' [but what I have seen I have seen] also negates the previous line's tentative 'kanske förlåter [jag] dej' [perhaps I will forgive you]: he positions himself as a witness to a crime he cannot forget or keep quiet about, running counter again to the 'I'm glad you stood in my way' of the source text. Even the line 'Om Anne var ett misstag för dej så har du ändå begått det' seems to move in the direction of understanding before negating it: it might have been a mistake, but it was still made.[18] Indeed the tone of the speaker's address is much more antagonistic generally in this version: 'Nu sover din fiende' suggests a possible cessation of hostilities, but this is again negated by the final line ('Och du har hennes famn'), so that there is a sense that the speaker can be betrayed again while he is sleeping, and that the relationship between Anne and the rival might continue.[19] If the Danish version is superficially the most faithful to the source,

---

17 'Det säjs at du bor i en stuga nu, långt ute i skogen'.
18 'If Anne was a mistake for you, it was one you still committed'. And he continues: 'Du slog aldrig slaget mot mej. Ända har jag fått det' [You never hit me but I still felt the blow]. The suggestion is that the rival did not deliberately set out to injure the speaker by having an affair with 'Anne', but it was still a blow – and one that he has never quite recovered from or forgotten. The change of name, from 'Jane' to 'Anne', is perhaps less important: Jane is both a particular name and a generic name, suggesting 'Jane Doe' as much if not more than an individual, and Anne is similarly personal and neutral.
19 'Your rival is now sleeping/and you have her embrace'. The animosity appears to be mutual: 'Sist när vi sågs/Var du stängd och fientlig' [The last time I saw you/You were closed and hostile]; even the song itself can be seen as an animated riposte to the journal that the rival is filling with memories from the past.

the Swedish is the least: the geographical relocation aside, two of the verses are almost completely new in terms of content, with little relation to Cohen's original, and as such, the Swedish song can be seen as a crossover between a translation and an adaptation. The mood of conciliation is either played down or altered, and in its place, an unredeeming sense of bitterness, loss and lack of forgiveness permeates the lyrics.

Gikk du noen gang fri?

The Norwegian version of the song is one of twelve lyrics by Håvard Rem, a well-known poet, biographer and translator, for a tribute album of Cohen songs entitled *Hadde månen en søster*:[20]

> Det er fire om morgenen, det er sent i desember.
> Jeg skriver for å spørre deg hvordan du har det.
> Det er vinter i Oslo, men for meg er det stedet.
> Det er musikk fra kaféen i Pilestredet.[21]

> Jeg har hørt at du flyttet til en øy ute ved kysten.
> Kan du leve for ingenting nå?
> Syns du skal føre et slags regnskap.[22]

Written by a Norwegian poet in Norwegian, set in Norway and performed by one of Norway's leading female singers, the song seems like the ultimate act of cultural appropriation: it takes an English-language original and transforms

---

20   Leonard Cohen, *Hadde Månen en Søster: Cohen på norsk*, C.C. Cowboys et al., trans. Håvard Rem, (Kirkelig Kulturverksted, FXDC 128, 1993). The title means 'If the moon had a sister', a reference to a line in 'The Law', the third song on Cohen's 1984 album *Various Positions*. Interestingly, all of the songs are performed by a selection of Norway's finest women recording artists, including the Northern Norwegian Kari Bremnes. Among the (many) highlights of Bremnes's performance is how well she brings out the metrical accents and rhyming couplets in Rem's translation.
21   'It is four in the morning, it is late in December./I am writing to ask you how you are doing./It is winter in Oslo, but for me it is the place./There is music from the cafe in Pilestredet'. Pilestredet is a major street in Oslo.
22   'I have heard that you moved to an island out by the coast./Can you live for nothing now?/Think you should keep some kind of record'.

it into something that is not only linguistically but possibly also culturally very un-American. The versification mainly remains the same – there are few changes to the metre.

The most obvious changes are to the place names and geographical setting of the text: New York and Clinton Street become 'Oslo' and 'kafeen i Pilestredet'. In one way, these transpositions of place are equivalent to planting a Norwegian flag on Cohen's text and claiming it as Norwegian territory – a perfect domestication and appropriation of the text. But they are consistent with, and in many ways prepare us for, the other shifts in the translation, most of which are cultural: the house in the desert becomes an island off the coast, an image which is suggestive of a different kind of sanctuary – more relaxational and personal than monastic and in the service of divinity. The effect of these changes is very interesting: by transferring the settings, the song's origins in a foreign culture and language become less visible, and Rem succeeds in creating something which on the surface at least seems as if it might have been originated by a Norwegian.

Perhaps the simplest change, in the sex of the singer and possibly also the speaker, is also the most significant. First of all, the shift influences the religious imagery and reflections in the song. The alteration from 'my brother, my killer' to 'min søster, min morderske' doesn't eradicate the association with Cain and Abel entirely, but it does necessitate an extra hermeneutical step in its recovery: generally speaking, as in Swedish culture, the Old Testament is not a significant presence in Norwegian culture.[23] But it also has a series of other consequences: 'Jeg skriver for å spørre hvordan du har det' for example, is not necessarily occasioned by the knowledge of an illness or depression as it is in the original, and therefore suggests a slightly less confrontational relationship.[24] For while much of 'Famous Blue Raincoat' defines Jane primarily as the site of competing claims of ownership (she is 'my woman' and, later,

---

23   In the Jennifer Warnes version, this biblical reference is completely removed. The main sentence of the line 'oh what can I tell you' is repeated and replaces the vocative phrase 'my brother, my killer'. The reference to brother by a woman performer could suggest a love triangle of a different and more complex nature. The Warnes version appears to have a female self, and this changes the text in many regards and the motif of rivalry is no longer dominant in the text.
24   'I am writing to ask how you are doing'.

when the singer appears to speak of himself in the third person, 'his woman'), the Norwegian speaks of 'hans liv [var ikke] mitt', which suggests a closing off, a refusal to share intimacies or confidences, rather than the sense of a life that is no longer possessed.[25] Perhaps the greatest shift in the translation then is from a 1960s worldview where men are perceived as primary (and where the speaker's greatest regret, arguably, is the loss of his former 'brother') to a 1990s post-feminist landscape where women are no longer spoken about and of and for.

The other changes relate to this first one: the rival woman no longer wears the masculine raincoat but the more generic and vaguer 'klærne' [the clothes]. In fact, the famous blue raincoat is not present in the Norwegian version at all; the love object is not given a name; and finally, Lili Marlene is out of the picture, and James Dean has taken her place. As with the Swedish version, the ties to the hypotextual Lili are severed, but some of these (now disconnected and possibly reconnected) elements are retained in the translation. The gypsy is retained – but now in the form of a temptress, a seductress with a rose between her teeth, and the associations are considerably altered: instead of the soldier's dream version of love and lover, a promise of the future, there is James Dean, the poster boy rebel without a cause, an accident waiting to happen, and a symbol of eternal youth. One can argue that both Lili Marlene in the source text and James Dean in the Norwegian version represent a foreign element: Lili Marlene has clear associations to the German popular song from the war, performed by a German, Marlene Dietrich, in English; James Dean is a symbol of American pop culture, youth culture and the silver screen. However, where the English language readily picks up and assimilates, both culturally and phonologically, names and words from other languages, Lili Marlene being no exception, James Dean is phonetically foreign to the Norwegian language and phonological system (in much the same way as Jane, New York and Clinton Street are foreign elements in the Danish version), and as such stands out and signals foreignness. But it seems unreasonable to claim that James Dean culturally speaking is a foreign element in the Norwegian version. If the rest of the lyrics can be seen as some form of appropriation and domestication of the cultural references, then why in this case is one global, cultural refer-

---

25 'his life [was not] mine'.

ence substituted with another – what exactly is the link between James Dean and Lili Marlene? On closer inspection, there is perhaps more that unites the two than separates them. First, as cultural entities, both work on a global and local level in their respective contexts – James Dean in Norway and Norwegian and Lili Marlene in North America and in American English. Although the reference of the names, at least in the non-fictional James Dean, may remain the same across languages, culture, and time, all connotations do not. Second, and related to their connotations and mythical status, they can both be seen as icons/symbols of desire for the opposite sex: James Dean featured on young women's walls decades after his death, and Lili Marlene represents an object of desire and longing in the song Lili Marlene, and also via association with the artist Marlene Dietrich, who popularised her in English and is known as something of a femme fatale. In other words, both can be construed as sex symbols – objects of desire, unattainable for most people, what we want but never can have. This crossing of fictional and non-fictional realms, the interplay of the global and the local, the tension of denotation and connotation, places these elements as hybrid elements, who, as soon as they enter a new context, will adapt to or change that context.

It is interesting how many of the overt religious references are slightly downplayed or removed in the Norwegian and Swedish translations. This applies to both the Old Testament references and the possible reference to Scientology. However, the ambiguity in the original phrase 'living for nothing', which can suggest that the rival was and is a spiritual seeker seeking liberation from all things material, is retained in the Norwegian version ('Kan du leve for ingenting nå'), and with it some form of spiritual elements.[26] The switch from a 'little house deep in the desert' to 'en øy ute ved kysten' is also interesting: islands off the Norwegian coast – such as Munkholmen outside Trondheim, or Selja in Sogn and Fjordane – could sometimes be sites of religious seclusion, so Rem's choices do not absolutely preclude the possibility of a religious retreat. But in a modern and secular society, such a relocation is more likely to be understood by a Norwegian audience as occasioned by the inheritance of an old family property, by a desire to return to a more traditional Norwegian lifestyle, or out of a need to recharge the batteries.

---

26 'can you live for nothing now'.

Conclusion

'Famous Blue Raincoat' offers opportunities for geographical transposition, and personal and cultural appropriation, something we see reflected in the history of its performances in English and the Nordic languages, which show a shifting back and forth between male and female singer-narrators, and the crossing of cultural, religious and gender-based borders. This eminently social process of the song's transmission over decades by Cohen and by others is a constituent part not only of its reception, but of its meaning. The cultural elements that travel are never the same in a new context, when they arrive at the new destination.

The German language Lily Marlene who makes her way, via Mack David's English language translation and Leonard Cohen's 1971 allusion, to Denmark, Sweden and Norway is not the same one who set out on her journey in 1914 – there are times, indeed, when she is almost unrecognizable. It is not only the language of her different appearances which alter, but also their cultural settings and the set of associations which the figure of Lili Marlene generates. A good example of these transformations is the reference to 'blommande park' in the Swedish version, because it appears to carry no trace of the original reference to a specific rose, but exists in a synecdochal relationship to it – a rose is a flower, and the park is full of flowers. Another example is the retention of the gypsy and the rose, but the dropping of any mention of Marlene in the Norwegian version, where the switch in the gender of the singer enables a switch in the gender of the object of affection: like Marlene, or Marilyn Monroe, or countless other stars, James Dean is the embodiment of a desire that is endlessly deferred, endlessly wished for. If successful translation involves transferring a collection of verbal and semantic objects from one time and place to another, it has to be recognized that the transference also gives rise to transformation, to a set of objects that are similar but also altered and integral. None of these objects are ever culturally pure and hermetically sealed: they always carry the imprint of other idioms and ideas – so that (*pace* Gertrude Stein) a rose is not always a rose, but a lover's request for a rose from his beloved, which becomes a rose in the gypsy mouth of another lover's rival, which becomes a rose in the mouth of a gypsy woman who is another woman's rival. Or a flower in a Stockholm park, its national origins almost, but not quite invisible. Cohen's song, of course, is itself a powerful example of how striated or marbled the creative enterprise is by other works of art, other languages and cultures, with the multiple religious references – which all are migratory in their different ways. The performance of the song by others continues but also impacts on that dissemination, producing new layers of cultural mélange in the process.

Bibliography

Cohen, Leonard, *Songs of Love and Hate* (Columbia, C 30103, 1971).
Cohen, Leonard, *The Best of Leonard Cohen* (CBS, 69161, 1975).
Cohen, Leonard, *Hadde Månen en Søster: Cohen på norsk*, C.C. Cowboys et al., trans. Håvard Rem (Kirkelig Kulturverksted, FXDC 128,1993).
Cohen, Leonard, *På Danske Læber: Leonard Cohen – Sange i Danske Fortolkinger*, Swan Lee, trans. Anders Dohn (Auditorium, TRBL 112, 2004).
Leibovitz, Liel and Matthew Miller, *Lili Marlene: The Soldiers' Song of World War II* (New York: W.W. Norton & Company Ltd., 2008).
Li, Chris Wen-Chao, 'Foreign names into native tongues', *Target* 19.1 (2007), 45–68.
Lundell, Ulf, *Sweethearts* (EMI, 1361401, 1984).
Nederveen Pieterse, Jan, *Globalization and Culture: Global Mélange* (Maryland: Rowman and Littlefield, 2009).
Simmons, Sylvie, *I'm Your Man: The Life of Leonard Cohen* (London: Jonathan Cape, 2012).

Contributors

Anja K. Angelsen is Assistant Professor of English Language at the Norwegian University of Science and Technology, Trondheim. Her research interests include translation, language learning and acquisition, especially issues related to vocabulary. She has extensive experience translating academic texts, the most notable published translation being *In the Beginning is the Icon* by Sigurd Bergmann (translated from Swedish into English). Her most significant non-academic translation to date is a collaborative translation of the first version of the screenplay for the film *Every Thing Will be Fine* (screenplay by Bjørn Olaf Johannessen, directed by Wim Wenders) which had its premiere at the Berlin Film Festival in 2015.

Christiane Fioupou is Professor Emeritus of English at the University of Toulouse-Le Mirail (Jean Jaurès), and specialises in African Studies, particularly Nigerian and Ghanaian literature. She taught English and African Literature at the University of Ouagadougou (Burkina Faso) for twelve years. Her publications include the French translation of Niyi Osundare's volume of poems, *Waiting Laughters/Rires en attente* (Présence Africaine, 2004). She has published a monograph on Wole Soyinka, *La route: réalité et représentation dans l'œuvre de Wole Soyinka* (Rodopi, 1994), and translated three of his plays into French: *The Road* [*La route*] (Hatier, 1988), *King Baabu* [*Baabou roi*] (Actes Sud Papiers, 2005), and *Opera Wonyosi* (Présence Africaine, 2014).

Annjo K. Greenall is Professor of English Language at the Norwegian University of Science and Technology, Trondheim. Greenall has published articles and chapters within the fields of pragmatics, sociolinguistics and translation studies. Her current research interests broadly include the role of English as a global language in Norway and the translation of song lyrics. She has translated (and performed) a selection of songs from the repertoire of the American jazz singer Billie Holiday, some of which have been released on a CD entitled *Eg vandrar langs kaiane* [*I Cover the Waterfront*].

Marius Warholm Haugen, PhD, is Senior Research Librarian at the University Library of the Norwegian University of Science and Technology, Trondheim. He is the author of *Jean Potocki: esthétique et philosophie de l'errance* (Peeters, 2014), and editor of the anthology *Dévier et divertir. Littérature et pensée du XVIIIe siècle* (L'Harmattan/Solum, 2010), together with Knut Ove Eliassen. He has previously published two articles on the travels and fiction of Jean Potocki: 'Morze, niebo, wyobraźnia – Jan Potocki o przestrzeni morskiej' (in *Autoportret* 2009, 28.3), and 'Jean Potocki et le plaisir de l'errance' (in *Dévier et divertir*).

Anne Karine Kleveland is Associate Professor at the Norwegian University of Science and Technology, Trondheim. She has published several peer-reviewed articles, book chapters and textbook texts within her specialization, Latin American contemporary literature. Her current focus is on multilingualism in literature, with special emphasis on Spanish language and Latin American literature in Norwegian-language prose. Some of the results of this project have been published in the book chapter 'Y el júbilo secreto de esta forma: las huellas de Julio Cortázar en la obra del escritor noruego Kjartan Fløgstad' (in *Rumbos del hispanismo en el umbral del Cincuentenario de la AIH*, 11, Bagatto Libri, 2012).

Domhnall Mitchell is Professor of Nineteenth-Century American Literature at the Norwegian University of Science and Technology, Trondheim. He has published two books on Emily Dickinson with the University of Massachusetts Press: *Measures of Possibility: Editing Dickinson's Manuscripts* (2005) and *Emily Dickinson: Monarch of Perception* (2000), and edited another on the *International Reception of Emily Dickinson* (2009). In addition to articles on Bob Dylan, Robert Browning, Henry James, and Fenimore Cooper, he has written on Dickinson for Cambridge University Press, *American Literature, Nineteenth-Century Literature, Notes and Queries* and *Legacy*.

Ritta Oittinen teaches translation at the Universisities of Tampere and Helsinki, Finland. She is the editor and author of several books on translation and more than 100 articles on translating fiction and translating for children as well as translating the verbal, the visual and the aural. Oittinen is also a translator and visual artist who has produced over 30 animated films. Her current interests include multimedia and translation and the translation of picture books, as well as translation teaching.

Priscilla Ringrose is Associate Professor at the Departments of Language and Literature and Interdisciplinary Studies of Culture at the Norwegian University of Science and Technology, Trondheim. She is the author of *Assia Djebar: in Dialogue with Feminisms* (Rodopi, 2006) and co-editor of *Fundamentalism and Communication: Culture, Media and the Public Sphere* (IB Tauris, 2011) and *Paid Domestic Labour in a Changing Europe* (forthcoming Palgrave, 2015). She has published in journals including the *Journal of Scandinavian Cinema* and the *International Journal of Communication*.

Inger Hesjevoll Schmidt-Melbye holds a PhD in French literature from the Norwegian University of Science and Technology, Trondheim. Her main research interests lie within the field of translation studies, and in her 2013 PhD dissertation she examined Francophone African novels in Norwegian translation. Her publications include the following papers: 'L'image du lecteur dans les stratégies d'adaptation du traducteur – Le cas du Pauvre Christ de Bomba' (in *Actes du XVIIIe congrès des romanistes scandinaves/Actas del XVIII congreso de romanistas escandinavos*, Acta Universitatis Gothoburgensis, 2012) and 'Ambigüités et hybridité – de la subjectivité dans le domaine de la traduction' (in *Synergies Pays Scandinaves*, 7, 2012).

Henrik Smith-Sivertsen is a Danish popular music scholar who works as a research librarian at the Royal Library of Copenhagen. He wrote his PhD on Danish translations of popular music and has worked with Scandinavian popular music history from a wide range of perspectives including value, technology, music industry and not least cover practices. His current focus is on how the different Scandinavian countries reacted to the Anglophonization of popular music in the region from the end of WW2 and onwards.

Nelly Foucher Stenkløv is Associate Professor of French Linguistics at the Norwegian University of Science and Technology, Trondheim. Her work focuses on temporal semantics, stylistics, translation studies and second language acquisition. She is currently developing an e-learning program for Norwegian-speaking students in French, based on contrastive linguistics/phonetics.

Sophie Vauclin is Assistant Professor of French Linguistics at the Department of Language and Literature at the Norwegian University of Science and Technology, Trondheim. Her research interests lie mostly within the field of sociolinguistics, with a special focus on the integration of words from others languages into French. She has published two articles, both of them in the journal *Språk og språkundervisning*: 'La valeur de la parole de la femme dans la société française actuelle' and 'Ya Rabbi que ça passe'.